Cyclone
Country

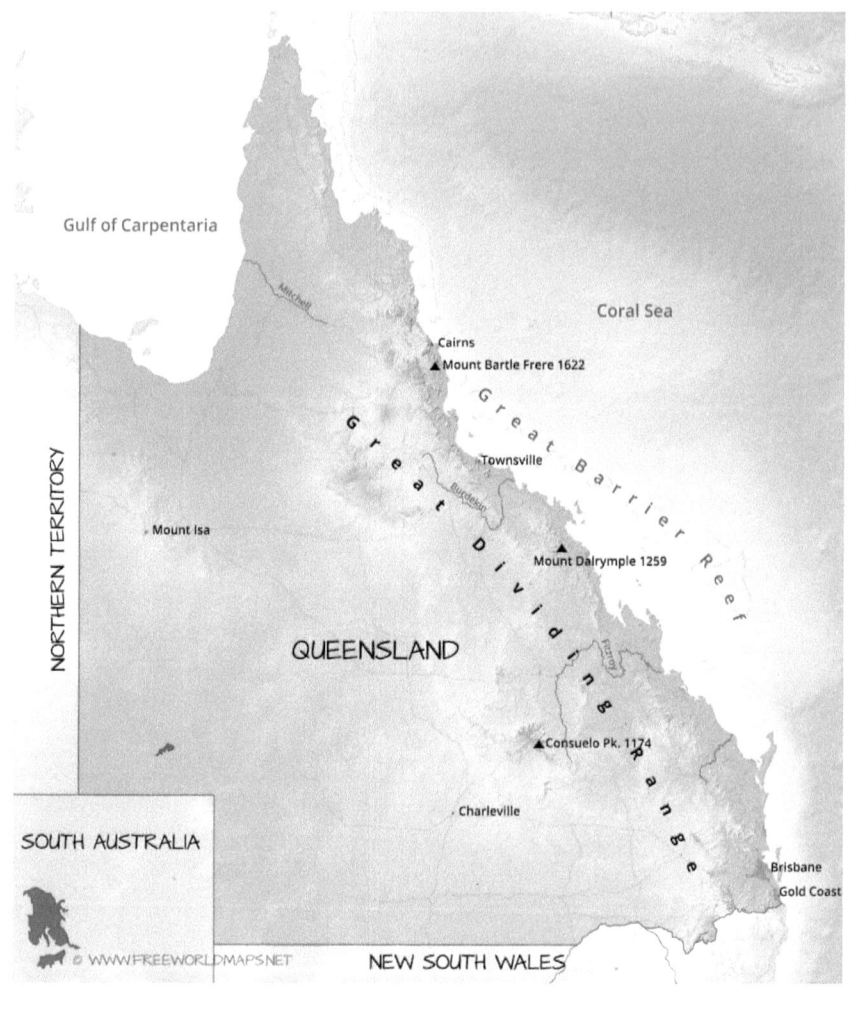

Cyclone Country

The Language of Place and Disaster in Australian Literature

CHRYSTOPHER J. SPICER

Foreword by Stephen Torre

McFarland & Company, Inc., Publishers
Jefferson, North Carolina

ALSO BY CHRYSTOPHER J. SPICER
AND FROM MCFARLAND

*The Flying Adventures of Jessie Keith "Chubbie" Miller:
The Southern Hemisphere's First International Aviatrix* (2017)

Clark Gable, in Pictures: Candid Images of the Actor's Life
(2012; paperback 2020)

Clark Gable: Biography, Filmography, Bibliography (2002)

ALSO BY CHRYSTOPHER J. SPICER AND
MARTHA CRAWFORD CANTARINI

Fall Girl: My Life as a Western Stunt Double (2010)

Frontispiece: Map of Queensland (freeworldmaps.net).

LIBRARY OF CONGRESS CATALOGUING-IN-PUBLICATION DATA

Names: Spicer, Chrystopher J., author. | Torre, Stephen, 1952– writer of foreword.
Title: Cyclone country : the language of place and disaster in Australian literature / Chrystopher J. Spicer ; foreword by Stephen Torre.
Description: Jefferson, North Carolina : McFarland & Company, Inc., Publishers, 2020 | Includes bibliographical references and index.
Identifiers: LCCN 2020034198 | ISBN 9781476681566 (paperback : acid free paper) ♾
ISBN 9781476640501 (ebook)
Subjects: LCSH: Australian literature—Queensland—History and criticism. | Cyclones in literature. | Disasters in literature. | Place (Philosophy) in literature.
Classification: LCC PR9605.5.C97 S65 2020 | DDC 820.9/994—dc23
LC record available at https://lccn.loc.gov/2020034198

BRITISH LIBRARY CATALOGUING DATA ARE AVAILABLE

**ISBN (print) 978-1-4766-8156-6
ISBN (ebook) 978-1-4766-4050-1**

© 2020 Chrystopher J. Spicer. All rights reserved

*No part of this book may be reproduced or transmitted in any form
or by any means, electronic or mechanical, including photocopying
or recording, or by any information storage and retrieval system,
without permission in writing from the publisher.*

Front cover: Satellite image of Severe Tropical Cyclone Yasi approaching Queensland, Australia on 2 February 2011 (NASA photograph)

Printed in the United States of America

*McFarland & Company, Inc., Publishers
Box 611, Jefferson, North Carolina 28640
www.mcfarlandpub.com*

For Marcella,
who survived her cyclone

Acknowledgments

I would like to thank some people for their help and encouragement during the writing of this book. First, I would like to thank my wife, Marcella, whose constant belief that I could accomplish this project, while she was learning to live with her own personal trauma, encouraged me to persevere with this project at times when the tide of my own belief would ebb. I could not have come this far without her faith in me and her determination to journey with me on this path.

I would also like to thank my supervisors for my original doctoral research, Professors Stephen Torre, Richard Landsdown, and Sean Ulm for their valuable support, constructive criticism and suggestions during our work together. They, too, had faith from the beginning in this project, although our situations by the end of the project had changed far more than we could possibly have foreseen.

The manuscript for this book would not have taken its final clearly formatted, correctly punctuated, reference-checked and organized shape without the efforts of my friend, colleague and reader, Jennifer Francis, who has my undying thanks for her fearless expeditions into the jungle of my prose and her consequent suggestions for clarification. Finally, for their friendship and moral support during my work on this project, I would like to thank Associate Professor Hilary Whitehouse and Dr. Jennifer Gabriel.

Table of Contents

Acknowledgments vi
Foreword by Stephen Torre 1
Introduction 5

ONE. The Cyclone Written into the Language of Place 9
TWO. The Naming of the Disaster 44
THREE. "Big wind, he waiting there": Vance Palmer's Cyclones of Apocalypse and Their Power of Revelation 64
FOUR. "Touching the edges of cyclones": Thea Astley's Cyclones of Revelation 84
FIVE. Threading the Eye of the Cyclone: Elizabeth Hunter's Epiphany in Patrick White's *The Eye of the Storm* 98
SIX. Earth Breathing: Susan Hawthorne's Cyclone Within 117
SEVEN. The Apocalypse and Epiphany of Cyclone in the Land of Alexis Wright's *Carpentaria* 135
EIGHT. The Word Becomes the Cyclone: Revelations of the Literary Storm 155

Appendix A: Fiction and Poetry Written and/or Set in Queensland Featuring Cyclones 173
Appendix B: Selected International Novels and Poetry Works Featuring Cyclonic Storms 176
Bibliography 179
Index 193

A story has no beginning or end.
—Graham Greene, *The End of the Affair* (1951)

Foreword
by Stephen Torre

In Book Five of *The Odyssey*, Poseidon summons up the four winds in a maelstrom intended to frustrate the homeward journey of Odysseus:

> Odysseus' knees shook and his spirit failed.... For two nights and two days he was driven by the heavy seas. Time and again he thought he was doomed. But in the morning of the third day, which Dawn with her beautiful tresses opened in all her beauty, the wind dropped, a breathless calm set in, and Odysseus, keeping a sharp look-out, caught a glimpse of land close by as he was lifted by a mighty wave. He felt all the relief that a man's children feel when their father, who has been in bed wasting away with a long, painful illness, in the grip of some malignant power, passes the crisis by the gods' will and they know that he will live. Odysseus' happiness was like that when he caught that welcome glimpse of earth and trees. He swam quickly on in his eagerness to set foot on solid ground [*The Odyssey*, trans E.V. Rieu, Penguin, 2009, pp. 70–73].

This pattern, from order, to disorder, to the return of order, is a common storm trope in classical literature. Not only does the storm disorient and re-orient the physical world; it also has a cathartic effect on the individual's psyche—Homer likens it to the recovery from a "malignant illness." In Ovid's *Metamorphoses*, the catastrophic storm in Book One is integral to the creation of the world, and then its destruction, so that then "a new race of miraculous birth, unlike the people before it" might be bred (*Metamorphoses*, Book One, Trans David Raeburn, Penguin, 2004, p. 17). In Book 11, Ovid projects the psychological and emotional turmoil of the lovers Ceyx and Alcyone onto a tempestuous storm. This use of storms (or more generally the weather) as a literary trope in the objectification of both environmental and psychological trauma and recovery, is pervasive, examples being found in Horace, Lucretius, and Virgil, and of course in post-classical literature, as in, for example, Shakespeare's *The Tempest*, where the storm dis-orients society as a prelude to its re-orientation.

Despite centuries of scientific and meteorological analysis of storms, their cultural and mythical significance and symbolic affectivity in literature have not been diluted. Although Chrystopher J. Spicer's *Cyclone Country* focuses on the literary representation of a particular type of storm, the cyclone, which seasonally occurs in the Australian tropics, his introductory chapters survey the imaginative response to nature catastrophes historically and globally. In particular, he shows how these events impact on "people, place and self," eventually contributing to a sense of *terroir* in particular landscapes. Most importantly, this complex of interactions comes to be mapped into narratives of place, into the "the texture and structure of stories" forming part of the imaginative inheritance of the local inhabitants.

The powerful anthropomorphic associations of these phenomena, and the human attempts to frame their sublimity, are evident in the polemics surrounding the naming of them. In Chapter Two, "The Naming of the Disaster," Spicer gives a fascinating account of the history of naming storms, winds, hurricanes, tornadoes, and so on, with special emphasis on the naming of cyclones, and the work of the pioneering Clement Wragge, who initiated the practice in Australia. Spicer shows that fundamentally, naming serves a hermeneutic purpose: "we gender the cyclone, characterize it, give it a personality ... so that we can figure out how to deal with it, cope with it, and relate to it." An original contribution of this study is the case Spicer makes for the unique *habitus* of the Far North Queensland tropics. A fusion of topography and climate creates a distinctive way of life in which cyclones are integral to the understanding of place and the lived experience of *terroir*. This conceptualization and contextualization of place becomes embedded in history and culture, and ultimately expressed in imaginative understandings of the tropics, in art, and especially in literature.

The deep and comprehensive analysis of the opening chapters provides the basis for Spicer's more specific study of a selection of canonical Australian literary works and their imaginative representation of tropical cyclones. Each of the works analyzed provides compelling material which enhances the historical and global corpus of disaster literature, while defining the unique literary imaginings of the tropics. In his account of Vance Palmer's novel *Cyclone* (1947), Spicer shows how the author "uses the mythical monster Leviathan as a trope for the cyclone and for those connotations of danger and fear of the unknown associated with it" in a narrative whose shifting shape itself reflects the misshapen serpent-monster. Against this, the characters' lives play out patterns of "apocalypse and revelation, and of death and resurrection." Similarly, in Thea Astley's fictions set in the Queensland tropics, particularly *A Boat Load of Home Folk* (1968), the outer cyclonic events are presented as both instruments of destruction as well as catalysts of revelation, serving to objectify the inner emotional and identity crises of the characters.

A cyclone is the fundamental catalyst for character transformation in

Patrick White's *The Eye of the Storm* (1973). The complex religious allusions in this novel form a grounding for the character study of Elizabeth Hunter, whose spiritual epiphany is achieved as a result of her revelations while engulfed in the core of a cyclone. Becoming aware of her flawed materialism, she is renewed by her experience in the cyclone to experience faith, love and humility. This experiential internalization of outer apocalyptic events is also fundamental to Susan Hawthorne's poem cycle *Earth's Breath* (2009) in which she says: "I am in with through the cyclone/which is inside with through me." Spicer draws widely on other (non–Australian) poetry about storms, concluding that Hawthorne's vision resonates with other poetry on the subject in finding that the forces in the ecosystem and the human system are cognate: "The experience of Hawthorne and other writers in the cyclone has opened them to the nature of being, of *who* they are in terms of *where* they are."

Spicer's finely detailed and authoritative reading of Alexis Wright's ground-breaking *Carpentaria* (2006) shows how apocalypse and epiphany are central to the functioning of cyclones in Australian indigenous people's cultural and spiritual understanding of origins and existence. The physical nature of cyclones as well as their seasonal recurrence constitute a cyclic pattern which is inherent to the non-linear Aboriginal understanding of the nature of time. The cyclic pattern is also infused in the cyclic multi-dimensional narrative structure, which Spicer shows is Wright's way of creating "an authentic form of Indigenous storytelling." In the spiritually animate world created in *Carpentaria*, cyclones are "spiritual voices and messengers … whose purpose is 'not only to punish and destroy but also to transform.'" In this, they resonate with the ancient classical stories in which storms are incarnations of the gods.

Spicer's study affirms the complex architectonics of cyclone imagery and symbology in literature, where it may function as a trope of place, of apocalypse, of cultural mythos and story, and of people and spirituality. It establishes that imaginative conceptions of the tropical cyclone contribute in an original and inspiring way to a universal trope in the literature of crisis, revelation and transformation.

Stephen Torre, Ph.D., is an adjunct professor in the College of Arts, Society and Education at James Cook University, Cairns, Australia. He is the founding editor of eTropic: Electronic Journal of Studies in the Tropics, *and the convenor of the "Tropics of the Imagination Conference."*

Introduction

As Severe Tropical Cyclone Yasi, an immense Category 5 storm system, made violent landfall on the Far North Queensland coast in early February 2011, my wife and I and our two mastiffs huddled in the hallway protected by mattresses. Although we seemed to have chosen to shelter for some hours inside the turbine of a large jet engine, we and the house fortunately survived. In the aftermath, I took down from a shelf my well-thumbed copy of Kerry Emanuel's *Divine Wind: The History and Science of Hurricanes* (2005), which seemed appropriate under the circumstances. As I began to read it once again, the words took on a new relevance. They were no longer just words, but an experience to which I could relate. As the title suggests, Emanuel examines not just the science of hurricanes but also their significance in history, literature and art, exploring an integrated appreciation of cyclonic weather events as part of human culture. It occurred to me then, with my own interaction fresh in my mind, that Emanuel was posing some significant questions about the interaction between violent weather and our environment, our place, and our imagination. Because my background as a cultural historian in both Australia and America, I am interested in answers to questions posed by stories of these weather events that we tell or write as prose fiction or poetry, such as in what way do violent, chaotic, destructive, life-threatening weather events provide inspiration for the literary imagination? What do their literary interpretations of these events say about people and societies in tropical places like North Queensland as they cope with regular visits by chaotic and disruptive weather events like cyclones? While the weather events may be catalysts for the literature, does the literature itself provide a means by which individuals and societies can cope with and integrate these events into their lives, culture and place? Do we name and character cyclones (and other tropical storms) as part of that coping and integration process? Finally, in what ways do such weather catastrophes as cyclones speak of our relationships with place and the people in it? After all, we do not have to stay in that place; we could move somewhere else.

In this book, I attempt to explore and suggest some answers to these questions because I consider that such investigation and discussion are important in a world where we have become so much more aware of our relationships to weather and climate. As a writer living in North Queensland, a tropical region prone to cyclones, I wondered how other writers either living in Queensland or writing about Queensland may have responded to these regular, seasonal, catastrophic weather events, and so I embarked on a doctoral research program at James Cook University in order to seek out some answers, and this book has been developed from that research. As the first extensive study to be carried out in Australia that explores the influence of the cyclone as a trope in the Queensland literary imagination, this book breaks new ground in exploring the relationship between people, place, the weather environment, and literature.

Although I do refer to storm literature from other places around the world in this work, I have drawn my primary examples of regional writing about cyclones as a nature disaster from Queensland literature because of the intimate relationships in this Far North Queensland area, where my research has been based, between cyclones, place, people, and writers. I've listed most of the major literary cyclone works in Appendix A, and from that list I have selected works for discussion that I consider exemplify various unifying themes and tropes, such as the wind, the serpent, and the spiral, that weave them into a body of work. I was also interested in the discourse that these works might prompt between the reader, cyclones, and Queensland place in terms of exploring what the writers of Queensland literary works that feature cyclones may be attempting to say about creativity, meaning, and order, and our approach to coping with nature disasters in a world where our environment can at times seem randomly destructive and meaningless.

I should take this opportunity to clarify that in this book I use the term "nature catastrophe" or "nature disaster," rather than the more commonly used "natural" disaster, which I have always thought is a rather dismissive term that carries implications of the ordinary and commonplace, which these events are not (although some Far North Queenslanders like to give the impression that they are). We should always bear in mind that such violent weather events as cyclones are inherently of nature and from nature and so, rather than an aberration, they are always potentially inherent in nature's cycle. If we want to live in their path, then it is we who need to be prepared to accept them as part of this place.

Any major research project requires some boundaries, or it would never be completed, just as every publisher has their deadline for a book or authors would never allow them to leave the house. Clint Eastwood's Dirty Harry once said, "A man has got to know his limitations," and so this book is not intended to be an historical, geographic, or meteorological study of cyclones, nor is it a study of the effects of climate change on them. Although I do refer to many of them, this is not by any means a complete history of cyclones in Queensland. The closest to that at present, as has been the case since it was written, is Hector Holthouse's worthy, but long outdated, *Cyclone* (1971, 1977). Neither was there the time nor space here to consider every work of literature in Queensland that might feature a cyclone. Instead, I have endeavored to focus on a selection of written fictional and poetic works that I consider are a representative sample of literature either written in or set in Queensland that together demonstrates the scope of the cyclone as trope across the authors, styles and chronology of Queensland literature. My chapter sequence reflects this sampling in that I am moving along an approximate literary timeline in order to discuss and establish stylistic and thematic connections and development between works.

While I explore here what the literary cyclone experience may reveal about the regional search for meaning amid the meaninglessness of disaster and what that disaster may reveal to the individual and to the shared community, I am also conscious that Queensland cyclone literature is very much a subset within the broader global literature of cyclonic storms in other tropical, as well as cooler, climate regions, and similar relationships between weather and culture have been explored in works pertaining to other places, such as Alexandra Harris' *Weatherland: Writers and Artists Under English Skies* (2015), and Liz Skilton's *Tempest: Hurricane Naming and American Culture* (2019). Although some elements of the cyclone trope are distinctly regional to the Queensland tropics, other elements are shared with cyclonic storm tropes across the broader tropical zone and even with global storm tropes. My objectives here are to explore how we integrate a violent, chaotic, and destructive weather feature into our culture through the use of storytelling and literature. At the same time, I hope to convey a sense of the connectivity and commonality of people's search for meaning amid the meaningless of chaos and catastrophe.

ONE

The Cyclone Written into the Language of Place

"Truly, at best, our apparent safety is but insecurity and our boasted power is but impotence. We speak at times as though we are conquering Nature, but the God of Nature speaks … and our scientific knowledge is of no avail to enable us to escape the gathering storm."—Mrs. Porter, a survivor of Cyclone Mahina, 1899

Tropical cyclones are an inevitable and integral part of the natural seasonal cycle right across the northern coastal area of Australia above the Tropic of Capricorn, although the effects of large cyclones can certainly be felt inland and further south. This coast includes the northwest coast of Australia around the Kimberley Plateau to Darwin and Arnhem Land in the Northern Territory, the Gulf of Carpentaria into Queensland and the Cape York Peninsula, and south down the east coast of Queensland towards the state capital, Brisbane. It also includes many coastal islands such as Bathurst, Melville and the Wessel Islands, Groote Eylandt, Mornington Island and the Wellesley Islands, the islands of the Torres Strait, Green, Fitzroy, Dunk, and Palm Islands, and the Whitsunday Islands. These violent and potentially catastrophic weather systems are a perpetual possibility there, reminding not only the inhabitants of these tropical regions but indeed everyone that, as Gloucester wisely observes in King Lear, "As flies to wanton boys are we to th' gods" (IV, i, l.36). As apocalyptic nature catastrophes that descend on us without invitation, cyclones are rather like unwanted guests that invade our homes and our lives, against whom we have to defend ourselves. In doing so, we can become aware of relationships between ourselves, our community and our place of which we might not have been previously conscious. Experiencing and surviving the cyclone might even encourage us to investigate our relationship with ourselves, to look within and ask questions about our personal responses to this kind of event.

Although cyclones can be anticipated by modern weather forecasting technology and their approach and predicted direction predicted and recorded on weather charts, they are not yet subject to actual human intervention: that is, we cannot control them. Their speed, eventual direction, severity and point of landfall are influenced by such meteorological elements as air pressure, humidity levels, water temperature, and ocean depths that may seem mysterious and entirely whimsical to the average person. The end result of this seemingly random coincidence of factors can be a catastrophic regional weather event that reminds humanity of its limitations when faced with the forces of nature. "Truly, at best, our apparent safety is but insecurity and our boasted power is but impotence," observed Mrs. Porter, having in 1899 endured the onslaught of Cyclone Mahina, or the Bathurst Bay Hurricane. She and her husband, captain of the pearling lugger *Crest of the Wave*, were among the few survivors of Australia's worst nature catastrophe in which some 350–400 people died in the region of Cape Melville in far northern Queensland, and her words are recorded in the first known major book about a cyclone published in Queensland, *The Pearling Disaster, 1899: A Memorial*. "We speak at times as though we are conquering Nature," she continued, "but the God of Nature speaks … and our scientific knowledge is of no avail to enable us to escape the gathering storm" (pp. 30–31). Like Mrs. Porter, North Queenslanders regularly experience an epiphany that cyclones can be greater than the sum of their parts. While these storms have the power to take lives, they can also recreate and change lives; they have the power to destroy place and community but also to reveal our relationships with place and with each other that can enable communities to bond and to rebuild.

Cyclones can be the chaos that devastates the structure of everyday life and so, in seeking to understand the reason for such chaos, people impart to the cyclone the qualities of apocalypse: the ultimate revelation. James Berger, author of *After the End*, a study of our cultural pursuit of the end and what follows, argues that to be truly apocalyptic an event must in its disruption clarify and illuminate "the true nature of what has been brought to an end." Yet, rather than being an ultimate end, Berger explains, an apocalypse in its true sense anticipates, reveals and explains the end (1999, p. 5). To see the cyclone as apocalypse, then, is to seek to understand what it explains and reveals, and in searching for the meaning of such chaos, writers have explored the literary Queensland cyclone as an apocalyptic event that reveals new opportunities and new understanding: an event that may destroy but may also explain and offer the opportunity to recreate. Some writers such as Susan Hawthorne in her poetry cycle *Earth's Breath* (2009) and Patrick White in his Nobel Prize–winning novel *The Eye of the Storm* (1977) explore the epiphany: the intensely personal, perhaps even deeply spiritual, apocalyptic cyclone experience that may reveal storms within as well as without. In Meredith Traherne's (1982) short story, "Cry of the Wild Wind," the apocalypse of

Cyclone Harry reveals to Lucy Morton, left home alone with three children, that she has the strength and courage with which to overcome her fears of her new North Queensland environment and deal with adversity. Having lost her father in an earlier storm, surviving a cyclone helps a young woman in S.G. Larner's "Chasing the Storm" (2014) to deal with her ultimate fear: the fear of death. For other Australian writers, cyclones in such novels as Thea Astley's *A Boat Load of Home Folk* (1968) and Vance Palmer's *Cyclone* (1947) reveal their flawed and anxious characters in the context of the broader world of their relationships, for better or for worse, with partners, family and community. We are all in this together, Astley proposes, because, "Everybody is living on a cyclonic edge" (Willbanks, 2008, p. 30).

Yet, while literary cyclones can expose hidden faults and fears, they can also inspire individuals to overcome those fears. In Astley's novel, a small group bands together at the height of the cyclone in order to survive, despite their animosity and selfishness. At the end of Hugh Halcro's short story, "Little Sigma" (1899), Jim Hardon realizes that he is a member of the common church of humanity as he defies racial barriers and vows to raise the Australian Aboriginal baby boy whom he discovers protected by the body of his dead mother on top of a hill after a cyclone. In Esther Knight's short story, "Monsoon Two," she observes that the days after a cyclone brought "a flood of compassion. Many local people, who had suffered damage themselves, left their homes and farms to help others. Armed with chainsaws and tools, they just quietly entered streets … and generally did what they could" (2008, p. 25). Like them, the citizens of Palmer's fictional version of Cairns also put aside their personal differences to work together in the aftermath of a cyclone to restore order to the town and to the community.

As part of their narrative search for meaning within cyclonic chaos, then, writers of Queensland literature reaffirm a communal cohesiveness within the regional cultural place. Those who survive cyclones are a unique community within the larger society, as is any other group who endures a catastrophe. Such experiences cause people to recognize a reality that encompasses trauma and chaos, a reality which they may not have encountered previously, and so their perception of events is transformed in a way that sets them apart from others who have not been through such events. "There is a vast gap," trauma studies scholar Kali Tal observes, "between those who have experienced the trauma and thus had reality disturbed and those who have not" (1996, p. 134). Where once we may have perceived an ordered universe, that structure and purpose may no longer be clearly apparent in the aftermath of traumatic events. "Fate and luck alone will choose what's taken, what survives," concludes poet Barbara Bufi after surviving Cyclone Yasi (Bufi, 2011, p. 27). In such circumstances we might agree with William's assessment in Umberto Eco's *The Name of the Rose*, "There was no plot and I discovered it by mistake" (1984, p. 599). Of course, there are those who would not agree with him and who would see some divine plan in it all, but by whatever means people have achieved it, their survival enhances a feeling of uniqueness and specialness, as an individual or a group, summed up in the memorable words of Ishmael in Herman Melville's *Moby Dick* (1851). As the sole survivor of the loss of the *Pequod* and her crew, Ishmael repeats the words uttered by those who survived catastrophic events in the Biblical story of Job: "And I only am escaped alone to tell thee" (1967, p. 470, and Job 1:15, 16, 17, 19). Like them, many survivors feel that the reason they have lived is so that they can tell a story that is an essential part of the human experience. After all, what could happen to one person could, at any time, happen to all.

When a catastrophe occurs, a society already has in place an explanation of the structure and organization of their world but, by their very nature, catastrophic events threaten to overturn and overtake these explanations and so disrupt that order. In the aftermath of the catastrophe, then, society needs to re-establish explanations of that catastrophe so that it can be quickly culturalized to enable the on-going maintenance of society's order and cohesiveness. Fatalities may be memorialized and remembrance days established, shrines built, recovery programs instituted, and stories of survivor experiences collected and published as a form of community expression of the catastrophe, such as the collections *Cyclone Larry: Tales of Survival* (2006) and *Cyclone Yasi: Our Stories* (2011) here in Australia, and Terri Merren's *Hurricane Ivan: Survival Stories* (2005) and Lola Vollen and Chris Ying's *Voices from the Storm: The People of New Orleans on Hurricane Katrina* (2008) elsewhere. On the other hand, stories may be created using fictional prose or poetry forms that also explore deeper cultural meanings of cyclonic events. In works such as these, the metaphor of the catastrophe is evident in our language as we seek to make use of the tangible to explain the abstract of destruction caused by an element we could not see: the wind, and so writers might personify the storm, giving it a human name, along with gender and other human characteristics, or they might employ zoomorphism and portray the storm as possessing animal-like characteristics such as pounding hoofs, claws, teeth, screams, or roars. In telling the story of the storm, we attempt to reduce vast weather events such as cyclonic storms to human size, to give them shape and character and intent, so that what they may reveal to us might be clearer and seem more relevant.

It is significant that these stories strengthen communal ties as part of the culturalization process because, "It is the community that offers a cushion for pain, the community that offers a context for intimacy, the community that serves as the repository for binding traditions" (Erikson, 1995, p. 234). In recounting and repeating these stories—to others, among themselves, and on through successive generations—storytellers continue to reveal and re-affirm relationships between the catastrophe and the community, between their place and their culture. In doing so, people are able to reconstruct into their lives that which could have been potentially destructive of them. This acceptance and integration of catastrophe into our life, or even of the likelihood of catastrophe, is an important recognition of the kind of personal relationship we have with chaotic events such as cyclones that are part of regional place and that, by their very seasonal repetition, perpetuate themselves within the culture of tropical regions such as North Queensland. Each type of tropical cyclonic storm, whether cyclone, hurricane, or the "divine wind" of a typhoon (Emanuel, 2005, p. 5), has an impact on the regional imaginary that is specific and unique to the nature, history and culture of that region. The stories of these storms are significant to our regional sense of tropical place, as well as to our personal understanding of and relationship with that place, including the people in it.

The Tropics and the Cyclone

In *Meteorologica*, Aristotle theorized that there were only two habitable areas of the earth: one near the northern pole region and the other near the southern pole. "The lands beyond the tropics," he claimed, referring to the Tropics of Cancer and Capricorn, "were uninhabitable" (II. v. 362a. p. 181). He also suggested that somewhere on the other side of the world in the southern hemisphere, "there must be a region which bears to the other pole the same relation as that which we inhabit bears to our [northern] pole" (II. v. 362b. p. 183). The passing of time and further exploration eventually proved the ancient philosopher right about a Southern continent, but he could not have been more wrong about that area between the Tropics of Cancer and Capricorn that is generally referred to as "the tropics." Contrary to those predictions, the tropical region is currently home to some 40 percent of the world's population and 80 percent of the planet's terrestrial biodiversity (*State of the Tropics*, 2014, p. 4), and it continues to develop; by 2050, approximately 55 percent of the world's population will live in the tropics (Harding, 2011, p. 2).

The climate of Far North Queensland is typically tropical, with a daytime temperature that may only vary an average of ten degrees Celsius all year and only two seasons: wet and dry. "The Wet," as it is usually known, is traditionally from about November through to May and coincides with the cyclone season. Despite postcard promises of blue skies, clear water and balmy breezes, tropical regions can be home to extreme weather conditions, and one of the most significant atmospheric phenomena affecting this region is the tropical cyclone which, through a combination of high-speed winds, heavy rain and storm surges, can be severely destructive. William Strachey, who was cast onto the virginal shores of the island of Bermuda in 1609 as a survivor of the wreck of the *Sea Venture* during a hurricane, later wrote in his *True Reportory of the Wracke* (1610) that "[t]hese Ilands are often afflicted and rent with tempests, great strokes of thunder, lightning and raine in the extreamity of violence: … which keepe their unchangeable round, and rather thunder then blow from every corner about them, sometimes fortie eight hours together" (Murray, 1991, p. 91). According to research into the impact of personal cyclone experience carried out by social anthropologist Hannah Swee, cyclones are "frequently recalled as sensory experiences," and some four centuries after the *Sea Venture* the impact on the senses can be just as traumatic, although the imagery is updated. Survivors interviewed by Swee recalled that when a cyclone sweeps onto land, the shrieking of the wind is if a jet engine is above you, punctuated by the snap and reverberating thud of trees breaking and hitting the ground (2017, p. 15). Survivors of Cyclone Tracy, which severely damaged the Northern Territory city of Darwin in 1974, also remembered the cyclone's sound as "a jet plane in your garden," and also as a banshee's scream, or "an express train going through a tunnel but one that went on for hours and hours" (Cunningham, 2014, p. 41). Then the noise suddenly ceases as the eye of the cyclone passes overhead, replaced by calm and silence until the other side of the cyclone arrives and the screaming and destruction resumes. As revealed by these recollections, and in literature such as Susan Hawthorne's *Earth's Breath*, the timeline of a cyclone can be absorbed through the senses as an extended, intimate and personal sensory experience that is essential to the knowledge that we assemble and retain about them.

Another form of sensory experience, however, and one that is becoming more relevant in the current media age, is visualization. A cyclonic storm, whether cyclone, hurricane or typhoon, is a rotating storm, with the direction of rotation varying according to hemisphere: clockwise in the southern hemisphere and counter-clockwise in the northern. Cyclones typically form when sea-surface temperatures reach above 26.5°C, sustaining gale-force winds and falling barometric pressure. Winds in these storms characteristically rotate around a center of low barometric pressure, known as the "eye," that is typically surrounded by a cliff-like "eye-wall" of dense weather, leaving the eye clear. Seas within the eye may be remarkably calm and even populated with birdlife. As satellite photography has developed in sophistication, we can now see images of these spiraling, rotating weather events in their entirety, allowing us to take in their beauty as we anticipate their terror, retaining in our imagination the image of that cyclic pattern that is so similar to the coil of a snake and the mystery of the labyrinth, both so important to our literary perception of the cyclonic storm as we will see later in the book. Some of the cyclonic storms that originate over tropical and sub-tropical oceans may eventually make landfall, generally increasing in size, wind speed and potential depth of the tidal surge as they move into shallower water, but some never do and remain entirely at sea, such as the one that features in Joseph Conrad's *Typhoon* (1903). Not only do cyclones rotate but they travel along a path that, as the years go by and technology improves, can be predicted with increasing accuracy. Nevertheless, cyclones remain notorious for their sudden changes of direction away from predicted tracks and for associated changes in speed and size.

Cyclones usually approach the Queensland coast from the east across the Coral Sea, whereas cyclones approach the northwest coast of the continent from across the Indian Ocean. In both cases, they may then track to the north or south, sometimes travelling into the Gulf of Carpentaria region before moving south. On average, approximately four cyclones develop in the Coral Sea off North Queensland every year; while not all of them make landfall, it is highly likely that at least one and perhaps two could strike the coast, creating a community context where severe, destructive weather is a regular, expected, and anticipated event, rather than being a singular or unusual occurrence. Australian tropical cyclones are classified by the Bureau of Meteorology from minimum strength of Category 1 to Category 5 on a slightly different scale that the U.S. Saffir-Simpson hurricane intensity scale. A Severe Tropical Cyclone is a tropical cyclone of Category 3 and above, Category 3 being an average sustained wind speed of 118 kmh. A Category 4 STC is above 160 kmh average sustained wind speed, and a Category 5 is above 200 kmh and strongest wind gusts of 280 kmh. Since Severe Tropical Cyclone Larry in 2006, another six STCs have made landfall in Queensland: Monica (2006), Ului (2010), Yasi (2011), Ita (2014), Marcia (2015), and Debbie (2017). However, it is not only wind speeds of cyclonic storms that cause loss of life and destruction of landscape and property, of course, but also heavy rainfall, high storm surges and associated flooding.

Occurring with cyclical seasonal regularity, cyclonic storms such as cyclones, hurricanes and typhoons are historically endemic to tropical regions and, consequently, they have been integrated into the life, culture and literature of those areas, even to the extent of naming the storms and endowing them with human characteristics. Like the people on whom they impact, these storms also have a life structure: they are born, live and mature, and then they die. In this way, cyclonic storms become yet another potentially dangerous life form with which one learns to cope when living in tropical regions: living with the potential threat of a tropical cyclone can seem like living next door to a bad-tempered neighbor prone to drinking bouts. In learning to live with such situations, we often discover personal resources that enable us to learn from those experiences and to then to be able to integrate the stories of those experiences into our lives. "People do not acquire their knowledge ready-made," observes anthropologist Tim Ingold, "but rather grow into it, through a process of what might best be called guided rediscovery ... each story will take you so far, until you come across another that will take you further." But, these stories do not come with meanings already attached nor do they mean the same for everybody, he notes. What they mean is something that readers and listeners "have to discover for themselves, by placing them in the context of their own life histories" (2011, p. 162). To live successfully in the tropics, North Queenslanders accept the context of destructive cyclonic storms that may arrive every year as an integral part of their life history, of their place, and of their regional identity, and this understanding and acceptance can be seen within their writing about those storms. In heeding the experience of the cyclone, we embrace new worlds that may be revealed by it and, in doing so, we may comprehend more about the relationship between person, people and biosphere in order to "better understand and better enable the tropical world" in which we live (Harding, 2011, p. 4).

Although generically referred to as cyclonic storms, these rotating storms that move along a track are usually known by different names according to where they are located. In the northwest Pacific, they are typhoons. In the Atlantic and North-East Pacific, they are known as hurricanes, an English word derived from indigenous Carib, Mayan and Aztec names for an evil god of wind and destruction, such as *hurucan*, *hunraken* or *jurukan*. To the Tainos of the Caribbean, he was Jurukan, son of the creation goddess Atabei. The early inhabitants of Cuba carved S-shaped images of their god Hurucan that consisted of a circular head with arms spiraling out from its sides, implying knowledge of storm rotation. This was long before amateur meteorologist William Redfield observed in 1821 that, after a hurricane struck Connecticut, trees had been blown down in a different direction on one side of the storm than on the other, eventually publishing his theories about rotating storms in 1838 (Emanuel, 2005, pp. 7, 18, and Schwartz, 2015, pp. 6–9, 139–143). Rotating Southern Hemisphere tropical storms in regions such as Australia, the Arabian Sea, the Indian Ocean and the Bay of Bengal, the Coral Sea, Torres Strait, and the South Pacific were generically, and somewhat confusingly, referred to as hurricanes or typhoons until the early twentieth century. Eventually, they became exclusively known as cyclones after Henry Piddington coined the term from the Greek word for the coil of a snake to distinguish a storm that had circular motion. Piddington—president of the Marine Courts in Calcutta—introduced the usage in his *Sailor's Hornbook for the Law of Storms* (1848, p. 8), the first widely accessible guide to successfully navigating a ship through a rotating storm. Although the word "cyclone" may have been in use in America as early as 1821 (Longshore, 2008, p. 115), Piddington was the first to publish the word as a proposed collective noun for all rotating storms as at that time, names such as gale, hurricane, and even typhoon were customarily used as descriptors of the strength of a storm, rather than to distinguish a type of storm. Even tornadoes, according to Piddington, had only been determined at this time to be "sometimes rotatory" (1848, p. 8). The new name was evidently quickly accepted: in his Third Edition of 1860, Piddington noted that "cyclone" had already been so readily adopted as a name for rotating storms that the term "cyclonology" had been suggested for the study of them (p. 12).

Given such historic cultural connections, and the propensity for cyclones to be intense, life-changing personal experiences, it is hardly surprising that cyclonic storms have featured for centuries in world literature, given the potential for their violence and dramatic form to inspire the imagination, just as they feature prominently as image and trope throughout the history of Queensland literature. Shakespeare's *The Tempest* (1975b, orig. 1610–11), for example, famously references that shipwreck of the *Sea Venture* in 1609 in a hurricane off the coast of Bermuda, some survivors of which eventually settled the island. Daniel Defoe's *The Storm* (2005, orig. 1704) provides an account of the savage North Atlantic hurricane that devastated the British Isles in 1703, and Joseph Conrad's *Typhoon* (1975, orig. 1902) is the tale of the Siamese steamer Nan-Shan's encounter with a storm in the China Seas. In Richard Hughes' controversial 1929 novel *High Wind in Jamaica*, children struggle to survive being seized by pirates after a hurricane destroys their home, and African American author Zora Neale Hurston's 1937 novel *Their Eyes Were Watching God* is based on events surrounding the Okeechobee Hurricane of 1928 in Florida. George R. Stewart's *Storm* (1941) is renowned for being the first American novel in which a cyclonic storm is given a personal name, Maria (pronounced Mah-rye-ah), and Jamaican author Diana McCauley's *Huracan* (2012) explores the author's family connections with Jamaica over several generations and the implications and contradictions of beauty and violence, slavery and independence. Cyclonic storms have also featured in such international poetic works as Anne Finch's "Upon the Hurricane" (1713), William Cullen Bryant's "The Hurricane" (1855), William Hamilton Hayne's "A Cyclone at Sea"(1900), Hart Crane's "The Hurricane" (1927), A.B. "Banjo" Paterson's "The Ballad of the Calliope" (1902), Adrienne Rich's "Storm Warnings"(1951), Edward Kamau Braithwaite's "Shar: Hurricane Poem" (1990), and Teresa Cader's "History of Hurricanes" (2009) (see Appendix B).

In this book, we will not only investigate the presence of the cyclone as a trope in Queensland literature (see Appendix A), but we will also examine the relationship between the cyclone trope and Queenslanders' sense of place as an example of the broader global relationship between people and place in time of catastrophe. In doing so, we will explore the use of the cyclone trope as a metaphor for epiphany and revelatory apocalypse, to which Professor Morton Paley refers as the "apocalyptic sublime" (1986, p. 1): a destructive event so terrible and terrifying that it is, as the English philosopher Edmund Burke argued in 1757 in his *A Philosophical Enquiry*, "a source of the sublime;

that is, it is productive of the strongest emotion which the mind is capable of feeling" (1992, p. 36). The term "apocalypse" derives from the Greek *apokalupsis*, implying an unveiling and realization of future events or meanings—a revelation—and in Queensland literature there is frequent reference to the literary cyclone as an instrument of fate or destiny, revealing to characters individually and collectively that they are part of the inevitable and uncontrollable cycle of death and birth, of change and renewal. The cyclone trope in Queensland literature is thus integral to the people and to the tropical place. Those caught up in the cyclone seek the meaning of it and in it, as they seek to integrate the experience as part of their lives within the tropical place.

Cyclone as Catastrophe

However, before discussing the significance of the cyclone as part of place and the literary imaginative response to it, we need to first consider the cyclone as a nature disaster or catastrophe in terms of its impact on people and place in order to appreciate the other part of Burke's equation: the terrible and the terror. The vast scope, yet personally intimate character, of the nature catastrophe means that those it effects may not readily understand it. "Disaster is, by definition, that which cannot be comprehended exactly," explains Martin Voss, head of the Disaster Research Unit at Freie Universitat Berlin. "It is a hopelessly hybrid entity: inextricably entangling the natural and the social, freighting objectivity with subjectivity" (Coen, 2013, p. 3). French philosopher Maurice Blanchot agrees that it is so difficult to define such events that he calls disaster "that which does not have the ultimate for a limit," he writes; "it bears the ultimate away in the disaster" (1995, p. 28). As events that can be so difficult to mentally envisage, nature catastrophes challenge attempts to contextualize, to tell or to write about them, or even to learn and heal from them as an individual or as a society. These events challenge the fundamental perceptions that we have of the world in which we live, perceptions that we might usually take for granted. Explorer and naturalist Alexander von Humboldt found his perceptions challenged during an earthquake, when he experienced a

> sudden revelation of the delusive nature of the inherent faith by which we had clung to a belief in the immobility of the solid parts of the Earth.... A moment destroys the illusion of a whole life—our deceptive faith in the repose of nature vanishes, and we feel transported as it were into a realm of unknown destructive forces ... and we no longer trust the ground on which we stand [1849, p. 212].

In effect, the nature catastrophe can unbalance the fundamental precepts by which we relate to our place, unbalancing our personal and material relationship with it.

In order to restore our faith in these precepts, we try to understand Humboldt's "unknown destructive forces" and the effect they may have on our place. As understanding develops, so does perception of our existence in that place, and in this way the relationship develops between people and place. Anything that impacts on and disrupts that relationship, physically or psychologically, disrupts our perception of existence there; we have to re-think that perception of our relationship between people and place and as we do that, it develops. We prefer to think that life has meaning and context, whereas on the other hand catastrophe often reveals the arbitrariness of life, an aspect we would rather not confront. "We would often prefer to generate comforting myths about traumatic experiences," argues Kali Tal, "rather than acknowledge the arbitrary nature of life" (1996, p. 134). Because we prefer to assume that life has purpose, rather than consider that it could be just a series of random events, we use myth and metaphor, trope and image to suggest that the catastrophe has meaning and significance, that it is not an aberration but part of a plan and integral to the relationship between us and the environment.

The ancient Greeks believed that the Fates eternally wove the threads of our destiny into the fabric of an ongoing text narrative of life. If a thread was cut, that only marked the end of one narrative thread, while the fabric of humanity's narrative continued to be woven. The death of any individual might affect destiny, but it was not the end of destiny. Their fate was merely the product of those mechanisms of destiny begun by their ancestors and it would, in turn, be part of the destiny of those in the future. With this philosophy in mind, we could perceive catastrophe in a different light. It might not be a sign of disorder or that our lives are undergoing a radical reversal: instead, perhaps catastrophe is woven into the tapestry of our fate as part of an ordered universe. Perhaps drastic events can reveal and confirm, through construction rather than destruction, the existence of another, alternative ordering of life.

In other words, we could perceive the nature catastrophe as truly apocalyptic in character: destructive, yet in its aftermath also presenting opportunities for renewal and reconstruction. Events like this can be "all-encompassing occurrences, sweeping across every aspect of human life, impacting environmental, social, economic, political and biological conditions" (Oliver-Smith, 2002, p. 23). It is because of this very comprehensiveness of their impact on the stability of our existence that catastrophes often reveal the deeper social grammar of people as we search for reasons for these events and for their meaning. We seek context for events that seem so out of context to our daily lives, even though such a search may never be entirely successful because, suggests anthropologist and disaster expert Susanna Hoffman, "No matter if the disaster stems from nature or from errant technology, no one, neither sage nor scientist, preacher nor president, can wholly tell the why or the where of a calamitous event" (2002, p. 113). Yet, we persist in attempting to write the why and wherefore of events that have taken place on a larger scale than we may be able to comprehend because, "without language, nothing can be shown" (Blanchot, 1995, p. 10).

Even if words may never be enough to address the true impact and scope of catastrophe, those events are still personally traumatic and deeply significant to us and so, individually and as a community, we typically find ourselves searching for ways by which to convey meanings beyond the scope of words. Consequently, "the belief systems of people experiencing or expecting calamity are rife with symbols dealing with their situation, and their cosmologies are vibrant with metaphor" (Hoffman, 2002, p. 113). Such tropes of catastrophe illuminate the event in the cultural mind, where they can act as a form of catharsis: a method of psychological survival for that society. "Literature of trauma is written from the need to tell and re-tell the story of traumatic experience," explains Kali Tal, "to make it 'real' both to the victim and to the community. Such writing serves as validation and cathartic vehicle for the traumatized" (1996, p. 21). Society recognizes and validates these experiences by telling and re-telling the story of them, and so it gives the catastrophe a reality of substance, shape, and remembrance that people can use as a focal point for the release of catharsis in an attempt to render the catastrophic unknown as known and so cope with it.

In remembering by telling the story, people seek to incorporate that event into the woven fabric of society. That story may take the form of a ceremonial story, for example, that is ritually re-enacted at regular periods to reinforce the significance of the event in cultural history. Survivors of the event may physically meet on the anniversary of the event to participate in public memorial ceremonies; they might erect shrines or monuments, or write poetry or prose by way of commemoration in the hope that the catastrophe might be explained and contextualized for the society on which it impacted and also, perhaps, for others outside that society. Ultimately, people seek the revelation of the apocalypse that will answer their questions about why their house and their street and their way of life was destroyed and, perhaps above all, they want to know why people died while they lived. If only they can find the right symbol, the right name, the right book or poem or word, then all those questions that have no answers will be encapsulated in something by which they will be able to grasp the meaning of it all. Naming the wind and the storm is an example of attempting to find that means by which the intangible can become tangible, by which the invisible can be made visible. Names play an important part in shaping our understanding of our environment, and by naming weather events such as cyclones, or hurricanes or typhoons, we attempt to not only identify them meteorologically, but we attempt to understand them culturally. As Queenslanders have interacted with cyclone names over the years in conversation, the media, and in literature, we have attached cultural associations, personal characteristics, histories, and expectations to them. In the next chapter, we will look more closely at naming because it is an important aspect of how we perceive and conceptualize them in our minds. As we do so, we distinguish the cyclone from other hazards of nature in that it becomes more than a name: it becomes an individual entity in our imagination.

In Dorothy Scarborough's remarkable 1925 American novel *The Wind*, air exerts an influence on the realm of the mind so tangibly that it becomes one of the story's characters, as well as being a primeval and ultimately irresistible natural force, reminiscent of the characterization George R. Stewart would give his storm Maria sixteen years later. "The wind was the cause of it all," Scarborough declares. "The sand, too, had a share in it, and human beings were involved, but the wind was the primal force, and but for it the whole series of events would not have happened" (1979, p. 1). Although settlers on the Texas plains in Scarborough's novel have sought to tame and reduce the power of the ever-present wind by planting trees and building houses, that wind resists as a force of nature demanding respect. It retains an animal power Scarborough likens to that of a legendary black stallion with hoofs of fire that races over the prairie at night, neighing wildly, "mighty in power, cruel in spirit, more feared than man" (p. 3). Calling to women "like a demon lover" (p. 4), this vengeful wind attempts to wear them down and drive them out, because it is for the women whom men are civilizing the plains. Here, the wind seeks vengeance on Lettie, newly arrived at her brother's homestead from the very different landscape of Virginia. Despite the efforts of her friend Roddy to warn her that the wind will prey on her mind, once Lettie is isolated at the remote homestead, she becomes convinced the wind is specifically seeking her out, determined to destroy her. She slowly succumbs to its insidious invasion of her mind, where it becomes "a force, a pitiless intelligence, as well as a power" that was the "evil mind" behind "all the evil that the sand did" (p. 199). Caught in a storm with Roddy, who offers to help her escape the area, Lettie is intimate with him and then blames it on the wind, claiming that it is deliberately driving her insane. She turns on Roddy and shoots him, but no sooner has she buried the body beneath a sand dune behind the homestead than the wind blows away the sand, threatening to expose the body and her as a killer. Finally, Lettie surrenders to the inevitable, running out into the storm that is calling to her, "borne along by the force of the wind that was at last to have its way with her" (p. 337).

Here the wind is both monster and myth, a primal force of nature in violent conflict with the power of humankind, like tropical cyclones. The wind's power in Scarborough's novel is as much psychological as physical: Lettie's mental decline is intimately associated with place, for it is the un-ending openness of the prairie in its natural form that provides this wind with the space within which to gather a power that in the end Lettie is unable to resist. For coastal Queensland situated on the edge of the vast Pacific Ocean, it is the un-ending open sea that provides the cyclone with the space to gather force and speed and power. While the natural elements of place can be vital and nurturing, implies Scarborough and other writers whose work we will discuss, they may also have the potential to be demonically destructive on a scale that can be difficult to comprehend. Conscious of the difficulty in conceptualizing the scope of nature catastrophes, writers seek a way of relating to such events through tropes because, "When trauma is written as text, it transcends the bounds of the personal. It becomes metaphor" (Kali Tal, 1996, p. 132). Symbols and metaphors are significant when attempting to understand a disaster such as a cyclone because they can be the only way of expressing events so chaotic, so out of the usual realm of experience, so incomprehensible that there is otherwise no way of adequately representing them. Literature incorporating those tropes is, as Chinese-American geographer Yi-Fu Tuan argues, "an articulation of life. It makes some experience visible and public.... Literature could be said, then, to code experience into words" (1976, p. 261). It is through the medium of literature, then, that we can seek to code into words and articulate visibly and publicly those unimaginable experiences such as cyclones.

As writers attempt to comprehend the scope and impact of these experiences, they are attempting an understanding of them that transcends the bounds of the individually personal. This is not an easy task because cyclones are uncontrollable phenomena that do not fit into our assumptions and expectations about ordered, controlled natural environments. Language can be a means by which people seek to grasp and contextualize weather events beyond the scope of their control; language can be a means of restoring order from chaos. As the acts of creating words, names, images, and meaning reinforce the connection of the weather event to place, they also reinforce the ownership of the event: it is not merely a cyclone that occurs in Far North Queensland, for example, but a Far North Queensland cyclone. This cyclone impacts on this particular place in a particular way because of its atmospheric conditions, weather conditions, geographic location and even the topography unique to this place, and so in a sense it "belongs" to the place. While the cyclone may destroy that place, at the same time it is part of it and confirms the identity of that place in the minds of the people in it. The language, literature and trope of that cyclone, like that of any nature catastrophe, become integrated over time into the very existence, fabric and life of the place because the trope is an important means by which people are able to conceptualize, contextualize, and integrate the nature catastrophe into the place. In linking the individual to the place, these literary elements encourage a sense of belonging: a sense of *terroir*. Without it, we wander lost in a place where we cannot conceptualize and contextualize that which befalls us and in which, consequently, we cannot find meaning. Although Blanchot (1986) argues that writing about the disaster is "the limit of writing," so much so that it "de-scribes" rather than describes (p. 7), he still affirms that "one must just write—in uncertainty and in necessity" (p. 11), for "it is dark disaster that brings the light" (p. 7).

People, Place and Self

The English philosopher John Locke proposed in his 1689 *An Essay Concerning Human Understanding* that a person was a thinking being capable of reason and reflection who was aware of the input from their senses and from their perceptions. Locke argued that it was this combination of thinking and consciousness that formed the individual self: an awareness of personal identity by which we as thinking, conscious human beings distinguish ourselves from others. This perception of self is related to time and memory, he argued, for to be conscious is to be aware of the past. We perceive that with which we come into sensory contact, he argued, and then consider those perceptions in relation to ourselves in time. In this way, we become temporally aware of who we are, not only as a result of present action but also as a product of past memory which, with perception, becomes "part of our selves: i.e., of our thinking conscious self" (Locke, 1984, p. 336). It was this conscious awareness of self and thus of personal identity that "makes a Man be himself to himself," Locke argued, and so "personal Identity depends on that only" (p. 336). Locke did not consider that identity might in some way be related to place, which he saw simply as a constant geographical point in relation to other points. Place, he declared, was "made by men, for their common use, that by it they might be able to design the particular Position of Things" (p. 170). It was plain, he declared, "That our idea of place is nothing else but such a Relative Position of anything" (p. 171).

During the late twentieth century, however, opinion changed about this point of view as various writers argued that there is more to place than being just a geographical location: there are in fact relationships between person and place. Geographical and social philosophers such as Edward Relph in his *Place and Placelessness* (1976) and Yi-Fu Tuan in *Space and Place* (1977) both emphasize the experiential aspects of place—place as experienced by human beings—rather than place being merely a geographical feature, and they argue that we are the product of place and the environment in which we live and that human awareness of self is closely connected to our experience of place.

"Place has human context," according to theologist James M. Houston. "Place implies belonging. It establishes identity.... Place is filled with memories of life that provide roots and give direction" (1978, p. 226). Place and self, rather than being separate, are in fact "essential to the being of the other," argues philosopher Edward Casey in *Getting Back into Place*. "In effect, there is no place without self and no self without place" (2001, p. 684). Place is more than a matter of geography: whether virtual, actual or imagined, place is constitutive of one's sense of self.

The relationship of self with actual place, in fact, can be strengthened by its relationship with imagined or virtual place because, "place is not only what is fleetingly observed in the landscape, a locale or setting for activity and social interaction. It is also what takes place ceaselessly, what contributes to history in a specific context through the creation and utilization of a physical setting" (Agnew, 1993, pp. 262–3). In being part of this "ceaseless" activity related to a locale, people develop through that creation and utilization, a "felt sense of the quality of life at a particular time and place." In short, they develop a "sense of place" that "reinforces the social-spacial definition of place from inside" (Agnew, 1993, p. 263). Place, then, can also be internalized; it can be a concept, a perception, a memory, or a product of imagination. While it always may be related in some way to the physical, a place may never actually be perceived physically or even be physical: it may be a place entirely within a person's mind but it remains, nevertheless, a place with which a person may have the same vivid and personal relationship as with a physical place.

The self may actually stand to gain by being able to move between places, whether physical or imagined, and perceive its relationship to and within those places. In answering the question of what connects the self to places, Edward Casey adopts Pierre Bourdieu's term *habitus* as a term for the connection point between nature and culture, consciousness and body, memory and imagination that constitutes the experience of place, the meeting place between lived and imagined place and geographical self. From that word, Casey then derives *habitudes* to describe our behaviors in that place that result from the quality of our experience in it (1993, p. 686). *Habitus* is, of course, linked to time and history in that we have various experiences associated with places during the course of one's life that may differ over time in terms of maturity, education and memory, for example. Those experiences, lodged within our memory, prompt attitudes or behaviors, *habitudes*, that collate to form the self, and so there is a reciprocity between self and place. We act on the basis of *habitus*: if the connection or relationship between self and place is positive, then our *habitude* is positive which reinforces the relationship, the *habitus*.

In other words, if we like the place, we want to stay there and inhabit it. As Casey contends, "The activation of habitus expresses an intentional and invested commitment to the place-world" (1993, p. 687). We make real our active commitment to place by inhabiting it, by establishing a psychological relationship as well as a physical one. The Latin root of inhabit is *habere*, to have or possess or to hold, and so to inhabit a place is to physically and mentally be in that place, to be holding it within one's purview. Place is not merely physical location; place is that which is also perceived and conceived in body and in mind, that which is actively lived in and experienced. Philosopher Martin Heidegger uses the word *dasein*, broadly translated as "being there" or "being in," to describe the relationship between people and place as "a relationship of dwelling—of inhabitation—in which there is a continuity between person and place": for him, being is "being-in-the-world" (Creswell, 2015, p. 27).

Evidently, experience of place can be a broad concept. Our lives are not necessarily limited to specific places, but are also "through, around, to and from them, from and to places elsewhere." One is not so much in the world but of the world, travelling through the world rather than across it, establishing during our lives a network or aggregate of places—what Casey refers to as "their intertangled skein" (1993, p. 689)—that form a broader personal landscape as much of the senses and the imagination as of rocks and dirt (Ingold, 2011, p. 148). Place is more than that in which we stand; it can also be that which is personally seen, felt, remembered, and experienced, as Marcel Proust demonstrated in his epic work *À la recherche du temps perdu [In Search of Lost Time]* (1913–1927) in which memory of place plays such a vital role.

Person, place, and the broader landscape interact as part of the co-relationship between *habitus* and *habitude*: place may be shaped by people, but people can be shaped by place. (Malpas, 2011, p. 17). That relationship with place is a fusion of function, feeling and meaning that professor of landscape architecture Anne Whiston Spirn argues can be expressed as a language of landscape that is derived from the mental shaping of it as well as the physical (1998, p. 3, 8). John Brinkerhoff Jackson, one of the great writers on the forces that have shaped the American landscape, maintains that in reading and comprehending this language, person and place mutually interact and in this way a bond forms between them, for places are not just a matter of aesthetics: they are also about sensory experiences of a familiar place that may include the "special kind of weather found nowhere else" (1980, p. 16). Commonalities of these experiences can be shared between groups of people, thus establishing communal bonds with places that can be psychological as well as physical. What such thinkers as Spirn, Jackson and Ingold are referring to here is a semiotics of place: place can signify deep emotion and connections for people who may have similar experiences, memories and stories of that place, and so they speak and mutually understand the language of that place.

In German, for example, the language roots for building, dwelling and "I am" are the same: we are because we dwell. Words such as the Danish *landskab*, German *landschaft*, Dutch *landschap*, and English "landscape" combine concepts of land as place and land as people, with *skabe* or *schaffen* meaning "to shape," as in the English "ship" as used in "partnership" and the Dutch *schappen* meaning to "materially shape" in the sense of Biblical Creation. Much of this original linguistic association between word and an active relationship with place was largely lost when "landscape" was assimilated into English from the Dutch as a painting term, *landskip*, referring to a framed representation of the countryside as seen by the artist (Schama, 1996, p. 10; Spirn, 1998, 16–17).

However, to see landscape as mere scenery gives precedence to appearance and risks trivializing it as decoration, as "landscaping." There is more to landscape as place than scenery because, as Spirn argues, it can also be an expression of ideas and actions that encourages an understanding of landscape as place, "as a continuum of meaning" (1998, p. 24). Rather than being a fixed point of view, landscape as place can be perceived as a concept that is continuously developing, fluent and malleable. We who inhabit it can shape its meaning in various ways, forming it as a *landschap* in which words are integral to place, as those words form meanings that in turn shape the people. To be open to such interactive meanings, though, we must be actively involved with place mentally as well as physically, such as through writing and reading about it, as every experience can be both an expression and a perception of our relationship to that place. "We have held these two things dear, landscape and memory," writes Barry Lopez.

> Each infuses us with a different kind of life. The one feeds us, figuratively and literally. The other protects us from lies and tyranny. To keep landscapes intact and the memory of them, our history in them, alive, seems as imperative a task in modern time as finding the extent to which individual expression can be accommodated before it threatens to destroy the fabric of society [1998, p. 143].

People and place should be considered in a holistic sense. We "cannot be understood as separate from the natural world" because we are "entwined with the natural world in a continuing process of co-creation" (Zapf, 2009, p. 190). The product of that process is a unique dynamic connection between place and people by which they form a particular relationship with that place, a relationship expressed in a language. Such a language, according to Spirn, may not be composed of only words. It might be spoken, written, read, or imagined (1998, p. 15); it might be a language of art, such as sculpture or painting, or music, or it could simply be a mutually agreed perception of what it means to be part of that particular place. In this way, we may be in place but also of place. Place can be a point on a map, but it can be a point within a landscape of memory or even a landscape of the imagination, urban or rural, village or city.

Such a dynamic perception enables place to "speak" both *of* us and *to* us. Spirn goes as far as to claim, in fact, that such a dialogue between humanity and landscape was the original language people learned as they evolved on the earth under the sky among plants and animals. It has *always* been present, she argues; everyone still carries the legacy of that original language people had to learn in order to survive. Clouds, wind and sun were clues to weather that could impact directly on one's life: being able to find a cave meant shelter, and navigating a river in the right place at the right time would ensure communication and continued existence (1998, p. 15). Riverboat pilot Samuel Clemens, better known as the great American writer Mark Twain, recognized that legacy of place-language when he observed of the river he was navigating in his *Old Times on the Mississippi* (1876) that "[t]he face of the water, in time, became a wonderful book." "It was a book that told its mind to me without reserve," he wrote, "delivering its most cherished secrets as clearly as if it uttered them with a voice. And it was not a book to be read once and thrown aside, for it had a new story to tell every day.... There never was so wonderful a book written by man" (1967, p. 26). Here, Twain is conscious of the dynamic relationship between himself and place, implying that he can read its language and understand its secrets as if it were a constantly changing story. In the same sense that Spirn claims understanding a relationship with place was essential to early people's survival, Twain learned to read the constantly changing pattern of hidden banks, snags, currents and bends of the Mississippi in order to successfully navigate the river. In other words, in order to maintain his relationship with place, Twain developed an on-going interactive relationship with the language of that place. While place may be a point of origin because everybody comes from somewhere, place is also where we are personally and currently, in our language and literature as well as geographically.

Sense of Place and Terroir

Ever since the ancient Greeks stamped amphorae containing foodstuffs with the seal of the region from which they came, the producers of goods such as wine, coffee, tea and cheese have recognized the existence of a regional alchemy that the French termed *terroir*: the combination of plant genetics with elements such as geography, geology, mineral compounds, soil quality and climate that imparts particular characteristic qualities to a product of that region. Like good wine and cheese, literature too can be permeated and characterized by *terroir* in that the very land on which and in which the literature is created and developed nourishes it and imparts unique qualities to that literature, imbuing it with a sense of regional place. More than the sum of its elements, place is not just a geographic location. It is "space imbued with meaning" (Vanclay, 2008, p. 3), such as the meaning inherent in our relationship with the weather.

Ultimately, it is these relationships between us and the elements of a region, whether that region be local or national, that create the meanings that give place its "sense." That sense of place can be individualized as well as nationalized, for the meaning of place is unique to the memory, history and association of the individual as well as the community. It is "the coming together of the biophysical, social and spiritual worlds. Simply put, place is space that is special to someone" (Vanclay, 2008, p. 3). For North Queenslanders, their sense of place includes the cyclones that have historically and continuously affected the individuals and the communities of that region. Because of their relationship with these tropical weather patterns, their place is a space special to them, and such affiliations can run deeper than connections to earth, rock and tree. Geologist and wine *terroir* expert James E. Wilson maintains that beyond the tangible habitat there is a "spiritual aspect that recognizes the joys, the heartbreaks, the pride, the sweat, and the frustrations of its history" (2001, p. 141). As Zapf professed earlier, our relationship with place extends to the air and water around us that constitutes, as Jackson argued, a "special kind of weather found nowhere else" that is an integral part of a familiar place, a special place. Our place. Our *terroir*.

Weather is part of that *terroir* because, "Weather is written into our landscape" (Harris, 2015, p. 9). We mutually constitute our weather into our intimate, interactive perception of place because, argues Zapf, "We cannot view the environment as something separate from and distinctly outside ourselves. The environment is part of us and we are part of it. Air and water are inside as well as outside our bodies" (2009, p. 71). Humanity may shape place, but so does wind and water and temperature. Our relationship with place is intimate for, "To inhabit the open is … to be immersed in the incessant movements of wind and weather" (Ingold, 2011, p. 121). Like any intimate relationship in which one is involved, we draw our meaning from place and place draws its meaning from us because our body and our place "are the effective epicenters of the geographical self" (Casey, 1993, p. 690).

We are centered in our minds, in our imagination, around a perception of our place-world in which our body exists, and the weather of place is fundamental to this perception because we do not so much perceive place but perceive *in* place. We see sunshine, hear rain, and feel snow; to live, we breathe air. We and our place are immersed in fluxes of weather within which we engage with each other as, "we breathe, think and dream in the regions of the air" (David Macauley, in Ingold, 2011, p. 135). Ultimately, "the wind is not so much embodied as the body enwinded" (Ingold, p. 139). As physical human beings, we are not merely surrounded by air: as living beings, we are *in* air, breathing it, taking air inside us to literally become an essential component of who we are. Without it, we could not be. Our breath and the wind are intimately related: inhalation is wind become breath and exhalation is breath become wind. Queensland poet Susan Hawthorne recognized this relationship in the aftermath of Cyclone Larry when she wrote: "I am in with through the cyclone/which is inside with through me" (2009, p. 78). As she so vividly understands, we exist in a weather world that is within us as well as without. It is part of our relationship with ourselves as well as with the world around us. Weather is part of *who* we are, as well as *where* we are.

Nevertheless, our perception of weather is largely a perception of its effects. We can see clouds but not touch them. We can feel the wind but not see it. We see what the wind *does*, rather than what it *is*, understanding places "through the marks the wind has made on them" (Harris, 2015, p. 9). In order to understand our relationship with weather as part of our place, then, we need to search for signs and clues of it in that place because weather is part of the language of our *terroir*. We as writers respond to weather using the words, images and tropes of that language as we attempt to understand and interpret in literature their cultural relationship to their place. "Literature endows common experience with significance," Spirn argues, and so as we respond to writers' interpretations, weather becomes integral and significant to our cultural perception of place (1998, p. 80). In this way, the literature of cyclone weather invites people in Queensland who have shared the cyclone experience to consider and respond to the significance of that experience as part of their cultural perception of their place, a perception that has always been important.

In *The Bible*'s Book of Job, God asks Job from within a cyclonic storm some profound questions that relate to his cultural perceptions of weather's origin and function. "Have you entered the storehouses of the snow, or have you seen the storehouses of the hail, which I have reserved for the time of trouble, for the day of battle and war?" God queries, before continuing to propose some of the most enduring questions in literature:

> What is the way to where the light is distributed, or where the east wind is scattered upon the earth? Who has cleft a channel for the torrents of rain, and a way for the thunderbolt, to bring rain on a land where no man is, on the desert in which there is no man; to satisfy the waste and desolate land, and to make the ground put forth grass? Has rain a father, or who has begotten the drops of dew? [Job 38: 22–28].

These questions are of course rhetorical: Job (and the reader) is expected to know that the answer to "who" will always be God. There is more to these questions than a single-word answer, though, for they are also intended to remind us of our relationship to nature as place. Rain, wind, light, and storms are all part of the weather, but these are elements over which we have no control. We have to accept, this passage suggests, that there might always be questions about nature and place for which there are no absolute answers.

Indeed, the power of weather as part of place lies in its potential to not only physically "be," but also to symbolize and evoke. It can be both tangible entity and metaphor: spring as life or winter as death, for example. While we can really only fully comprehend the force and feel of wind and weather by being in it, our appreciation of them can be enhanced through word and image which are then intermingled with our physical sensory response. In this way, we are constantly re-creating and re-imagining the weather. In *Paradise Lost*, for example, variations in the weather come about as a divine penalty when God punishes Adam and Eve (and future humanity) after Eve yields to temptation. Milton's pre–Fall Eden has a uniform temperate climate, but in the aftermath of Adam and Eve's fall from grace, the Divine Being employs his angels to alter the orbit of the sun in order to create temperature zones, introduces thunder as an instrument of terror, and sets the winds to "their corners, when with bluster to confound/Sea, air, and shore." Neither had there been any seasons, but God now bids the angels to physically push "oblique the centric globe ... to bring in change/Of seasons to each clime," and the effect is that,

> These changes in the heavens, though slow, produced
> Like change on sea and land—sideral blast,
> Vapor, and mist, and exhalation hot,
> Corrupt and pestilent....
> And snow, and hail, and stormy gust and flaw [1951, pp. 248–9, ll.651–706].

In Milton's imagination, weather has a moral dimension. Seasonal variations are not just a matter of meteorology and geography; they are the result of the fall of humanity into a state of sin. For Milton, the physical environment was a product of the spiritual environment.

In *Orlando*, on the other hand, Virginia Woolf uses weather imaginatively to evoke historic eras. On the last night of the eighteenth century, for example, Orlando leans out from the window of her London home amid "light, order, and serenity." As she watches, a small cloud gathers behind the dome of St. Paul's and rapidly spreads across the sky as the chimes of midnight begin to sound. By the eleventh chime, "a huge blackness sprawled over the whole of London," and by midnight a "turbulent welter of cloud covered the city. All was darkness; all was doubt; all was confusion. The Eighteenth-century was over; the Nineteenth century had begun." By daybreak, the cloud extends over the entire British Isles, and consequently the air becomes saturated with rain, damp seeps into buildings, people become cold, beards are grown, clothes secured tightly, furniture is covered, and ivy encouraged by rain grows profusely. As the climate changes, "stealthily and imperceptibly ... the constitution of England was altered" (Woolf, 1993, pp. 156–7).

Just as Woolf uses the characteristically gloomy weather of England to evoke place, Queensland author Thea Astley uses cyclones, an iconic element of tropical Queensland weather, to not only evoke a specific locale but to speak to the broader meaning of the relationship between person and place, between *habitus, habitude* and habitant. In her novels *A Boat Load of Home Folk* (1986), *It's Raining in Mango* (1989), and *The Multiple Effects of Rainshadow* (2010), the storm reveals the true nature of characters trapped within whirling vortexes of circumstances, teetering on the edges of their own personal cyclones. "Weather is one of the most powerful threads holding us together," Harris suggests (2015, p. 12), and weather interacts with person as part of the language of landscape in literature. In seeking an understanding of the tropical cyclone as part of that literary language of North Queensland place, we need to understand that place as tropical place.

Queensland as Tropical Place

Historically, we have perceived the temperate and tropical zones differently. The tropical zone has been traditionally characterized as the uninhibited, violent and primitive foil to the civilized and cultivated nature of the temperate. "It is to the inhabitants of the temperate zone," declared the otherwise enlightened naturalist, explorer, and philosopher Alexander von Humboldt in 1849,

> that the rest of mankind owes the earliest revelation of an intimate and rational acquaintance with the forces governing the physical world. Moreover, it is from the same zone (which is apparently more favourable to the progress of reason, the softening of manners, and the security of public liberty), that the germs of civilisation have been carried to the regions of the tropics [p. 15].

European imaginative engagement with the tropics has, over time, embraced the differences in perception. On the one hand, the tropics has been perceived as a place of paradise, where there could be, "A long sweeping curve of coast, fringed with tall plumed palms casting wavering shadows on the yellow sand as they sway and swish softly to the breath of the of the brave trade-wind that whistles softly through the thickly-verdured hummocks on the weather side of the island" (Becke, 2005, p. 228). On the other hand, tropical weather can seem like a hell where, "The rage and volume of that avalanche [of rain] one must have lived in the tropics to conceive; a man panted in its assault, as he might pant under a shower-bath; and the world seemed whelmed in night and water" (Stevenson, 1996, 17). On the one hand, the tropics has been perceived as a golden Eldorado of light; on the other, it is Joseph Conrad's *Heart of Darkness* (1899) inhabited by Mr. Kurtz sent mad by the jungle, a darkness that was then brought full circle back to Europe when William Booth extended Humboldt's analogy by likening the supposedly "civilized" living conditions of urban, industrial nineteenth-century England to those within the tropical jungle. "The Equatorial Forest traversed by Stanley resembles that Darkest England of which I have to speak, alike in its vast extent…; its monotonous darkness, its malaria and its gloom, its dwarfish, de-humanized inhabitants, the slavery to which they are subjected, their privations and their misery," Booth thundered in his 1890 work *In Darkest England and the Way Out* (p. 12).

Typically, North Queensland as imagined and envisioned tropical place has been perceived by writers in those same dualities of light and dark. For some, their experience is in terms of intensities of light and beauty. Australian science journalist Rosaleen Love writes in *Reefscape* that her experience on the Great Barrier Reef encouraged her to explore different perceptions of her relationship to beauty and to place. "From 'sense of wonder' at the beauty of reef life," she maintains, "it is a small step to the notion of the 'sense of the sublime,' the sense that here is something so wonderful that it transcends the existence of the individual caught up in this particular time and place" (2000, p. 222). Even if one is not a believer in a traditional God and thus does not feel a sense of awe in religious terms or that the "other-worldly nature of the reef experience is a glimpse of Paradise," she argues, "the beauty of the reef allows the non-believer imaginative space to take the notion of 'awe' seriously." In fact, she claims, diving on the reef actually changes one's perception of their place in the universe because, "Going underwater is a view from the bottom up," instead of the more customary view of life from "the privileged position of air-dwellers" (p. 223). Writing about her time living on Green Island, offshore from Cairns, writer and critic Nettie Palmer enthused that "[t]his gleaming little forest of vines and evergreens can seem at times more wonderful than the coral reef itself. There's a gentleness about it…" She was entranced by the "immense apparent nothingness of sea and sky" (1988, p. 82), and by "endless, subtle rich colours" of coral that caused "your eyes to swim with the heavenly tones" (p. 92). North Queensland is a place where the days are so rich in sensation that one can actually taste them, according to Thea Astley, who once described a tropical day as "a juicy fruit, warm, dripping with frangipani and an overlying tang of salt" (1993a, p. 215).

For others, however, such as journalist Robert Reid, an edgier North Queensland tropics can be, "a moody place, a canvas of wild beauty and drama, where exotic landscapes huddle together, juxtaposed in strange patterns as if they don't belong, yet exist as if for some mysterious, unknown purpose." To him, the ancient regional landscapes defy the usual perceptions of the tropical, varying between mountain ranges and rainforests to extensive savannah grasslands, delta mangrove wetlands inhabited by crocodiles and wild pigs, and many kilometers of white sand coastline. This is a place where destructive forces of "primeval nature," such as monsoon rains, floods, and cyclonic winds, constitute part of the tropical year, "the season of drama and danger," and so it is a place where "life blooms large and vibrant, but death strikes quickly, returning physical existence to the earth with savage finality" (2003, Introduction). The tropics can be a place of difference where beauty, danger and death co-exist.

The tropical place imagined by Queensland-born author Janette Turner Hospital is no heart of darkness for, "In the Sunshine State, we resist shadow," she claims. "We don't believe in darkness" (2011, p. 218). Nevertheless, some of the shadows of her childhood *terroir* lurk within Hospital's fiction. She characteristically structures her work as lantana-like puzzles in which the time scheme and narrative are fragmented and out of sequence, enticing readers to make their way into them as explorers in order to discover meaning. They are, according to critic David Callahan, "rainforest narratives" in which the "profusion and entanglements of the rainforest serve as a model for Hospital's fictional strategies" (2009, p. 2). Her characters become entangled in webs and nettings of association that "both invites symbolic exploration and confounds it," he argues, "just as the rainforest's exuberance can invite physical exploration and confound it" (p. 3). In Hospital's fictional tropical place, many of her characters inhabit a remembered, imagined Queensland. In her story, "You Gave Me Hyacinths," for example, it is "the pungent and fertile tropical landscape that suggests to Hospital the intertwined complexity of the world" (p. 112). The opening sentences of this story are some of the most evocative imaginings of landscape in any story set in North Queensland:

> Summer comes hot and steamy, with the heavy smell of raw sugar to the north-east coast of Australia. The cane pushes through the rotting window blinds and grows into the cracks and corners of the mind. It ripens in the heart at night, and its crushed sweetness drips into dreams [Hospital, 1995c, p. 15].

One of the ironies of this story, however, is that this richness is not reflected in the lives of the inhabitants but, instead, it is reflected in the unique Cooktown orchids.

Hospital's tropical landscape is an active example of the unruly and tangled moral universe of her characters but is also often evocative of loss. Her Queensland place is a homeland that Hospital left behind in order to live overseas and to which she frequently returns in her prose as a landscape of memoir, a "site of narrative and moral intensity in which both loss and gain, displacement and engagement are referenced" (Callahan, 2009, p. 135). Perhaps the one work of hers in which these elements are best collected is "Litany for the Homeland," in which she considers the connections and networks between places. "Where the St Lawrence is still mostly skating rink but part flow," she writes, "I have smelled and touched Queensland. I have woken, disoriented, to see orchids in snowdrifts.... I have smelled rainforest" (1995a, p. 422). Hospital recognizes that, as Ingold suggests, our lives ebb and flow "from and to places elsewhere" and so she perceives that "Queensland itself is fluid in shape and size, it ebbs and flows and refuses to be anchored in space.... It is always larger than would appear on the map." Her *terroir*, "where the evening star goes down, and where the first ones and the late-comers make temporary camp together under the violent stars," will always be part of her, will always be her. "Wherever I am," she believes, "I live in Queensland" (p. 422).

In that encounter between tropic environment and the senses, there is an intersection of what is known and what can be represented. "The tropics" as larger place is, in turn, a network of smaller places that are tropical in their own unique way, and human beings inhabit and represent these places according to their diverseness or similarity. The tropical North Queensland landscape is a unique place, whether envisioned by those within it or outside of it. As the American Deep South is different from the rest of the United States, tropical North Queensland is different from the rest of Australia. Yet, it can exert a magnetic attraction just by virtue of that difference and uniqueness, as it did for writer David Malouf, for whom it was the very fact that there was "a place that was uncontrolled and uncontrollable that first attracted me and attracts me still." After all, he asks,

> Isn't that what is meant by exotic? A hope that somewhere close there was a place that belonged to us and that was in a sense ours, but that had escaped the laws and the interpretations we like to impose and remained unknown within us. Darkly mysterious. Overgrown and hard to find our way into. Not yet mapped or fully described. Where we, too, when we entered it, might become other and unknown, even to ourselves [2014, p. 77].

As this kind of unique, exotic, tropical place with the power to transform people, North Queensland reveals Australian cultural uniformity to be a myth, perhaps suggesting that it might be time to forget likeness and instead be more inclusive of the many varieties of difference that Australians now exhibit.

North Queensland as a region incorporates that sense of difference into its very *habitus* so completely that in Hospital's story, "The Second Coming of Come-by-Chance," a reporter for the Melbourne *Age* newspaper wonders if indeed Queensland actually exists or if it is just a primitive state of mind from which most people have evolved, "our own Gothic invention, a kind of morality play, the Bosch canvas of the Australian psyche, a sort of perpetual

One. The Cyclone Written into the Language of Place   35

memento mori that points to the frailty of the skein of civilization reaching out so tentatively from our southern cities" (1995b, p. 220). Thea Astley, who was a great admirer of authors of the American South such as Flannery O'Connor, James Faulkner, Carson McCullers and Truman Capote, suggested that like them, "I'm very interested in people outside the mainstream" (Richey, 1986, p. 92). She proposed in her essay "Being a Queenslander," that it is, in fact, a similar sense to that which they had of being different from the rest of the country that distinguishes the Queensland cultural landscape. It is a sense of difference, she argues, that has developed over the years for various reasons, such as, "the isolation of the place, the monstrous distances, the very genuine suspicions of political neglect" (Astley, 1976, p. 252). Associated with those factors is a refusal to conform. The architecture does not duplicate that of the rest of the country, for example, with its "houses perched on stilts like teetering swamp birds," seemingly designed for occupants to live underneath them (p. 252). Some of these differences are not as apparent now as they were when the essay was written, but argumentatively they are still buried in the Queensland psyche. Nevertheless, as Astley observed, Queenslanders do still dress differently and their manners are laconic in tune with the high temperatures of the tropics. In fact, some of these tropical differences were observed as early as 1893 by a newspaper journalist who, in an article titled, "A Northern Pilgrimage," observed that "there are no people in the world who are more sanguine than those of North Queensland. Nothing crushes or daunts them. Out from every disaster they rise serenely and hopefully." These attitudes must be primarily due to the tropical weather, the reporter suggests for, "It is almost impossible to be otherwise in a land of blue sky and white light. Day after day the sun shines in unclouded vigour and its brightness and intensity creates, and perpetuates an optimistic spirit.... Under all circumstances, it is necessary to keep a stiff upper lip." Much like David Malouf, this journalist concluded that "[l]ife up here is freedom itself." (p. 750).

Yet freedom can imprison and constant beauty can eventually overwhelm and even seem dangerous. To the Antiguan-American novelist and essayist Jamaica Kincaid, for example, the Caribbean island of Antigua is,

> too beautiful. Sometimes the beauty of it seems unreal. Sometimes the beauty of it seems as if it were stage sets for a play ... all of this is so beautiful, all of this is not real like any other real thing there is. It is as if, then, the beauty ... were a prison, and as if everything and everybody inside it were locked in and everything and everybody that is not inside were locked out. And what might it do to ordinary people ... to live in such heightened, intense surroundings day after day? [2000, pp. 77–79].

The British writer Alec Waugh, elder brother of Evelyn, having "been told that so many things are dangerous in the tropics," agreed in his *Hot Countries* (1930, p. 98) that when it came to people living in such tropical surroundings, the tropics could actually be its own worst enemy. Tahiti, he wrote, suffered from, "The fatal gift of beauty," and was consequently betrayed to the invasion of European society "by her loveliness, her own sweetness, her own gentleness" (p. 73). In his novel of life on the Queensland Gold Coast, *A Night at the Pink Poodle* (1995), Matthew Condon's protagonist looks down on the city from a helicopter and senses the same danger of that fatal gift lurking within the paradise below him. His sense of insecurity increases as he marvels at "how watery the whole place was, how precarious." The buildings are just "tenuously stacked on fingers of what were nothing more than strips and nodules of sand" (p. 101). Abruptly aware that the level of the sea would only have to rise slightly for it to wash all this away, he now perceives the canals as a threat, the surf as "a killer in waiting," and the Nerang River as a serpent. "Perhaps it was what made the coast so mad," he decides. "Here it was, teetering on the edge of the Pacific, leaning towards the sea" (p. 101). As an island continent, all of Australia leans towards the sea, towards the coast where most of the population lives, and Queensland along with it. Janet Turner Hospital places Queensland in perspective: "The world spins in the margins of space. Australians float in the edges of the world. Queenslanders live in the rind of Australia" (1995a, p. 422).

For many Queenslanders, although certainly not all, place is coastal place: littoral place. No other nation except Russia looks out onto three great oceans as Australia does. This country is, as the national anthem suggests, "girt by sea": the Pacific Ocean, the Southern Ocean and the Indian Ocean. The continent is bounded by some 36,700 km of coastline, which includes approximately 10,685 beaches and 1800 islands (Huntsman, 2001, 5). While Australia has traditionally celebrated "the bush" in its eternal, desperate search for lasting stereotypes of "Australian-ness," it was in fact the coast which in the early decades of settlement was the focus of trade, exploration, transport, industry and encounter, and in many ways it remains so. "The littoral is a place of encounter, where new waves must reconcile with old waves, where things can flow in two directions at once," maintain Australian literature researchers Sue and Rick Hosking (2009, p. vii). However, by the latter part of the nineteenth century, the bush of the country's interior had taken on significance in the minds and hearts of Australian writers and there was relative indifference to the coast and beach. As the nation's sense of self emerged and developed during that period, it was the idea of the bushman pioneer as a national type that became influential. The pervasive presence of the bush led to a view that Australia lay somewhere out west, somewhere that was a different country than the coast, somewhere that had to be tamed, subdued, owned, cultivated, and developed as explorers and pioneers were drawn inland by their expectations of what they could observe and find.

Perceived as a place with no such promise, on which nothing could be built or grown, the coast was left out of the general nation-building until the early twentieth century when it began to develop importance as a place of recreation, of freedom, of physical well-being and, eventually, as a place of communion with nature. Eventually, too, people came to appreciate that it could be occupied, built on and developed, and so the coast became part of the national economy as a community with a particular life-style into which was interwoven and perpetuated those traditional cultural themes of love and desire, loss and death. Whereas the coast as place, where the land ended abruptly at the sea, was previously considered the edge, the margin of Australia, it is now perceived as a significant place of creativity and potential. The edge is being recreated and redefined; the coast is now where things happen, and discoveries are made. "It has now become clear," argues Philip Drew in *The Coast Dwellers*, "that the coast, not the outback, is central to the Australian imagination" (1994, p. xi). It is the coast, he continues, that "replaces the centre as the chief spatial and symbolic focus in our culture" (p. 3). However, at the same time, the coast remains an unpredictable place. It can be a place of license and freedom but it can also be a place that is sinister and threatening: crimes take place on the sand and there are sharks and poisonous jellyfish in the water. The coast is a place of flux: it "never is, is always becoming" (Huntsman, 2001, p. 173). Changing size and shape with wind and wave, the Australian coast is not just leaning towards the sea, but also towards the weather coming in from a sea that is constantly attempting to wash the coast away.

The North Queensland Cyclone

Cyclones are historically endemic to the Australian tropics. A study of sand beach ridges formed by storm surges on the northern Queensland coast carried out by Jonathan Nott, Scott Smithers, Kevin Walsh, and Ed Rhodes (2009) found evidence of the impact of severe tropical cyclones for over 6,000 years. Physical traces of them were immediately apparent to early European visitors. "The marks of such cyclones, and the tracks of tornadoes," observed nineteenth-century explorer and historian Ernest Favenc during his early visits to North Queensland, "were plainly visible in what were then practically virgin coast lands" (1903, p. 7). The earliest recorded cyclone to make landfall in Queensland after European settlement was the storm that in 1854 flattened the tent township that would become Gladstone and sank shipping there. However, "both Bowen and Townsville, during my stay of some 16 or 17 years ... were almost periodically visited and scourged by these visitations," recalled Favenc, who notes that "both these towns lie in a belt peculiarly liable to cyclonic influence," and that cyclones had been particularly prevalent during the 1860s and 1870s (p. 7). Most major towns and cities along the

Two children sitting with a badly damaged piano in the ruins of Port Douglas after the March 16, 1911, cyclone. Two people died and only seven houses were left standing in the town (Collection of John Oxley Library, State Library of Queensland).

Queensland coast, such as Rockhampton, Mackay, Townsville, Cairns, Port Douglas, and Cooktown have at some time been either destroyed or severely damaged by cyclones, some more than once, and the effects of some cyclones have been experienced as far south as Brisbane and into northern New South Wales. Historically, a cyclone was the cause of the largest loss of life to occur in Australia as the result of any nature disaster when Cyclone Mahina—also known as the Bathurst Bay Hurricane—struck the Torres Strait pearling fleet sheltering in Bathurst and Princess Charlotte Bays near Cape Melville, North Queensland on March 4, 1899, killing over 300 people.

North Queenslanders, then, necessarily forged an early, significant, and personal relationship with cyclones as individuals and as a regional community. So integrated have they become into the local coastal culture that the period between November and April is officially declared in the region as the "cyclone season." By their very nature unpredictable, uncontrollable, and ineludible, cyclones are an integral part of tropical Queensland life. In fact, it was a Queensland meteorologist who was the first person to systematically name cyclonic storms, when on September 20, 1894, Clement Wragge, the Queensland Government Meteorologist and Superintendent of the Chief Weather Bureau in Brisbane, gave the name "Beta" to a storm approaching Lord Howe Island. Wragge developed a chain of weather stations from which he gathered data that eventually extended off-shore as far east as New

Caledonia to enable him to detect potential cyclones as soon as possible. The well-read meteorologist then translated this data into forecasts and announcements of meteorological events (including storms and cyclones) full of literary flourishes and allusions published in Australian newspapers, making Wragge the earliest known European Australian to publish cyclone literature, which we'll discuss further in Chapter Two.

By its very nature, the cyclone is unpredictable, uncontrollable and unavoidable. Those who live in North Queensland realize that "cyclone knowledge is by default about the condition of tropical life" (Collet, McDougall, and Thomas, 2017, p. 10), and in order to live that life Queenslanders have historically considered that their duty is not to surrender in the face of such extreme weather. "Our townsmen, however, do not intend to give in," wrote a Cairns journalist after the cyclone of 1878, pointing out that rebuilding work was already underway for, "this sort of thing is of the north. 'Hard work' is the motto for nearly everyone above Cape Palmerston." With no small quota of parochial pride, they added, "We have no idlers; when we want rest, we come amongst you southerners" (Destructive Tornado at Cairns, 1878, p. 3). Those sentiments have not changed over the years. Referring to Cyclone Leonta that had devastated Townsville in 1903, a newspaper journalist reporting on the Mackay cyclone and storm surge flood of 1918 amid chaos "hardly describable in language," wrote that

> what one relates as actual facts must beget a scornful jeer from people who have only seen a strong southerly gale in Sydney. We hear a good deal nowadays of shell-shock. Men who have gone through a tropical cyclone on land realise what that is, but will not be persuaded that any terror that human ingenuity can invent is able to stand comparison for a moment with Nature in a mad mood [North Queensland Cyclone, p. 3].

A local woman echoed similar sentiments in a published letter after the same cyclone, writing, "You southern people can't realise what we pioneers of the North go through" (Chatty Mackay Letter, p. 3). Unlike those people south of the border, tough Queenslanders could survive anything. The Right Reverend George Frodsham, Anglican Bishop of North Queensland, recalled after the 1903 Townsville cyclone that "I was deeply impressed by the fortitude and spirit of the people in Townsville. I never heard a man or woman complain. They were hard at work the next morning trying to gather up the ruins of their homes" (The Townsville Cyclone, p. 6). Elevating the Mackay cyclone event to nobler heights of endurance than mere catastrophe, the editor of the *Cairns Post* made reference to World War I when he declared, "As if there was not already sufficient sorrow in the world, it has pleased destiny to write yet another chapter in the 'Martyrdom of Man'" (The Mackay Disaster, 1918, p. 4). Some ninety years later, after Severe Tropical Cyclone

Larry destroyed Innisfail in 2006, the Head of Operation Recovery Task Force, General Cosgrove, asserted, "I knew that the people of the Far North were built of strong stuff. They proved it yet again after Larry. They took an almighty body blow, but they dusted themselves off and got on with their lives as best they could" (Operation Recovery Task Force Team, 2007, p. 7).

Cyclones are an integral element of the littoral Queensland place and community, where these annual severe weather events are part of the literary place as well as the physical place. Narratives of the Queensland cyclone have become part of the narrative of place, a narrative that is an indigenous force in that it gives a voice to those who live with cyclones. This narrative has become an expression of both a material and a mythic force that might, on the one hand, destroy. On the other hand, however, this narrative is also an expression of a force that can be a tool for survival and point the way to post-disaster restoration, because,

> Narratives of cyclones are not mere records of destruction. They also reveal liminal spaces between ocean and land, the textual and the imagined—spaces of rehabilitation where the cyclones are "heard" and acts of positive human interactions with nature are performed. Literature has the potential to provide a forum for those whose voices (nature's and human's) are not always heard [Ravi, 2017, p. 40].

In providing this forum for those voices, cyclone literature (whether drawn from the imagination or based on fact) becomes part of place. It is a narrative of the *terroir* that can be experienced by the one as well as the many: the *terroir* embedded in the senses and stories of the individual. As those stories are told and re-told, it eventually becomes the *terroir* of the community, for

> in telling stories about our places, we create and re-create; revise and adjust; confirm and re-confirm; affirm and re-affirm our connections to place. Storytelling is a way in which any place becomes "our place" or "our patch" where we assert some authority, or ownership, or at least some connection to a place [Vanclay, 2008, p. 5].

By telling their stories of the cyclone, the communities' connection with *terroir* is reconfirmed and reinforced. Compiling and publishing collections of stories, poems, and art-work by cyclone survivors reminds survivors of their collective and unique bonds with each other and their place. The great spinning wheel of the cyclone as a trope in Queensland literature is about more than the weather; it is about the cycle of life itself.

People and Place Mapped into the Texture and Structure of Stories

Stories are our way of attempting to understand our relationship with this cycle of life, with the people in it and with place. In effect, "we live within worlds of stories, and we use those stories to shape those worlds" (Potteiger and Purinton, 1998, p. 3). Stories tell of origins, causes, and boundaries that may be political, geographical or ethical; they tell of what is known while pointing towards future possibilities and explorations. It is through story "that we embrace the great breadth of memory, that we can distinguish what is true, and that we may glimpse, at least occasionally, how to live without despair in the midst of the horror that dogs and unhinges us" (Lopez, 1998, p. 13). Stories are more than a sequence of events; they offer "patterns of sound and association, of event and image" (Lopez, 1998, p. 13.). They are more than words: they can be an entire sensory experience. Stories have shape, too, and we need to select an appropriate format for the story that will reveal that shape as the story is told, for those patterns are important to meaning. Stories embrace multiple formats such as fiction, non-fiction, lived experience, myth, anecdote, oral history and legend. The story and the format are really a matching pair for which we use the collective term "narrative." Narrative is ultimately a language of time that selects certain events and links them together in a sequence to form a story with a shape. Altering the sequence would alter the shape and thus the meaning of the story, and so meaning resides not in just what is told, but in how it is told. The narratives that are there in that place, that shape people and place, are formed as a product of intersection with places; they accumulate as layers of history, tell of events associated with place, and are thus assimilated into the place and the people. In effect, the interplay between story, narrative, place and people forms an integral part of the *terroir*. As we remember, interpret, plan and dream through such stories and narratives, they give form to our lives.

In this way, both people and place become mapped into the texture and structure of the narrative of place. "Every narrative ... plays a critical role in making place," argues Potteiger and Purinton. "It is through narrative that we interpret the processes and events of place. We come to know a place because we know its stories" (1998, p. 6), and so those stories become integrated into our memory and perception of that place. They are written into place, as it were. For example, we may know a site or visit a location not only because of its association with our own life but because of its association with a film or novel or historical event. Our understanding of that place is then in part because of that association we have or sense, but it is also in part because that location is then enhanced because of that association. For example, when visiting Silverton, out beyond Broken Hill in New South Wales, do we see the beauty of the striking outback scenery, or do we see the place that was a backdrop to the adventures of Mad Max? If we visit Monument Valley in the United States, do we marvel at a remarkable desert vista or do we have in our minds a mental image of John Wayne riding through it? As the superimposition onto place of our experience with film may add to or detract from the quality of our narrative of place, the superimposition of our experience with weather on to place may enhance or detract from our perception of that place narrative.

If a cyclone (or any other nature catastrophe) destroys a town, for example, then that event and the experiences of those caught up in it becomes part of the narrative of that place, just as Mad Max's car parked outside the Silverton hotel or John Ford's Point overlooking Monument Valley have become part of the narrative of respective film locations. The coastal towns of Bowen and Airlie Beach, in North Queensland, will dedicate a memorial in 2020 to mark the fiftieth anniversary of the destruction of their towns and the deaths of fourteen people by Cyclone Ada, and the town of Cardwell further north along the coast has installed a memorial pathway to commemorate the destruction of most of the town and adjacent marina by Cyclone Yasi in 2011. Those memorials will visibly remind residents and visitors that a destructive weather event, a cyclone, is integrated into the story of this place and the people in it. For some of us, however, that story may not be one which we can successfully integrate into our own. It may detract from the narrative of that place so significantly that eventually we might leave that place, never able to live there again. On the other hand, that weather catastrophe may provide an impetus for change in that place, perhaps for an improved lifestyle in a re-built town. It may even lead to changes in warning systems and emergency services. Either way, that place narrative can develop into a very tangible, personal and relative story that not only forms that place but also eventually becomes the individual and the collective place. Every time we walk the streets, we might hear the wind, feel the rain, and sense the fear that is still within us of that traumatic cyclone experience. The weather event has in effect formed us: shaped who we are as individuals. On the other hand, in the aftermath of the cyclone we might collectively celebrate the community's triumph of rebuilding, and so the event can also form the community, shaping who they will be in the future.

In either sense a narrative of place, inclusive of us as a person or as people, develops that in some way binds us to that place, whether we physically remain there or we don't, because human existence is not "fundamentally place-bound ... but place-binding" (Ingold, 2011, p. 148). The lives of people and places unfold along paths that intertwine, maintains Ingold, binding in a knot where they intersect. So, we move through the world rather than across it, tying knots of place woven from lines of movement to form a weave of landscape narratives that contain different meanings for different people: a meaning we have to discover for ourselves. "People do not acquire their knowledge ready-made," he declares, "but rather grow into it, through a process of what might be called re-discovery.... each story will take you so far until you come across another that will take you further" (p. 152). As we learn about and grow into our narrative of place, the better we come to know it in our mind and the greater the depth and clarity of our perception of our environment. "Landscapes of place reflect upon landscapes of the mind," according to James M. Houston. "Land is the palimpsest of human need, desires, meaning, greed and fears" (1978, p. 225). He refers to Paul Tournier's contention that man has a personal need to live in particular places because, "All our experiences, emotions and feelings are indissolubly linked in our memories with places" (p. 227). Our relationship with place is not solely a response to the physically tangible, but is a holistic relationship that consists of everything we incorporate into us, even cyclones.

Ultimately, "whatever place we wish to define as ours is inextricably interconnected with every other place" (Prieto, 2013, p. 179). All places in the world meet up with each other. Any border around the place that we might wish to consider our own is highly permeable, and that home place becomes suffused with, and enriched by, our relationships with other places. Our sense of our place in the connected world is intensified, not only by our exploration of the immediate environment around us, but by a willingness to explore and to look outward into those other places as we experience the ebb and flow of interchange between us and our greater world. These relationships between nature and culture, between people and weather, between language and art, between life and natural environment, are expressed in people's narratives. "Because literary texts operate, for the most part, within the hypothetical, metaphorical register of fiction and poetry," comments Prieto, "they may … change the ways their readers view the world around them, making possible new ways of understanding what is actually there and catalysing new ideas about what might be…. they help to make possible the emergence and establishment of new kinds of places" (p. 9). The relationship between story and place can thus be one of revelation and re-creation. Stories of our place, of the people and the environment of that place, help us understand our relationships with place, people and environment and with the greater world to which we are connected as the stories reveal them to us. In understanding and coping with the challenges of our place that may include catastrophe and chaos as well as order and beauty, apocalypse as well as creation, storm as well as calm, we are at the same time developing our relationships and responses to each other and to our community. Our stories can enable the resilience and continuity of culture during times of catastrophe and in the aftermath, helping to restore balance by reminding us that these are shared experiences. In doing so, our stories develop our understanding of our *terroir*. They are no longer merely about our community and us: they *become* us.

Two

The Naming of the Disaster

>What's in a name?—(*Romeo and Juliet*. Act 2, Sc.II)

Caught up in the shriek and whirl of wind and debris, and the pounding of relentless rain as the cyclone wreaks havoc on your environment, it is easy to feel that the storm is directing its attention at us personally. Being within a cyclonic storm is an intimate, emotional, and personal experience, during which we no longer feel in control of our lives or our destiny; instead, we seem to be helpless in the path of this fearsome and violent force of nature. The cyclone experience is both invasive and pervasive, as poet Susan Hawthorne realizes in the aftermath of Cyclone Larry when she acknowledges that "[t]he wind has entered/some inner part of me/and I cannot wrench it out" (*Earth's Breath*, 2009, p. 77). The British and Argentinian naturalist, William Henry Hudson, felt the wind's influence on his creativity when he wrote,

> My experience in a high wind was as if, blowing through me, it had blown away some obstruction, some bar to a perfect freedom of mind; or as if the two minds in us, the conscious, slow, laborious mind, and the mind that works easily and swiftly in the dark, and only from time to time gives us a result, a glimpse, of its secret doings, had become merged in one, the thoughts coming and going so rapidly that it was like the flight of a bird, every wing-beat a thought, spontaneously clothed in an appropriate expression, coming and vanishing, to be instantly succeeded by others and still others [1923, p. 37].

Caught up in an inner turmoil as the cyclone reduces our outer world to chaos, we attempt to seize back some control and to seek to make some sense of it all by establishing a personal relationship to the event, and so we name the storm and then relate to the name as if we were trying to know them as a person, like "Larrikin" Larry or Hamish, the "kilted hammer thrower" (Hawthorne, pp. 23, 75).

Australian academic George Seddon, who popularized the concept of sense of place, argues that our language of landscape and environment is "inescapably anthropocentric" (1997, p. 16), in that the words we use for our geological or meteorological environments are all about how *we* relate to our environment. To Hudson, for example, the wind beating around his house is

> hissing, whispering, whistling, muttering and murmuring, whining, wailing, howling, shrieking—all the inarticulate sounds uttered by man and beasts in states of intense excitement, grief, terror, rage and what not. And as they sink and swell and are prolonged or shattered into convulsive sobs and moans, and overlap and inter-weave, acute and shrill and piercing, and deep and low, all together forming a sort of harmony, it seems to express the whole ancient dreadful tragedy of man on earth [1923, p. 16].

Hudson hears humanity in the wind; he creates the human tangible out of the natural intangible as he likens the sounds of the wind to those uttered "by man," and in doing so he takes control of any fears generated by noises in the night. By bestowing characteristics and names on natural elements like wind and storm, we are humanizing them and in doing so we are demonstrating our power to do that. The act of naming the storm positions *us* at the heart and center of it. We recall where *we* were when the cyclone struck, what *we* did, what *we* heard, and what *we* felt, by association with the name. As geographer Yi-Fu Tuan asserts, "Naming is power—the creative power to call something into being, to render the invisible visible, to impart a certain character to things" (1991, 688). In bestowing names on the cyclone, the hurricane, and the typhoon, we attempt to reduce these vast weather events that threaten us with chaos to a more ordered, coherent, visible human scale that we can readily comprehend and over which we can attempt to assert some power of control, which ultimately enables us to feel more physically and emotionally secure.

Much like the name of a physical topographic feature, such as a mountain, as we continue to use the name of the cyclone and refer to it in different contexts, the storm accumulates character qualities and becomes humanized. Eventually, the name not only identifies the cyclone, but with frequent use that name ultimately *becomes* the cyclone in our country of the mind as we form associations of memory, place, and activity with it, endowing the cyclone with character according, perhaps, to its scope of destruction, or its strength, or even whether its path was direct or particularly circuitous. As we continue to make these associations, the names of the storms become part of us as well as part of our place, remaining in our personal geography like the names of mountains and rivers. Their names "affect our perception and reaction to them," writes Liz Skilton in *Tempest*, her ground-breaking study of hurricane names and American culture, from when they first appear on weather forecaster's maps to long after they have dissipated (2019, p. 2). Over time, we develop our own personal history and geography of named storms that we have experienced, and so we are likely to respond to each new storm according to comparisons we make with the existing features of that personal map, much as we compare new people we meet with members of our existing social group. We may even choose to evacuate or remain in a storm's path depending on assessments we make according to that prior experience (p. 219).

In the aftermath of the storm, we make similar comparisons about personal and material damage, comparing this latest named storm with previous ones and perhaps looking ahead to what may be in the future. As we have these conversations and tell these stories, our perception of the storm is "shaped by the present moment, ghosts of the past, and fears of the future" (p. 2). As these moments interact in our mind, these named storms develop individual character in terms of their behavior and scale of damage, much as if they were uninvited guests who invaded your home and misbehaved. As they develop these character attributes, they assume a place not only in our personal history but also in regional cultural history, our *terroir*, and in our identification with it. In other words, when you ask yourself the question about where you belong, is your answer that you belong here in the potential path of cyclones, hurricanes or typhoons? If so, then these named tropical storms have become part of your personal, regional identity.

We compose our narrative of that identity from a number of differing elements that we bring together in context over time, such as perceptions of our landscape, our natural environment, our built environment, our culture, our community, and of our relationships to all of these. When we seek to express our experience of a named cyclone in words, whether they are spoken or written, heard or read, the names and the words associated with them form that storm in our minds in the present moment as we assemble and use those words. Then, as we tell and write the stories of these cyclones, hurricanes and typhoons, those words form the storms in the imagination of listeners or readers. Although those words are created in our time for us to hear and read in the present, they are also for those in the future to hear and read. Yet, they are words often drawn from previous experience, and so the names bring with them the ghosts of the past as well as the fears of the present and the future.

Because winds have always played a major role in cyclonic storms, they have names as old as those of *huracán*, perhaps as old as language. Like naming a cyclone, naming the wind is our attempt to discover a means by which the intangible can become tangible and the invisible become visible for because the wind is moving air, we do not actually see it. As landscape writer Jan DeBlieu suggests, "the wind yields its greatest influence not in the realm of the body but in that of the mind" (1998, p. 177). We may feel the wind touch us, but we cannot touch the wind. Instead, we see the effects and impact of it or we see something caught up in it, like snow, leaves, or sand, which may prompt the illusion of seeing it. In fact, our experience of wind is primarily a sensory, personal interaction between body and mind that many cultural names for the wind reflect, as revealed in anthropologist Lyall Watson's list of over 400 cultural names for winds in his book, *Heaven's Breath* (1984, pp. 330–344). The many and diverse names that we bestow on the wind speak of our association with our place and our culture and in this speaking, they become infused into our *terroir*.

For the Australian Aboriginal Euahlayi people in the Narran River region of northwest New South Wales, for example, *Yarragerh* is the male spring wind who woos the three trees who are his wives: Budtha, Bibbil, and Bumble. When he breathes on them, they burst into shoots and buds, then flowers and fruits, showing that their lover has arrived. The hot, rain-bringing north wind is *Douran Doura*, who woos the coolabah and kurrajong trees that burst into flower after he has kissed them (Parker, 1905, p. 100). The Gidjingarli speaking people who live at the mouth of the Blyth River on the north coast of Arnhem Land define their seasons by referring to the dominant wind occurring at that time of year: *balmarrk wana*, for example, is big or strong wind, while the Wet season is *djambirr*, and the northwest monsoon is *barra*, depicted in their *Djambidj* song cycle as a warrior going into battle. Damage during the wet season from winds or floods happens when Modj, the rainbow serpent living in the river, has been angered (Jones R and Meehan B, p. 15). To the northeast of them, the Masigalgal people of the Masig Island archipelago in the central Torres Strait rely on the direction and type of winds to indicate the seasons of the year: *kuki*, the Wet season, is driven by the hot and humid northwest wind; *zei* is the nesting turtle season of the southwest wind; *woerr* or *sagerr* is the season of the predominant southeast wind; and *naigai* is the season of hot, dry weather and calm seas when you prepare for the Wet. Far to the east, the Enata (meaning simply "the people"), the indigenous inhabitants of the Isles of Hiva, or the Marquesas Islands, also centered their lives around the direction of the winds that came from different points around the horizon. For them, there was no north, south, east or west: instead, they had thirty-two names for the winds such as *Tua to Ha*, the wind from the southeast that was most constant during the three breadfruit seasons from April to October and which dropped rain on the eastern sides of all the islands, and from November to March there would be *Tiu*, the wind from the north and east. (Dening, 1980, p. 60).

Away from the Pacific region, North Africa has the suffocating, hot, dry and dust-laden *simoom*, a name derived from the Arabic for poison, while in Morocco the southeasterly wind is the *mezzar-ifoullousen*, from the Berber language and meaning "that which plucks the fowls." The northeast trade wind of the Sahara region, famous for its heat and dust, is known as the *harmattan*, or "doctor," because to colonists on the Guinea coast it brought relief from the humid wind off the sea. In Egypt there is a wind known as the *khamsin*, from the Arabic for fifty, because it traditionally blows for fifty days. The northeasterly wind of the Aegean is the *malteme* or bad-tempered. The Rhone valley has its famous *mistral* (masterly) wind, while Switzerland has its crop-ripening *trauben-kocher*, or "grape-cooker," and Argentina has the fast, dry *zonda* that from May to November can descend from the mountain crests down the eastern slopes of the Andes to the lowlands at speeds of 240 kph (DeBlieu, 1998, p. 173). As we can see, these words for the wind do have the power "to call places into being" (Tuan, 1991, p. 686), as they relate nature to culture. In applying words such as names to natural force such as the wind and the storm, we are attempting to integrate nature into our human place and so comprehend it as part of "our" place.

As we interact with these names in conversation, the media, and in literature, they become more than identifiers. Studies of media reaction to the 2017 extra-tropical Storm Doris in the UK, for example, reveal that the volume of published newspaper material and social media discussion increased as soon as the storm was named: the volume of newspaper publication about the storm's impact was double that of storm forecasting, for example (Charlton-Perez, p. 9). Within this interaction, we attach layers of reference to the cyclone, hurricane, or typhoon, such as cultural associations, histories, expectations, and personal characteristics. We have traditionally gendered storms, whereas that tradition has not been so evident for other nature catastrophes such as earthquakes, floods, fires or avalanches, for example, and we often refer to those gendered storms in terms that current cultural mores would not allow us to use when referring to each other. Another study of just one form of communication revealed that Twitter users gendered their language when discussing Storm Doris, "taking cue from the storm's female associated name." They reconceptualized the storm "as a sexually aggressive and lewd woman … revealing underlying sexist patriarchal attitudes of how a woman should act and how sexual she should be." The researchers found it "fascinating" that in this current age that emphasizes equality, "Twitter users were using gender-coded pejorative terms for women towards a storm openly in both an intentionally humorous and serious manner" (Ablett, 2018, p. 87). There comes a time, then, when our perception of the cyclonic storm can change. It can become more than a meteorological weather event for us: largely because of associations we make with the name of the storm, it can develop into an individual entity.

Examining some of the history of tropical cyclonic storm naming is particularly relevant to the cultural context of this book because the naming of tropical cyclonic storms using an officially designated system originated in Queensland during the latter part of the nineteenth century. Consequently, the first appearance in published literature of cyclonic storms that had been personally named according to an official system also occurred in Queensland, and so this Australian state has led the way in the cultural adoption, adaption and assimilation of cyclonic storm names. This leadership resumed in the late twentieth century, when Queensland became the first place in the world to officially change a gender-specific (female) cyclonic storm naming system to being gender equal, once again proving that the cyclonic storm naming process and the names themselves can "serve as fingerprints for cultural change" (Skilton, p. 3).

The man responsible for originating the systematic personal naming of storms was Clement Wragge, at that time the Director of the Chief Weather Bureau in Queensland's state capital, Brisbane. Born in England in 1852 and orphaned by the age of five, Wragge was raised by his grandmother in a rural area of England, where he developed early interests in natural history, geology, and meteorology. However, his grandmother died unexpectedly when he was twelve and Wragge's relatives sent him to boarding school in London, from where he eventually went to work in a law firm. Nevertheless, he continued to maintain his interests in the natural environment and, although he sat for his intermediate law exams, he found he was spending more time at the British Museum that in the law library. When he inherited some money on his twenty-first birthday, Wragge invested it in travelling widely throughout Europe and the Near East, before visiting Australia and then America. After such a journey, England evidently seemed much too quiet when Wragge returned, because he promptly gave up law to study navigation and seamanship, quickly signing on as a midshipman to work his passage back to Australia. There, in 1876, he gained a position with the Surveyor General's Department in Adelaide but upon marrying, he went back to England in 1878 with his new bride, Leonora, and resumed his interests in meteorology. Establishing his first weather station under the guidance of Robert Scott, the Director of the London Meteorological Office and of the Royal Meteorological Society, Wragge proceeded to establish a number of other weather stations, including one on the summit of Ben Nevis, and for his efforts received the gold medal of the Scottish Meteorological Society.

However, apparently Wragge could not forget Australia for in 1883, he and his wife, their three children, the cat, and Robin Renzo the dog, packed up yet again and returned to Adelaide, where Wragge immediately established the private Torrens Observatory, from which he was able to begin publishing his first weather forecasts, and then founded the Meteorological Office of Australasia. When his work attracted the offer of a position with the government in Queensland, which was still a colony and had no central weather office, the ambitious Wragge saw an opportunity to establish the first national weather forecasting service in the country, and so in January 1887, he began work there as Director of the Chief Weather Bureau in Brisbane. Soon, Wragge was publishing inter-colonial weather forecasts in newspapers employing information received twice a day from a widening network of subsidiary weather stations throughout Queensland, as far east (1,469 km) into the Pacific as New Caledonia (for whom he was providing reciprocal forecasts), from an altitude of 2,228 m (7,310 ft) at the summit of Australia's highest mountain, and as far south (1,789 km) as the 1,271 m (4,170 ft) summit of Mt Wellington, behind Hobart on the island of Tasmania. By 1891, his work was so highly regarded that he was the Queensland delegate to the International Meteorological Conference in Munich, a role he repeated in 1898 and 1900 in Paris (Mr. Clement Wragge, 1894, p. 7).

For many years, the historic tradition had been to name major storms not by a system but in memory of significant loss, or the day or place they made landfall.

Portrait of Clement Wragge (1852–1922) by Sir Harold Nicholas (Collection of John Oxley Library, State Library of Queensland).

In England, for example, the Royal Charter Storm of 1859 was named after the ship, *Royal Charter*, that was driven onto the east coast of Wales by that storm with the loss of 450 lives. Puerto Rico has had at least three hurricanes named San Roque, because they arrived on the feast day of that saint, August 16, in 1508, 1788, and in 1893. An early European catastrophe, among the earliest involving named storms, was the First St Marcellus' Flood, a devastating storm and associated flood surge that on the Feast Day of St Marcellus in 1219 destroyed a large part of the Netherlands coast, killing an estimated 36,000 people. Like in Puerto Rico, this was perhaps a day to be somewhere else entirely: in 1362, a massive southwesterly gale swept across England, striking the same area of the Netherlands coast on the same day as in 1219, and then continued up into Northern Germany and Denmark. Towns such as the English port of Ravensor Odd and the Dutch port of Rungholt disappeared, as well as entire parishes, with the loss of perhaps 100,000 lives, a tragedy memorialized in the evocative name of the storm: Gross Manndrenke (or Grote Mandrenke), the Great Drowning of Men (Blackbourn, 2007, p. 117).

However, as Wragge's wealth of information accumulated, it quickly became apparent that he would need a more precise system by which to distinguish multiple low-pressure storm systems that his constantly improving network and advanced meteorological instrumentation was now detecting, well before they made landfall in Australia. In fact, he could now detect these weather systems even if they never made landfall but remained entirely at sea, meaning that he could now issue weather forecasts for shipping. More particularly, Wragge needed a system to identify cyclones, "in order that people who may encounter them or suffer by their conditions may, therefore, the more readily associate their experience attaching to any particular storm" (Mr. Wragge's Disturbances, 1895, p. 6). Consequently, he announced in March 1894, that he would be initiating a system of naming northern tropical storm systems using the letters of the Greek alphabet (Meteorology, *Courier*, April 1894, p. 3).

Typically, the impatient Wragge had already pre-empted his own announcement by naming Cyclone Beta on February 19 as it neared Lord Howe Island, the first tropical cyclonic storm known to have been named according to an officially declared system. On the same day, he gave the name Gamma to what was probably a large tropical low forming to the north of Fiji (Meteorology, *Courier*, February 1894, p. 3). On April 6, 1894, Cyclone Zeta struck the Queensland eastern coast in the vicinity of Cape Tribulation, tearing off some roofs in Cooktown and causing flooding inland and further south, becoming the first of Wragge's named cyclones to make landfall. Two years later, Cyclone Sigma became the first named cyclone to cause serious damage and loss of life when it destroyed much of Townsville during Saturday and Sunday, January 25 and 26, 1896, as well as the surrounding countryside for hundreds of kilometers. Some eighteen people died as the town was severely flooded, buildings were flattened, and ships were driven ashore or lost at sea (Holthouse, 1977, p. 41). Even this early in the history of named cyclones, the non-gendered Sigma evidently acquired some character traits, for at least one journalist noted that Sigma was "spoken of as if it were a personality—some being of a higher race, wreaking vengeance on mankind for some failure in reverence and worship." In tune with this treatment of the cyclone as if it were a god, the storm was described as "stalking" along the coast, tossing boats around "as if playing with them in sport, before hurling them to destruction" (Current Notes. February 1896, p. 19). Seven years later, in March 1903, Townsville was again devastated by another storm named by Wragge, Cyclone Leonta, the eye of which passed directly over the town. At least a dozen people died, many when the wind tore down the thick, solid brick walls of the local hospital and the Grammar School in which people had sought shelter. So many churches and pastoral residences in the area were destroyed by the cyclone that the Anglican Bishop of North Queensland, Dr.

Frodsham, toured Australia in the months afterwards to raise money for rebuilding (Holthouse, 1977, pp. 46–47).

Within a few weeks of naming Cyclone Beta, Wragge realized that he would need to differentiate between low pressure systems and circulating storms approaching from the colder south and southwestern latitudes and the northern tropical storms, and so he announced on April 26, 1894, that he intended "to christen the Antarctic storms in Hebrew, thus avoiding confusion," and that the first of these would be christened Aleph (Mr. Wragge's Forecasts, April 26, 1894, p. 3). By the following year, however, he had worked through the Greek and Hebrew alphabets and so he moved on to other languages, such as Sanskrit and Arabic, as well as names of people, including women and the occasional politician. In June 1902, for example, he named an Antarctic storm after the current (and first) Australian Prime Minister, Edmund Barton (The Weather, June 3, 1902, p. 3). Shortly after, he named another storm in honor of the Australian Attorney-General, Alfred Deakin, who would become prime minister the following year for the first of his three terms in office (The Weather, June 7, 1902, p. 8). A few weeks later, a New South Wales member of the Federal Parliament, Alfred H.B. Conroy, made the mistake of angrily describing Wragge in a parliamentary debate as a "gentleman who pretends to be a scientist" whose forecasts made with no scientific data were "almost invariably wrong." Yet, Conroy protested, alluding to Wragge having spent time with Australian Aboriginal people "under the impression that they possessed a knowledge of storms the white man did not," people regarded him with the reverence of a "Hottentot rain god" (Tit-Bits from Hansard, 1902, p. 1). He should have known better. Wragge promptly gave the name Conroy to a southern storm off the Western Australia coast. "Perhaps," he added with tongue firmly in cheek, "his name will become familiar as an antipodean meteorological curiosity to the scientists of the civilised world" (*Telegraph*, August 2, 1902, p. 6).

Mr. Conroy MP quickly became Wragge's favorite person of the day to tease in print: a few days later, he observed that "Conroy is looking foxy and ugly" (Meteorology, *Courier*, August 8, 1902, p. 3). Evidently, Conroy was something of a self-important egotist, and the press and other politicians soon took up the joke. Needless to say, Conroy was not amused. While "politically as well as meteorologically," he may have been "an extremely stormy and long-ranging 'disturbance,'" *The Age* newspaper commented to its Melbourne readers, "he apparently has strong objections to being called one" (Federal Political Notes, August 21, 1902, p. 5). Conroy seized his chance for revenge when objecting to a Bill being debated in Parliament that would enable meteorological information to be telegraphed free of charge to and from Wragge's weather office. Conroy ranted for almost an hour in a speech against the Bill and that was criticized for taking advantage of parliamentary privilege to attempt to damage Wragge's reputation. Instead, a number of parliamentarians supported Wragge and passed the Bill.

Although Wragge rather ingenuously plead the case that he named his cyclones and storms simply "for the sake of public convenience and utility" (Mr. Wragge's Disturbances, 1895, p. 6), his use of personal pronouns and qualities when referring to weather features in his lyrical and literary published forecasts imbued those weather systems with gender, personality, and character far beyond mere utility, and he was well aware of this. Commenting on a tropical cyclone that he had named Eline (*El-ee-nie*), for example, to which he constantly referred in reports as "she," Wragge unabashedly observed that

> we are now calling these tropical storms by the soft dulcet names of the dusky beauties of the South Sea Islands. That the names prove softer than the storms goes without saying; but they will have their uses, we trust, not only by associating any given storm with its particular name, but also by possibly inducing some fond mothers to call their infant girls by the pretty bubbling names of the maidens of the "Summer Isles of Eden" [Meteorology, February 2, 1898, p. 5].

Wragge later further defined the name of this cyclone, which would severely damage Mackay, as being derived from the names of women of the Line Islands, an extended chain of eleven islands and atolls (some of which are part of the present nation of Kiribati) that stretches over the Date Line and across the Pacific for some 2,350 km (Hurricane at Mackay, 1898, p. 2). A few years later, he was still christening storms with "quite a set of charming names culled from the palm groves and coral reefs wherewith to delight the hearts of interesting young mothers of pretty baby girls." He urged the mothers to consider using such names as Aceta, which he had just used to christen a tropical low approaching New Caledonia, that "scans with a lullaby soft as Lydian measures" (The Weather, December 28, 1901, p. 8). Wragge even applied these same ideals when naming the cyclone that ultimately killed more people than any other in Australian history. "Mahina is a girl's name, culled from fair Tahiti," Wragge extolled, "with its coral strand, waving palmgroves and mountain peaks, the loveliest of all the lovely islands in the wide Pacific; and mothers will agree no infant daughter can bear a softer or prettier name" (Meteorology, March 7, 1899, p. 3). If there was any cyclone that was neither soft nor pretty, it was the deadly Cyclone Mahina that caused well over 300 deaths when it destroyed the Torres Strait pearling fleet sheltering in Bathurst Bay on the Cape York Peninsula. That Wragge's custom of bestowing names on weather patterns was rather paternalistic did not escape notice: one journalist referred to them as Wragge's roughly playful "storm pets" (The Ravages of Nerva, 1899, p. 847). The act of naming implied that Wragge had a right to do it, as if he owned storms or had even fathered them, and that he was attempting to impose his own order on weather that threatened chaos. In effect, these were "his" storms.

However, we must not forget that Wragge also had very practical reasons for naming low-pressure zones, storms, and cyclones. Exposed as we are in this century to constant, real-time, weather forecasting visually portrayed for us on brightly colored maps, we readily forget that Clement Wragge was pioneering weather forecasting at a time when even diagrammatic maps drawn on paper could not be readily published in a newspaper, let alone transmitted to other places. Wragge could put up a weather forecast map outside of his weather office or the post office in Brisbane, but from then on the effectiveness and clarity of his weather forecast to people around the continent was entirely reliant on the power of his prose and the receptiveness of their imagination. For example, he once described a monsoonal weather pattern named Petrus as "having taken the form of the letter C with a broken back, and other deformities,—such, in fact, as might be executed by a tyro in the art of writing at an infant school" (Meteorology, *October* 23, 1897, p. 3). By using these unlikely metaphors, Wragge was appealing to readers' imagination so that they would be able to "see" that weather pattern in their minds.

In writing so evocatively about weather, including naming cyclonic storms, an experienced writer like Wragge would have been aware of the impact of his words and images on his readers' imagination and on their perception of meteorology and thus their environment. "It is idle for us," he once wrote,

> to ignore the wonderful lyrics of meteorology there enunciated to those who will but only listen. Every bend in the isobars, every segment of the high and low pressure systems, expresses the musical emotions of its own special recitative, and none but the callous—or we should have said the stoic—can fail to be impressed by the remarkable picture displayed by our chart [Meteorology, October 23, 1897, p. 3].

He regarded his weather reports as an opportunity by which he could educate readers not just in readings of temperature and rainfall but in the literacy, metaphors and beauty of weather. As the effects of the southwestern edge of Cyclone Sana, "so suggestive of Samoa, coral reefs, and tete-a-tetes under the coconuts," were about to be experienced along the Queensland coast near Bundaberg in February 1898, for example, Wragge predicted that "a grand performance on the meteorological organ of Australia is in store for us! How the isobars, like the strings of the harp, will vibrate and shiver, each to its respective note!" Although he does not name the person specifically in this case, Wragge's cyclone would have been named for Princess Sana Sola, who by this time was Mrs. Sana Jardine. The niece of the King of Samoa and renowned for her beauty, Sana was only seventeen years old and a missionary teacher when she was kidnapped from a mission launch at gunpoint by a besotted Frank Jardine, the magistrate and senior government official at the outpost of Somerset at the tip of Cape York. Barely a year later, they married and over the years created a family of four children and their own pioneer port settlement at Somerset, which Wragge visited in late 1885 on a trip to investigate locations for weather stations. Perhaps because he'd met the woman in question, this storm in particular seems to have inspired Wragge's imagination, as he continues to use musical metaphors for weather conditions throughout the rest of the report: some "isobaric strings" would be *allegrissimo*, for example, the tropics would be *tranquillamente*, and the very hot temperatures in South Australia would be *lacrimoso* for the people there (Meteorology, February 19, 1898, p. 3). Meteorology was a new science to the average person, who still tended to view forecasting weather conditions with suspicion and skepticism, if not being only a step removed from the black arts. Wragge knew he needed to sell this new concept to people, which is why he put so much effort and talent into his published weather reports and then went on stage to talk about weather in public lecture tours throughout the country. During the next few years, although undoubtedly a controversial figure, he was just as undoubtedly Australia's most heard and read spokesperson for meteorology.

Over the following days, Cyclone Sana developed in Wragge's imagination from a mere organ recital to a full-scale theater performance. "What a grand meteorological opera is in progress," he enthuses in the *Brisbane Courier*, suggesting that people between Bundaberg and Ballina should regret they could only hear part of the storm concert, whereas those in New Caledonia would be able to be present for the full event:

> The sea in sympathy adds its stentorian bass to the whirring of the wind, anon roaring around some cavernous bluff, then lashing the cliffs in angry tones with supernal cascades of majestic beauty—while modulating the sonata, in turn, to the hissing, seething notes of bubbling foam. But … in New Caledonia … will "Sana," the storm empress of the Pacific, soon perform her marvellous evolutions, and dance her wildest step…. Sana will give music of a very different type, wielding her baton to the delirious chords of Nature [Atmospheric Disturbances, February 24, 1898, p. 5].

Wragge endows his "storm empress" with emotive and personified allegories of music and dance, associating both with the sublime in tune with Edmund Burke's interpretation some 140 years earlier in his *A Philosophical Enquiry into the Origin of Our Ideas of the Sublime and Beautiful* (1757), in which he proposed that,

> Whatever is fitted in any sort to excite the ideas of pain, and danger, that is to say, whatever is in any sort terrible, or is conversant about terrible objects, or operates in a manner analogous to terror, is a source of the sublime; that is, it is productive of the strongest emotion which the mind is capable of feeling. I say the strongest emotion, because I am satisfied the ideas of pain are much more powerful than those which enter on the part of pleasure [p. 36].

Both Burke and Wragge were aware that nature has two sides: beauty and pleasure, terror and pain. Like Burke, Wragge knew that cyclones can provoke emotion and imagination; he too could see the sublime within that whirling storm.

Only two years after the various colonies joined to form the Australian nation in 1901, Wragge resigned from his position. He'd dearly wanted to become head of a national weather service or bureau, but the forthright and outspoken meteorologist had made too many jealous enemies during his career to be able to generate the political support and funding necessary to establish such an organization, despite having established the most extensive and best-equipped network of weather stations in Australia at that time. He spent the years until his death in 1922 travelling, lecturing and writing. His naming system was not retained, and by the time of his death it had already been largely forgotten by Australians, remembered if at all as merely a curious eccentricity.

Yet, Wragge had had faith in his system of storm naming. "The practice will become universal," he once declared confidently, and so it did (Clement Wragge at Home, 1894, p. 491). Someone on the other side of the world did not forget his innovation. In a section on cyclones in the second volume of his *Manual of Meteorology*, published six years after Wragge's death, the eminent British physicist and meteorologist, Sir William Napier Shaw, noted that because of unique characteristics such as moving along a track, and changes in size, shape and wind speed, while still preserving their identity, cyclones give "the impression of definite entities, subject to travel and to change, yet preserving a kind of individuality." So marked was this impression of a cyclone's individual character, Shaw continued, "that Clement Wragge in Australia used to give names to those that appeared on his maps, and for the few days of their transient visit referred to them by name" (1928, p. 345). It was this reference to Wragge, the meteorologist who had "felt storms to be so personal he had given them names," that was discovered some ten years later by an English professor in northern California, George Rippey Stewart, while carrying out research for a novel that would feature a massive storm. He had originally intended to model his book on the plot structure of Vicki Baum's *Grand Hotel* (1929), in which a group of characters with individual stories of generally equal significance are connected by a unifying event (all being in the same hotel at the same time), but as he read those lines about Wragge, Stewart had an epiphany about this storm: that "[h]er birth, growth, adventures, and final death were to be the main vortex of the story" (*Storm*, p. viii). His human characters would only be there because of their connection to the storm; rather than build the novel around them, he would structure it around the life cycle of the storm as if it were the life of a person. That person, like Wragge's tropical island belles, would be a woman with a lyrical name: Maria (as in *Ma-rye-ah*) (1947, p. ix).

Stewart moves his characters into the storm's path rather as if they are chess-pieces on a giant topographical board. To reduce their individual significance and keep the reader focused on the storm, Stewart merely identifies some of his human characters with initials or job titles, whereas all the storms have names such as Antonia, Cornelia, and Maria. These are not official names, but female names bestowed secretly on these weather events by the Junior Meteorologist because he perceives each of them as individuals, and because he finds referring to a storm by a single name easier than referring to it as a low-pressure area at a particular latitude and longitude (p. 12). Having used all the names of women he has known, the Junior Meteorologist is now beginning to use names "ending in *–ia* which suggested actresses or heroines of books rather than girls he had ever known" (p. 13). However, with just a touch of irony, he bestows on this menacing meteorological threat the gentle name of Maria (p. 18).

Developing his storm as a life cycle allowed Stewart to build plot tension and to build the storm as a character to which his readers could relate. The JM names her "as if he had been a minister who had just christened a baby" (p. 18), and while at first "young and undistinguished," she develops personality as she grows "in healthy fashion" like "a normal child" (pp. 43–44). A few days later, she is no longer a baby but "more like a middle-aged person who has grown too individualized, not to say crotchety, to fit any rules" (p. 147). As the storm grows in size and complexity, the Junior Meteorologist now feels like a father whose child has become famous, "his affection mingled with awe" (p. 147). Maria even births another smaller storm: Little Maria. For most of the novel, the Junior Meteorologist never speaks his storm names aloud, reinforcing their privacy and imbuing them with mystery. When he does eventually let a name slip, however, he discovers that the Chief Meteorologist has in the past also given some storms names, but in his case these were the names of his historical heroes, such as Hannibal and Genghis Khan, hinting that Stewart's storm-naming concept may not necessarily have been as gender-selective as readers have since assumed. Nevertheless, significantly, Stewart has incorporated imagination into the science of meteorology. "Perhaps," the Junior Meteorologist theorizes, "there was something about the human mind itself which made it feel comfortable to think of a storm as a person, not an equation" (p. 236). On the other hand, we cannot ignore that Stewart's protagonist storm is not just any person. Stewart's Maria is a destructive woman: one who becomes more destructive as she matures. She is the ultimate meteorological *femme fatale* that became the model for people's perception of violent storms for many years to come, normalized by Stewart's treatment of Maria in *Storm* and further impressed on popular memory by the subsequent inclusion of the name in the title of the song, "They Call the Wind Mariah," included in the stage musical *Paint Your Wagon*.

Storm was first published in November 1941, and immediately became a best seller. In 1943, a special reprinted Armed Services Edition was included in American military kits, and so it is highly likely that Stewart's novel influenced the standardized, secret, all-female naming code for hurricanes and tropical storms introduced by the United States Army and Navy in 1944, and continued into 1945, to enable discussion of specific Pacific weather patterns by military weather personnel and during military briefings. Although the system was officially phased out after World War II, the issue was given new life when a new edition of Storm was published in 1947, with an introduction by Stewart explaining the origins and circumstances of the novel. Four years later, in 1951, lyricist Alan Lerner collaborated with Frederick Loewe in the stage musical Paint Your Wagon to remind audiences that, while fire might be known as Joe and rain might be known as Tess, the name of the wind was Mariah. Pronounced the same as Stewart's storm, Mariah's name was repeated throughout the hugely successful and often-recorded song, "They Call the Wind Mariah," which was subsequently re-recorded by a number of artists. Consequently, the practice of naming and gendering the wind quickly became indelibly stamped in the popular mind. In 1951, the United States Weather Bureau began using the phonetic alphabet to name hurricanes, as in C for Charley, F for Fox, T for Tango, but in 1953 they officially introduced an alphabetical list of female names for hurricanes and tropical storms. In 1969, "They Call the Wind Mariah" appeared again in the equally successful movie version of Paint Your Wagon, reinforcing the behavior pattern of personalizing and gendering the wind.

Although in a different hemisphere on the other side of the world, someone in Queensland may have been influenced by the 1951 introduction of alphabetical code-naming of storms in the United States to revive Clement Wragge's original idea. In March 1955, the name Annie was given by either an unknown journalist or an equally anonymous weather bureau employee to a cyclone that struck the east coast between Mackay and Rockhampton on March 7, causing much destruction and wide-spread flooding. The naming of these cyclones appears to have been a localized practice (cyclones in northwestern areas of Australia do not appear to have been named at all) that was not noted by the national media nor commented on widely by people. Referred to in the press as both "A-For-Annie" (*Central Queensland Herald*, March 10, 1955, p. 1) and "Ungentle Annie" (March 17, 1955, p. 3), this was the first cyclone to make contact with the Australian coast to be given a human name since Wragge's system had been abandoned. Only a few days later, on March 27, Cyclone Bertha made landfall in the area of Gympie and Maryborough. The next major cyclone to make landfall in Queensland, severely damaging Cairns and Townsville on March 6, 1956, was known as Agnes, the first Australian tropical cyclone to be tracked on radar, to be followed by the offshore Cyclone Clara in February 1957. But, when a cyclone destroyed much of Bowen in early 1958, it does not appear to have been named, and when another cyclone devastated the town barely a year later, it was only incidentally referred to as Connie. After that, the practice appears to have been abandoned, apparently because of objections lodged by women to the Queensland weather office (In Queensland This Week, February 7, 1963, p. 2).

Nevertheless, in October 1963, the Commonwealth Meteorological Bureau in Australia (now known as the Bureau of Meteorology or simply as "the BOM") announced that they would be instituting a nation-wide system of naming cyclones with female names in alphabetical order from December 1 that year. Although acknowledging that there had been protests from women, the Bureau excused the official adoption of the system as merely "following overseas practice" (In Queensland This Week. October 10, 1963, p. 2). Australia's first officially named cyclone was Cyclone Bessie, which made landfall in the north of Western Australia on January 10, 1964, and Queensland's first officially named cyclone, Cyclone Audrey, arrived soon after, striking the south of the state on January 14. From the very beginning, people added personal character to the names. Cyclone Audrey's name was quickly modified to "Little Audrey," referring to a female character famous for her post–World War I appearances in jokes about catastrophes, as well as comic books and in post–World War II Paramount Pictures cartoons. The punchline of a Little Audrey disaster joke customarily used the phrase, "she just laughed and laughed," which would rather fit in with the typical droll Queensland attitude to violent weather events. That year of 1964 was a busy cyclone year: Cyclone Dora drenched the west of Cape York Peninsula in February and in April, Cyclone Gertie drenched the Whitsunday Islands, while Cyclone Flora flooded Cardwell in December. But, the winds of change and progress were soon blowing around the world for cyclone names.

In November 1975, the United Nations' International Women's Year, the Bureau of Meteorology in Australia announced that in future the names of cyclones within the Australian weather district would be drawn from a list consisting of an equal number of male and female names. The specific reason given by William Morrison, who was Minister of Science earlier that year, pointed back to the recent total devastation of the Northern Territory city of Darwin by Cyclone Tracy on Boxing Day. "Women should not have to bear the adium [sic] associated with tropical cyclones," he declared (Men Join Women, 1975, p. 1), but it is quite likely that Morrison's decision was also prompted by the changes in attitudes by women and about women that were taking place world-wide. Six years earlier, in December of 1969, feminist Roxcy Bolton had attended the National Organization for Women conference in New Orleans, where she raised the issue of the appallingly derogatory references to women inherent in media commentary about recent Hurricanes

Camille and Debbie, such as being "witches," "angry," and that they needed to be seeded to be calmed. "I am sick and tired of hearing that Camille was no lady," she fumed (Skilton, 2019, p. 81, 83). The National Organization for Women agreed with her that hurricanes should no longer be named exclusively for women and in March 1970, Bolton delivered a letter in person to the National Hurricane Center director, Robert H. Simpson, demanding that the current naming system be changed. It began a struggle that would last for nearly eight years. Having been belittled, derided, and abused for her stance, Bolton put aside the hurricane-naming debate in 1972 to become involved in other women's rights issues, and it was not until President Carter appointed the first female U.S. Secretary of Commerce, Dr. Juanita Kreps, in January 1977, that the argument was finalized. The National Weather Service came under Kreps' jurisdiction and, aware that modern attitudes towards women had changed and that Australia had led the way in moving to an equal-gender cyclone naming system, she ordered that the American hurricane naming system be altered accordingly, which it was in May 1978.

Yet, although our Queensland cyclones might now be gender-equal in name, we still customarily characterize, gender, and personalize these catastrophic weather events as we seek to relate to them because of their potential to impact on our lives. There comes a time when the size and complexity of the event goes beyond human visualization and comprehension, although satellite photography has helped with visualization in recent years, and the cyclone just becomes lists of statistics about wind speed and rainfall with which it is all too easy to lose personal touch. Writers of the disaster, especially those who are writing in the first person having been through the disaster, play a vital role in keeping us in touch with our relationship to these events as they add stories and evocative word images of our environmental challenges to the scientific data, evoking subjectively the personal lived experience. Writing about the disaster, whether using poetry or prose, reveals our personal, embodied, empathic relationships to weather events, and it is the telling, the writing and the reading of these experiences that brings people together as a community in a joint understanding of their responses to them. Personifying the disaster in that writing enables us to perceive the intangible as tangible and to define the undefinable. In writing it, we work out a relationship with this chaotic, destructive monster that will help us to live with it as we define our relationship with the natural community of our environment.

On March 20, 2006, the destructive chaos monster was Severe Tropical Cyclone Larry that extensively damaged the Queensland town of Innisfail and the surrounding area. The first severe tropical cyclone to make landfall since 1999, Larry maintained cyclone strength for several hundred kilometers inland, causing damage and flooding along its path. Although we have been focusing on female-named cyclones, the way in which survivors refer to this male-named cyclone in their writing provides an excellent example of how we gender and character storms regardless of whether the name is male or female. In her poem, "Innisfail, my poor Innisfail," Barbara Bufi interprets the cyclone's descent on the town as a personal attack carried out by a man who has "ripped and torn and ravaged" it. Bufi portrays this "mongrel wind" as an animal-like mugger stalking a victim on whom it descends, wailing, clawing and tearing as it attempts to find a vital organ (2007, p.15). In their "Cyclone Larry Rap," the Years 5–7 students at the Good Counsel Primary School in Innisfail also see Cyclone Larry as a violent male who enters their town and tears down their houses. Their lyric humanizes the dramatic and life-threatening confrontation between cyclone and survivor on an intimate level: "He came to MY house and scared me to death,/I'm telling you, he took away my breath/And I thought for a while/I'd be Dead! Dead! Dead!" (Students Good Counsel, 2007, p. 32). Student Gurpreeth Singh writes of a Cyclone Larry that "lashes his anger upon us" with "aggressive winds raging ferociously" (*Cyclone Larry: Tales*, p. 67), while Sinead Cristaudo recalls the "high-pitched scream" of that violently destructive rage (p. 84). These children perceive Cyclone Larry as uncaring about the havoc he wreaks and about their consequent suffering; he has invaded their place uninvited and destroyed it in anger with no reason.

A few years later, on February 2, 2011, the much larger and more destructive Category 5 Severe Tropical Cyclone Yasi made landfall in the area of Cardwell and Mission Beach, passing between the two major coastal cities of Cairns and Townsville. However, the system was so large that it affected most of the North Queensland coast. Having formed within the area monitored by the Fiji Meteorological Service, the cyclone was named by them as Yasi, or sandalwood, because their naming system includes objects, unlike that of Australia which consists of only male or female personal names. The most powerful cyclone to strike any of the Australian coastline since Cyclone Mahina in 1899 and the Mackay and Innisfail cyclones in 1918, Yasi developed maximum wind gusts of up to 285 kph across a front that extended for hundreds of kilometers. The regional situation was regarded by authorities as so serious that, as the cyclone system approached, patients from the Cairns Hospital were moved out in the largest hospital evacuation in the country's history. The eye of this cyclone alone was 35 kilometers wide, and over the next twenty-four hours the system tracked some 900 km inland; the body of the weather pattern was so large that it could only be truly appreciated in satellite photos. Yet, although STC Yasi was the worst cyclone in Queensland history in terms of the number of people affected, there was mercifully only one indirect fatality. Nevertheless, the damage to homes, farms and infrastructure was profound, and the trauma of surviving the event is evident in how people wrote about their experience. Most people were unaware at the time (and in my experience are still largely not aware) of the origin and translation of the name and that Yasi was thus the first cyclone to make landfall in Queensland to have officially been given a gender-neutral name. While writers did struggle to gender it, they nevertheless continued to characterize the cyclone: "an unwelcome tourist" was a typical example (Lawson, 2012, p. 97).

In her poem, 'Tropical Cyclone Yasi,' Linda J Vaughan speaks to the cyclone personally as 'you' on behalf of 'we,' the small community of Mission Beach for whom this is 'our' shore. Their experience of this disaster is a shared one, she suggests: the fears and trauma of the one here are those of the many. While on the one hand the community is terrified by the cyclone's size and its potential to damage and destroy, they are at the same time amazed and awed by its terrible beauty, Nevertheless, she accuses, this storm is an uninvited guest who invades the town in the night with deliberate intent to do them harm and proceeds to vent its anger. Like a vengeful child having a temper tantrum, the cyclone carelessly destroys everything in its path (2012, pp. 53-5). That metaphor of the cyclone as thief and home invader who steals elements of our lives away also pervades Chelsea Ball's poem, "A New Beginning." Forced to hide in the cold rain and the darkness as the wind rips away her roof and then her home to steal her memories, she laments that her heart has been broken by such a deep personal loss (2011, p. 9). For some writers, such as Barbara Bufi, the rampaging cyclone takes on the qualities of a clawed mythical beast that shreds all it can seize (2011, p. 27). Others recognize that the damage to people can be more than physical: that the "cyclone of our mind" can feel as real as the one outside (Callandar, 2011, p. 123). Ultimately, the perception of the cyclone can be so intimate and personal that its very sound can live "etched in the DNA" of our bodies and souls (Campbell-Lloyd, 2011, p. 85).

Yet, throughout the attempts by Queensland writers to come to grips with the traumatic cyclone experience, there is a constant sense of triumph in a personal battle with a very real adversary who attempts to take and destroy your home, your possessions, your pets, your family, and ultimately even your life. Writers speak of their encounter with the cyclone as a personal and intimate encounter between human being and nature that is inherently violent and during which nature teaches us the uncomfortable harsh lesson that we do not actually control the natural elements. Much like a video camera gradually pulling back, enabling the lens to see more, Maureen Clifford's poem "Yasi Tried" begins with a close-up on the individual who has lost home and possessions. Then, the view broadens out to take in the community, as if the subject of the poem is gradually recovering from the shock and becoming more aware of their surroundings. Like poets such as Bufi and Vaughan, Clifford also suggests that this cyclone has attacked Queenslanders personally and tried to defeat them, but they are tough and though battered will not surrender and despair. They may be down, but they are not out. Though he is rendered homeless by the cyclone, the poem's subject recognizes that he is still alive and determines that he will rebuild and replant because this is his land, his country and his home and here he will stay (2012, p. 104). As school student Jade Amess declares in "'Cause of Larry," rather than cry about the damage, they will channel their energy into rebuilding the town. (2007, p. 44).

Likewise, although the people of the small coastal town of Mission Beach might be bruised after the cyclone in Vaughan's poem, they are not broken (2012, p. 54). Although buildings have gone, along with some sources of income, there were no fatalities. Although Cyclone Yasi has arrived like an uninvited and potentially dangerous nightmare guest that has frightened and traumatized the town, Vaughan triumphantly concludes that it has not won because their Australian spirit endures and they will go on (p. 55). Ball's "A New Beginning" also turns into a declaration of triumph in the face of adversity. After such a night of destruction, a new day dawns in which she will begin again because, although the storm might have threatened to break her, she is stronger and will not give up. Home is more than a building, she declares; home is also of the heart (2011, p. 9).

In naming the cyclone, we are doing much more than just labeling it with an identifying proper noun. We are attempting to explain, both to ourselves and to others, something bigger than us, something that could threaten our lives and which may attempt to steal that which we hold dear from us. Consequently, we gender the cyclone, characterize it, give it a personality, even make jokes about it to give it shape and heft so that we can figure out how to deal with it, cope with it, and relate to it. Yet at the same time, the weather chaos that periodically descends on us with apparent randomness or as the fickle finger of fate, depending on your philosophical persuasion, is an integral part of place. We cannot remove the cyclone from the coastal Queensland environment any more than we can control it; in fact, by its very presence the cyclone reminds us how little influence we as human beings have on the elemental forces of nature and even how little we may understand them. Yet, the name and the words can also bring people together, enabling us to laugh at the same jokes, to share the experiences of violence, terror, and loss, and to share courage and determination to renew and rebuild. By relating creatively to the experience of the cyclone, then, those who write about it bridge an important gap. They open a dialogue between insiders and outsiders, between those who have been in the eye and those who have not, but they also open a conversation between those who have been through the cyclone together as a common experience in the only realm that such a dialogue can occur: the imagination.

Three

"Big wind, he waiting there"
Vance Palmer's Cyclones of Apocalypse and Their Power of Revelation

> "What tongue does the wind talk? What nationality is a storm?"—Tom Fury, lightning rod salesman

In his short stories based on the 1934 Cape Tribulation cyclone that culminate in his 1947 novel *Cyclone*, Vance Palmer explores the ebb and flow of interchange between people and weather, nature and society, myth and spirituality. In *Cyclone*, Palmer works closely from a historical and environmental background with which he was familiar from his six-month residence with his wife Nettie in Cairns and on Green Island through the middle of 1932. Although based on historical people, places and events, Palmer's novel is more than "faction." In seeking to explore the deeper elements and meanings of relationships between those people, nature, and place, rather than just recounting history, Palmer creates a novel unlike any other that he wrote. Although critic Harry Heseltine dismisses the novel as merely "a slight tale of the North Queensland coast, competent but undistinguished" (1970, p. 118), Palmer's characters in *Cyclone* are motivated by a search for meaning that is deeply related to their tropical place and to their lives there. It is a search even more meaningful today in the light of current concerns with environmental messages.

While Palmer bases *Cyclone* on historic events in early 1930s North Queensland, he deliberately repositions those events in order to reinterpret and rework them, moving the arrival of his fictional cyclone eighteen days beyond the historic date to Easter weekend: a period associated with resurrection and renewal that gives Palmer scope for a number of symbolic implications. In attempting to tell this story, Palmer would have had to confront the personal tragedy of his good friend Bill Millard's death during the 1934 cyclone and perhaps this explains the delay in completing the novel: *Cyclone* was not published until 1947, some thirteen years later when Palmer was in his early sixties. Palmer advocated that a writer spend some time thinking about a subject because, he maintained in *The Rainbow Bird*, "Most good stories have not been invented; they come from something in the author's experience." That "something," he elaborated, while admitting it was an old metaphor, was like a grain of sand that irritated an oyster until it was turned into a pearl. However, he argued, the writer's experience "is not so external to him as the grain of an oyster; he has thought over it; it has become a minute but integral part of his inner life. What he really wants to do is to give it a shape and significance that will make it communicable to others" (1957, p. 123). This was never an easy task, Palmer concluded, because "each subject has its special problem and the right angle of approach to it has to be sought painfully and discovered" (p. 124). Palmer's special problem with *Cyclone* was more than likely that he and the late Bill Millard had been good friends, and that working on this novel meant coping with some painful memories.

Portrait of Vance Palmer (1885–1959) by Alfred Hughes, c. 1935 (Collection of John Oxley Library, State Library of Queensland).

We can see that Palmer was actively attempting to find his approach into the novel over many years because drafts of his ideas about scenes and characters for it are revealed in three of his short stories: "The Big Wind," published in late 1932; "Cyclone," which appeared in March 1936; and "Tempest," which was published in September of that year. In the earliest of these stories, "The Big Wind," Palmer seems to be sketching out an early draft of the character of his female protagonist in *Cyclone*, Fay Donolly: the fearful left-at-home wife made stronger by her cyclone experience. In this story, the woman made stronger is pregnant Mary Shenton, who survives childbirth during the cyclone to realize in the aftermath that she has defeated the source of the fear that has haunted her like some monster looming in the shadows. "I won't be afraid of wind again. Afraid of anything else either," she declares afterwards. "You just clench your teeth, and at last you come out the other side" (1932, p. 13). The second story, "Cyclone," contains a version of part of the novel's plot in which a boat captain feels duty-bound to take a load of supplies north in the face of an approaching cyclone. In "Tempest," Palmer is working out his visualization of the cyclone as monster, as "leviathan," as well as drafting an early version of the Randall character as the disfigured and embittered pilot Gessler who has an epiphany in the cyclone regarding his self-worth. It is as if the emotions and memories engendered by the tragedy of Millard's loss blocked Palmer from immediately writing the longer work and so he attempted to contextualize those events using short story form in a search for the meaning of the tragedy. Writing as a form of catharsis evidently worked for Palmer on this occasion, for he was ultimately able to complete the larger, more profound novel.

Much of the context of *Cyclone* is associated with the place in which it is set: the North Queensland coastal region around Cairns, where Palmer and his wife Nettie lived for a short time some two years before the events of the novel. Consequently, *Cyclone* is grounded in Palmer's intimate knowledge of, and association with that tropical place, an intimacy of *terroir* apparent in detailed descriptions of local backyards, plants and weather, for example, and in his accounts of characters' largely positive relationships with them. "His characters represent living people," Deborah Jordan points out, "in whom the spirit of place becomes expressive and individualized" (2010, p. 156). However, it is by no means a fixed expression. As Mrs. Porter aboard the *Crest of the Wave* during the 1899 Cyclone Mahina realized, cyclones not only have an impact on place but on our attitude to it. After surviving her cyclone, Fay Donolly also realizes that "[s]he wouldn't be so sure of her own little world again … a window had opened up in her mind, giving her a glimpse of the terror and mystery lurking behind the stolid face of things" (Palmer, 1947, p. 194). Yet, while the destructive power of the storm in *Cyclone* may indeed engender terror, the mystery of the storm lies within its power to change and to reveal. The cyclone of Palmer's novel "purges the human conflicts it has both intensified and symbolized" (Heseltine, 1970, p. 119), and so it acts as a catalyst for change by revealing mistakes and presenting new futures. These character's lives will never be the same again and, in this way, Palmer's cyclones fulfill the true nature of apocalypse.

The English word "apocalypse" is derived from the Greek *apokalupsis*, meaning literally to uncover or reveal, which is why the word was originally associated with revelation rather than with the world-ending violent event for which the word tends to be used currently. In its original sense, while an apocalypse may certainly be a catastrophe, it happens for a reason. James Berger maintains in *After the End* that a truly apocalyptic event must "in its destructive moment clarify and illuminate the true nature of what has been brought to an end." An apocalypse is not the end in itself, then, but anticipates, reveals and explains the end (1999, p. 5). By extension, a destructive weather event such as a cyclone can be apocalyptic in the sense that it also reveals and explains. In the aftermath of the cyclone, survivors are offered choices and opportunities to start again, to perceive previously unseen aspects of themselves and so renew their lives. It is through these revelations that the event explains the reason for its existence, that the catastrophe becomes apocalypse, enabling the incomprehensible to be comprehended and the randomness of violent weather be seen to have a reason after all. This is why throughout Queensland literature the trope of the cyclone appears as both destroyer and re-creator, as an instrument of both divine will and of the will of nature, as an instrument of fate and of destiny. Palmer uses the cyclone trope in his work as a true apocalypse that reveals to characters through its violent chaos that they are part of the inevitable and uncontrollable cycle of death and birth, of change and of renewal. Consequently, from destruction revelations emerge: old things are wiped away and new worlds revealed.

Vance Palmer was aware of the power of cyclones to change people's lives physically and spiritually through having listened to survivor's stories; he knew that people could discover the strength to transcend that whirling storm. He and his wife Nettie, by now established writers and critics, experienced tropical life and environment and heard about the dangers of North Queensland cyclones while on a prolonged visit to the Cairns area in 1932. They negotiated a permit to set up camp on Green Island, a small, forested coral cay surrounded by a lagoon and reef that is located about 27 kilometers off-shore from Cairns. Proclaimed a nature reserve under council control in 1906, the island's only permanent occupants at that time were a ranger/caretaker and his wife. Seeking a peaceful and quiet respite from life in Melbourne, Vance and Nettie remained on the island for some six months through the middle of the year during the tropical winter. Nettie always appreciated that "[t]here is a good deal to be said for letting the mind rest in one spot, small enough to hold the affections and, perhaps, to be understood" (1988, p. 484), and so while they were seeking to have a break from city life here, they looked forward to developing an understanding of this tropical place. Although claiming to be resting, Vance and Nettie did not stop working completely, being the perennial writers that they were. They kept up with reading and their work on various projects: Nettie was working on a collection of essays that would be published on their return to Melbourne as *Talking It Over* (1932), and Vance was working on a novel and various short stories. While on Green Island and after they left, they both also wrote a number of articles for papers and magazines about life in the tropics. Vance and Nettie wanted to learn about the tropics as place, rather than fiction in which no one reached coral islands "except by being neatly wrecked on them," Nettie wrote. Instead, they wanted to discover "something about the mystery of coral reefs, not as scientists but as seekers after the world's wonders" (1988, p. 527), and they endeavored to enhance that mystery in their articles by some subtle literary manipulation. Though only a short boat trip from the coast on an island regularly visited by tourists, fisherman and guests, the Palmers did like to give the impression in their letters and articles that they were on a remote coral island within "the immense apparent nothingness of sea and sky" (1988, p. 82). In reality, Vance and Nettie socialized with the crews of the fishing boats and luggers that dropped anchor at the island, while they sheltered from bad weather or rested on their journey along the Reef, listening to their stories of the sea and storms. The Palmers had never previously been to North Queensland or that part of the Barrier Reef, and so their residence on the island for such a prolonged period was a new and exciting immersion for them into North Queensland culture and place. "I never knew it before," Nettie wrote to a friend about North Queensland, "but I feel its fascination" (Palmer & Palmer, 1977, p. 72).

Much of that fascination for the Palmers was with the region's paradisiacal environment. Nettie referred to living on Green Island as being miraculously transported into a green forest that reminded her of Shakespeare's Forest of Arden in *Midsummer Night's Dream* (1932, p. 9). She felt that to live on such an island was "almost a domestication of Fairyland"; it was a place, she thought, where "every tree has personality, ... where every bird is a delight" (1932, p. 13). Adding to the mystery, Vance observed that they seemed to be living on an island within an island: when the tide receded, it revealed a reef island around them that was "ten times as large, teeming with its own kind of life" (1932, p. 20). Despite its actual close proximity to Cairns, the couple felt transported on this island into the original Paradise. Their camp on the leeward side of the island faced the shore, and their view across the water towards the jungled mountain escarpment behind Cairns seemed to Nettie as if they were "looking at the originals of ancient engravings of the Garden of Eden" (1932, p. 9). That Biblical Eden had been under God's protection and she felt this place, too, was "a beautiful, safe jungle ... even more wonderful than the coral reef itself." There was "a gentleness about it—no thorns, poisonous reptiles, stinging insects. Instead, there are the unafraid birds ... and the bright, flickering butterflies, all seemingly sure of being in some forest fastness," she recorded in her journal (1988, p. 82). Like any Eden, there were no snakes in this brilliantly colored, naturally lush environment that was so different than anything to which they had been previously exposed.

Yet, there is menace even in Eden, and Nettie and Vance were aware that this paradise did not remain safe and peaceful for the entire year. The cyclone season returned annually to these Wet Tropics, with the potential to render this apparent haven a very unsafe harbor indeed. Although they had wisely timed their stay outside of the cyclone season, Nettie was acutely aware of the inherent danger lurking beyond the horizon, graphically describing a cyclone as an "insane bird with incredible force," in an echo of Vance's later description in *Cyclone*. She imagined the storm as "an unnamed and unnameable giant" that was "like some colossal animal darkly furred with cloud, each 'blow' of its paw a hundred miles an hour" (1934, p. 4). In fact, only a few months before the Palmers had arrived, on January 18 and 19, a cyclone had crossed Cape York Peninsula from the Gulf of Carpentaria to the west, a little south of the town of Coen. It had then travelled south down the coast beyond Cairns, causing major flooding around Tully and Innisfail where a child had drowned. Nettie noted astutely that such violent weather events became landmarks in regional memory; local people still recalled where they had been, she wrote, when previous severe tropical cyclones had struck, "as people who were in Europe remember where they spent the first days in August, 1914" (1934, p. 4). She praised the endurance of the fishermen she and Vance met with whom they discussed the dangers of working in the vicinity of the Great Barrier Reef during the cyclone season, a necessity because housewives still wanted to buy their fish. There was, the couple quickly became aware, profound peril lurking beneath the beauty of this paradise. "Every Eden has its serpent," Vance wrote, prefiguring his treatment in *Cyclone*, "and in the coral islands of the Great Barrier Reef the cyclone provides the chief menace to life—the one thing that mars an existence that would otherwise be idyllic" (1938, p. 4).

During their stay, the Palmers became good friends with two men and their families from the local maritime community: Bill Millard, who captained the nine-meter fishing and supply ketch *Mossman* on voyages north to Cooktown and south to Palm Island and the Hinchinbrook Channel, and John Demos (also known as Tinos), who was captain of the fishing boat *Quest* that often fished the waters around Green Island (Nettie Palmer, 1988, pp. 102–104). Both men were experienced seamen. Millard was a former Royal Navy officer who had served in World War I, and Demos had sailed the Mediterranean and the North Sea. Vance would often sail with Millard on his supply trips north up the coast to the villages of Daintree and Bloomfield, and on the return voyage they would usually stop to fish among the Low Isles. When Vance and Nettie left Green Island in November 1932, it seems fitting that they sailed south in the *Mossman* with Millard and his wife and children, who had decided to coincide the Palmers' departure with the Millard's first holiday In years, island-hopping from Fitzroy to Dunk to Hinchinbrook Islands, camping ashore at night, fishing and exploring.

After they returned to Melbourne, Nettie recorded in her diaries that during the following months she and Vance often discussed their experiences on Green Island and the Reef and their travels with the Millards (Jordan, 2011). Eventually, they decided that their trip had been so enjoyable they began to plan for a return visit to the Great Barrier Reef in the middle of 1933. They estimated they could put together a group of about thirty people who would be willing to share the cost of the venture and then, between June 21 and July 21, they would sail north from Townsville aboard the *Mossman* with Bill Millard, camping at Dunk, Palm and Green Islands and exploring the Reef (Barrier Reef Expedition, 1933). However, according to Nettie, these plans never succeeded in being completely watertight (1977, p. 82). Apparently, some of the leaks could not be sealed because the expedition never eventuated, and the Palmers remained in Melbourne. Nevertheless, they always retained fond and unforgettable memories of their association with the *Mossman* and Millard, whom Vance would later describe as a "good seaman, good comrade," a man he considered to be of "uncommon character and ability" whom people, whether Aboriginal or white Australian, trusted implicitly because "his most careless promise was his bond" (Palmer, 1934, p. 6).

Understandably, the Palmers were devastated to hear the news less than a year later that their good friend had been drowned when a cyclone had struck Far North Queensland near Cape Tribulation on March 12, 1934. Destructive winds, along with a nine-meter storm surge, had caused widespread damage and the loss of between fifty and sixty lives along with many boats, including Millard and the *Mossman,* and John Demos and the *Quest.* The wreckage of the *Mossman* was identified by Tom McDonald, pilot of the only aeroplane in Cairns at the time, who flew along the coast between Cairns and Cooktown after the cyclone to search for survivors of the various boats that had gone missing, landing at various places to identify wreckage and guide survivors to safety (McDonald, 1934). What he did was so helpful "as to make aviation seem a form of human effort able at last to mitigate, by warning and observation, the persistent peril for those at sea in these cyclone months" (1934, p. 4), Nettie wrote later.

Vance apparently agreed, effectively memorializing McDonald as the character Randall in *Cyclone*. His wording of Randall's flight to Cooktown closely follows McDonald's own published account in which McDonald reports that the cyclone had cut a visible swathe of destruction through the jungle of the then lightly-settled Cape Tribulation area, essentially destroying Daintree and the settlement of Bailey's Creek, now known as Cow Bay (McDonald, 1934). There was also some structural damage and flooding in Mossman and Cairns, and Nettie was indignant that newspaper journalists seemed more concerned about the property damage than the loss of life. She lamented their good friend and seaman Millard, with whom they had spent so much time on that long trip down the Reef, whose "courage, his camaraderie, his love of independence, and his enthusiasm for that lean, rich life of picking up a pittance with a small boat," whom they both remembered so fondly (1988, pp. 128–9). Vance was deeply affected by Bill's death, she wrote, as he had only recently lost another friend, Jimmy Throssell, the husband of author Katherine Susannah Pritchard. When Bill's frail and penniless widow,

Lillian, had to move to Melbourne with their two children, the Palmers took them in and comforted and cared for them (Jordan, 2011). Despite the Edenic memories that Vance and Nettie retained of their 1932 Green Island sojourn, the island and the Reef were not the same without their beloved friends, and the Palmers never returned.

However, Vance Palmer did return there in his imagination, fictionalizing events surrounding the 1934 cyclone over a decade later in his novel, *Cyclone* (1947), as well as in two short stories he wrote during the intervening years, "Cyclone" (1936a), and "Tempest" (1936b). In 1932, however, Palmer had touched on the theme of defeating fear of a storm in another short story, "The Big Wind," that he probably wrote on Green Island before leaving North Queensland, in which the protagonist and his wife live on Cowrie Island, which is off the Queensland coast near Hamilton Island in the Whitsundays. Although Palmer does not actually name the small port in which his protagonist lives in the short story "Cyclone," and his destination of Sharon River does not appear on any maps, there are certainly clues it is located in an Australian tropical region, such as paw-paws, frigate birds, coral reefs and a cyclone season in February. He also refers to Old Woman Island, a rather distinctive name that he apparently transplanted from an island (also known as Mudjimba Island) off the Sunshine Coast further south near Maroochydore. "Tempest" is clearly set in the same estuary port, with similar tropical features, but this time Palmer links the town more closely to Cairns with additional references to the Great Barrier Reef and the off-shore meteorological station northeast of Cairns on Willis Island.

In the novel, *Cyclone*, Palmer mingles the drama of the storm with other violent events that occurred while he was in the area in 1932, known as the "Battle of Parramatta Park." This bloody altercation exploded on Sunday, July 17, when approximately one hundred unemployed people who wouldn't leave their camp at the Cairns show-grounds were surrounded and severely beaten by between 1,000 to 2,000 local vigilantes, encouraged by police and local business owners and armed with iron bars, clubs, and fence posts wrapped in barbed wire. While by some miracle there seems to have been no fatalities, some 80 combatants were injured, some severely enough to be hospitalized. Although Palmer fictionalizes actual people and places in the novel, his models for some of the major characters and settings are thinly disguised. More importantly, though, Palmer brings the date of the historic cyclone's arrival forward some eighteen days to Easter Sunday, which fell at the beginning of April in 1934, for no obvious plot reason. Only the general time of the year would have made a difference to the setting, rather than a calendar month, because in the North Queensland wet tropics there are only two seasons rather than four: Wet and Dry. Setting the novel during "the Wet" obviously allows Palmer to use the increase in humidity and air pressure to enhance the build-up of tensions in the novel, but if he had only that purpose in mind he could have set it at any time between Christmas and Easter. For that matter, he could have had his fictional cyclone arrive on the same date as the historical one and it would not have made any difference to the novel's plot. Clearly, Palmer made a deliberate choice to set the novel's events predominantly on Easter Sunday and that choice will be explored later.

As we have already noted, Palmer did not return to the 1934 cyclone events in extended fictional form until many years later, yet *Cyclone* still seethes with tensions and conflicts, meteorological and personal, of that period. As a cyclone nears land, the humidity and temperature increases. The air feels heavy and stifling while the wind can actually fall away and an ominous silence prevail because birds will have left the area. In the stillness, even an isolated sound like a loud voice or a dog bark can travel a long way. Palmer's novel revolves around three men, Brian Donolly, Ross Halliday and Clive Randall, and the developing tension in the relationships between them are embodied in that build-up of atmospheric tension ahead of the on-coming cyclone. Donolly and his wife Fay have rented out their farm and come to the North Queensland coast with their family to establish, in partnership with Brian's old army friend Halliday, a coastal shipping business primarily financed by Randall, another army mate. However, their dreams of developing a thriving shipping business do not work out in the face of Depression-era economic hardship and the loss of their first boat in a fire, leaving them to struggle along with a battered old launch, the *Gannet*.

Afraid that the business will fail and leave her family stranded, Donolly's wife Fay becomes increasingly unhappy, remembering their farm as a place where they lived and worked together and where they were economically and socially secure compared to the overgrown property on the edge of a swamp where they now live. Here in this port, their financial and domestic security is at risk and, to make matters worse, Donolly is constantly away from home. With a cyclone approaching the coast, he has decided to sail north with Halliday because no one else is available to crew the boat, and he and Fay argue over his decision. Fay's state of mind is not improved by her suspicions that Randall is having an affair with Halliday's wife, Bee, nor by the actions of her brother, budding writer Tod Kellaher. For reasons that she does not understand, he has abruptly abandoned his job aboard the *Gannet* to live in the encampment of unemployed at the town show-grounds, seemingly prepared to risk both his reputation and his physical well-being to stand in solidarity with them in the face of threats of violence from local business people.

Palmer tightens the tensions between his characters as the cyclone nears, drawing together the potential damage from human conflicts with that from the surrounding epic, elemental forces of nature. The very wind becomes one of the animal-like, mythic beasts of air, land, and sea lurking within the landscape. "Big wind, he waiting there, jus' over skyline," a Murray Island man says to Brian Donolly in a bar. "Big wind, he bunch himself up, all ready to spring. I know. Feel 'm in head here, feel 'm in belly, feel 'm in bones" (Palmer, 1947, p. 104). Palmer's townsfolk will need to combat these beasts and monsters of chaos in order to restore order in their lives and to rebuild their place in a struggle that is legendary in its age-old scope. "Literature," proposes literary critic and theorist Northrop Frye, "is conscious mythology: as society develops, its mythical stories become structural principles of storytelling" (1970, p. 295), and in the literature of *Cyclone,* Palmer is developing his own conscious mythology of the tropical storm as he uses the serpent monster Leviathan as a trope for the cyclone and for those connotations of danger and fear of the unknown associated with it.

The Leviathan is a structural principle of Palmer's storytelling in *Cyclone*: the shape of the natural event becomes that of the misshapen unnatural. "In myth and literature, the monster is best understood as an embodiment of difference," argues Susanna Hoffman. "Monsters such as Caliban, Frankenstein, Grendel, Dracula, refuse to participate in and be part of the civilized order and as such are a threat to it" (p. 128). Every ordered civilization has a monster, a Grendel, a white whale, a zombie, or a Leviathan, so that we can clearly comprehend the outcome of disorder. For the same reason, we give the names and characteristics of the monsters of myth to the monsters of nature: volcanoes become fire-breathing dragons, tornadoes become devils, floods become hungry creatures that devour and swallow. When we can find no name by which to define the scale of chaos, we fall back on generic terms of difference such as "freak of nature." Then, just when we think that we have imposed some order on nature and have it under control, that the boundaries between order and chaos are finally delineated, the monster of disaster and disorder shape-shifts into some other form to challenge our attempt at cultural order and to cause us to re-assess our hubris. Neither does the monster always show up on schedule, although people try to impose time frames on it by endeavoring to detect and define a schedule or a season for it, like Ahab attempting to find the White Whale by tracking his migratory route across the ocean. But, cyclones may arrive earlier or later outside the customary season, for example, or make landfall further south, or they may be of a size so that their effects are experienced further inland than their usual radius. We install weather radar, seismographs, barometers, ocean buoys, and underwater sensors in efforts to warn of the approach of the weather monster, but nature insists on not always knocking at the door.

In myth, literature and science, the monster is out there at the limit of knowledge and resists detection and capture. By its very nature, it is unpredictable and undefinable, and there lies its true threat to society. We want to know it, but it does not want to know us. We may think it is gone, but it is only sleeping and can always return. Despite all our technology and science, the nature disaster remains the monster that threatens our claim to dominion over nature and the superiority of order. In the mythic construct, the monster is there for a reason: in challenging order with chaos, it forces us to constantly re-think the motivation and construct of that order because even with the mere threat of a potential apocalypse, the monster tempts us with enticing perceptions and probabilities of a new world. In the aftermath, the ordered society that we thought we knew might never be the same again, and there is always the possibility that we might prefer it that way. Beauty could be the result of encountering the beast.

In *Cyclone*, Fay Donolly, as unsettled as the townspeople and the weather, is locked in a mental struggle with the monster of chaos that threatens the order of her life and family. "You get screwed up in this wet season, feel as if some particular person or thing is twitching at your nerves" (p. 8), she anguishes. Although she briefly visualizes the wind as a swooping sea eagle waiting to strike, the threat of chaos ultimately takes the form in her mind of the great serpentine sea-beast, Leviathan. She perceives that what should have been a new Eden for the family is now under threat from various sources. The success of her husband Brian's business venture with a charter boat for which they have sacrificed their former home and security is in doubt; the marriage of one of the business partners could be failing, and her brother cannot find his direction in life. "So many ghosts are set walking by the threats of the wind," she senses and for her, these threats persist throughout this Easter weekend. The house and its environs become metaphors of her mental condition: the wind "nags" at loose fittings, working iron sheets free from nails, and it seems to Fay as if the ramshackle house is being "worried to pieces" (p. 2). The children are attacked by fevers, because the house is adjacent to a small swamp. The yard has become a jungled wasteland in which outhouses are rotting, where rampant vegetation hides potential hazards of rusting tin and fencing. There is, she senses, "a touch of something sinister in that fecundity of the warm water-logged earth. You could almost feel in the thrusting pressure against anything that had been built by human hands the assertion of a blind, destructive will" (p. 13).

The chaos of her immediate environment is symbolic of the unrest that permeates the town. To Fay, it seems that during these wet months, something has been "nagging at people, wearing their nerves to a frazzle" (p. 19), so that the town has become a "stew of quarrels, small and big" (pp. 51–2). It has been invaded by unemployed people waiting for the cane-cutting and fishing seasons to begin in which they will find work; much to the angst of the town's tourism-conscious business people, those waiting for work have set up camp at the showgrounds and refuse to move on. The mood of the town seems depressed, while old feuds fester and violence appears ready to erupt at any moment (pp. 51–2). Fay's promised Eden has become a dark, threatening place in which she struggles to maintain order and to protect her family, including her brother, Tod, for whom this place has also become "a battlefield, the arena for a great conflict, a testing ground for himself" (p. 82). Her husband Brian, too, has a feeling that deep down, "beyond the circle of light that ringed them something was waiting that would test their strength and endurance to the limit" (p. 135). That "something" is the stalking cyclone.

This chaos and conflict are symbolized by serpents large and small that invade Fay's decaying paradise: first, the python invades her untended and overgrown Eden garden, and then the serpentine sea-monster, Leviathan, invades her mind from within the storm. When the python appears early in the novel, Brian estimates that the seven-meter reptile must have seemed like a dragon as menacing as any in her picture-books to their diminutive and terrified daughter who had stepped on it. As far as Fay is concerned, the python must pay the ultimate price for threatening her family, and she insists that Brian execute it. Worried by a folk legend that the headless snake will still not actually die until sunset, she also insists that Brian bury it immediately, declaring that she loathes "all the slimy growths" from out of the jungle (p. 17). Even after the snake's burial, it still has the power "to writhe through her thoughts" (p. 110). But, their previous home had been a farm where killing snakes was an everyday occurrence, and so Fay realizes that her uncharacteristic reactions are indications of deeper issues. She is associating the snake in her Eden with the oppressing disorder and decay that has been encroaching on her life and corrupting her faith in her family. She feels she is losing control of her relationship with her husband as they go their separate ways, and that their ordered lives are being pushed apart by this place like the spouting being pushed from the roof by the luxuriantly invading grenadilla vine. Fay wonders if these comparatively recent fears and doubts are haunting her because she has begun to question the security of her relationship and her life. Perhaps, she muses, she is subconsciously using her reaction to the snake as an attempt to influence Brian to also hate this place to provide justification for leaving it (p. 111). So, when Brian does ultimately decide to accompany his friend Halliday north in the *Gannet* into the mouth of the cyclone beast, it is with Leviathan that Fay does battle in her mind in order to save her husband.

As the cyclone rages around her home, Fay envisions it as the enormous sea-monster, mortally wounded like the python in her garden, rearing its scaly bulk "dripping with weed and wrack, from the waste of waters," thrashing and convulsing in a death agony during which lightning sparks from its forked tongue as it sweeps its tail over beaches and reefs, swamping rivers (p. 159). This is a snake resurrected in anger, so strong this time that Fay feels it cannot be destroyed because it is "in league with the dark forces behind the deceptive appearance of things" (p. 159), always waiting to "raise his dragon head and turn the known world to an evil waste" (p. 160). The poet John Milton described the Leviathan in *Paradise Lost,* that

> Hugest of living creatures, on the deep
> Stretched like a promontory, sleeps or swims,
> And seems a moving land, and at his gills
> Draws in, and at his trunk spouts out, a sea [VII, pp. 412–6].

Herman Melville, on the other hand, firmly associated the name "leviathan" with whales in the modern literary mind when he selected Milton's lines as the epigraph for *Moby Dick* and then constantly repeated that association throughout the work. However, Palmer's use of "leviathan" in *Cyclone* clearly refers to the word's earlier mythical and Biblical origins as the name for the serpentine and terrifying great sea-beast that is cosmologically, according to Northrop Frye, "the element of chaos within creation" (1982, p. 190). When the Biblical psalmist praises the strength of the God who "brakest the heads of leviathan in pieces" (Ps. 74.14), he is referring specifically to a deity who has the power to defeat the mythical Canaanite monster Litanu, or Lotan (a seven-headed chaos beast linked with the sea), because the Jehovah of the Old Testament wants to remind people that He possesses the greater power by which He can rebuild order from chaos. When He finally does speak from within a whirlwind to the afflicted and despairing Job, God reminds him of that superior power with a series of rhetorical questions about the great beast. "Canst thou draw out leviathan with an hook? Or his tongue with a cord which thou lettest down? … Wilt thou play with him as with a bird? Or wilt thou bind him for thy maidens?" God asks, rhetorically implying that it is He, not Job, who can do such things (Job 41: 1, 5). After all, He reminds Job, "None is so fierce that dare stir him [Leviathan] up; who then is able to stand before me?" (Job 41.10). No one, of course: it will be God who restores order one day by punishing Leviathan, "that crooked serpent … the dragon that is in the sea" (Isaiah. 27.1). As Fay discovers, Leviathan may seem powerful, but it is possible to defeat the beast.

In this sea-beast, Palmer amalgamates the literal, the psychological and the mythical serpent. In Fay's mind, the literal snake that she ordered buried before it had time to die is resurrected, transformed into this mythical Leviathan that is allied with dark forces. It rises angrily from out of a familiar landscape of backyards and coral seas under which it perpetually lurks, ready to lay waste to everything. However, in her dream Fay finds an inner strength with which to escape it. She experiences a vision of an upturned boat with two figures clinging to it, from which she wakes in time to save her daughter. As she re-discovers that woman who used to take charge in a crisis, Fay re-establishes control over her house and the children. She persuades Randall to take his plane up to find the men, thus saving her husband's life, all the while maintaining the strength of will to hold firmly in her mind the protective image of the boat securely tied up at a safe mooring.

Like Fay, other characters survive the cyclone while involved in relationships in which life itself, though blind and battered, is "yet moving to some pulse in its secret core" (p. 189). They have to make choices about these relationships and, in many ways, the cyclone reveals to them their options. It is only when Donolly finally relies on his intuition and sense of portent and chooses to leave behind his confrontation with Halliday, for example, that he can marshal his energies to survive the cyclone. Up until now, he has chosen not to recognize the change in Fay's circumstances: that she now feels more responsible because she is concerned about their children's future. He does not want to admit, either, that his business relationship with Halliday has now reached a crisis point and that he may have to accept defeat. While part of Donolly recognized the seriousness of their current situation, he has been stubbornly keeping Halliday and their business afloat, partly out of loyalty to his friend but partly out of loyalty to his dream of a life without the pressures of worrying about the future. In doing so, he has become Ishmael to Halliday's Ahab as they both chase the elusive White Whale of their respective dreams. It will only be Halliday's death in the cyclone that finally frees Donolly to move on, as Ahab's death freed Ishmael.

Northrop Frye (1982) argues that the themes of stories have mythic foundations, and so he uses the term *mythos* for the narrative principle on which they are based. When Donolly, presumed dead, is eventually cast ashore alive onto a remote beach from the depths of the sea like Jonah regurgitated from his leviathan, Palmer is writing his own version of a traditional *mythos*. Donolly is the hero returning alive, having slain the beast when all thought him surely dead. He is Theseus returning after slaying the Minotaur in a subterranean labyrinth. More significantly, he is Perseus rescuing the chained Andromeda by slaying the sea-monster, Cetus, which has been threatening her, for within this particular *mythos* there is an etymological chain of connection. The Greek word *ketos*, Latinized as *cetus*, means a large fish, whale, or sea monster, from which is derived the English word *cetacean*. Although the English version of the Biblical story of Jonah usually has him swallowed by a whale, the more accurate translation of the original Hebrew term for the creature, *dag gadol*, is the less specific "great fish" which translates into Greek as *ketos*. However, Jonah's story does not end with him being swallowed by the leviathan because, after much pleading with God, Jonah is regurgitated onto the beach a changed man. Later in the Bible, Jesus links the *mythos* of Jonah to that of his own when, upon being asked by the priests for a sign, Jesus replies that there will be only one sign: as Jonah was three days and nights in the belly of the whale, so he would be "three days and three nights in the heart of the earth" (Matthew 12.40). He leaves his audience to supply their own conclusion to what would have been a familiar story to this group of scripture scholars. As in the returning hero *mythos*, Jesus was implying that he, too, would defeat the monster of Death in the Underworld and emerge victoriously. The day that celebrates this event on the Christian calendar is Easter Sunday and it is on this Sunday that Palmer has Donolly, having been presumed dead, found alive.

Palmer is writing in *Cyclone* about the great mythic themes of the struggle of good against evil, of life against death, of the fight with great leviathans from which it is possible to emerge triumphant. Brian and Fay Donolly's story is one of death and resurrection, of destruction and renewal. While his wife Fay is doing battle with the sea beast Leviathan in her mind, Brian is physically struggling with the sea that threatens to destroy him. When, like Jonah, he is thrown into the sea, he fights the forces that threaten to overwhelm him with "a will to extract the last effort from the sources of life buried in him, to go on and on and not be destroyed" (1947, p. 147). He fights in a dark, hellish place where the known world has dissolved and time has ceased to exist, where "demon voices, some wailing, some triumphant, broke loose, bringing images of devils riding and hounds giving tongue" (p. 142), where "demon powers" are at war, "shouting in voices that shook the heart with awe"(p. 144). To defeat these demonic figures of darkness, he summons up in his mind images of his family and of his home flooded with a warm radiance that permeates his whole being. Although swallowed by the sea, Donolly is not destroyed; like Jonah, he is ultimately regurgitated onto the beach as a figure typifying "life itself ... moving to some pulse in its secret core" (p. 189).

Fay Donolly also prevails and defeats her Leviathan of chaos, the beast of doubt and fear that has threatened to destroy her life with her family. Her cry at the end of her vision awakens her in time to save her daughter from possible harm when part of the roof blows off. As she protects her family, Fay's small familiar world flows back to her and as her vision of the storm fades, the cyclone loses its hold on her and its power wanes to a natural force she can withstand. Fay not only survives her cyclone experience, she transcends it. As she sees behind and beyond the mundane rituals of everyday life to the "terror and the mystery lurking behind the stolid face of things," she experiences an epiphany that enables her to gain access to a new dimension of understanding (p. 194). This apocalyptic cyclone reveals to her aspects of herself that she had forgotten, and she will never again be the person she was prior to its arrival. Fay's insights into the spiritual aspects of her cyclone experience reveal Palmer's interest in developing deeper emotional and psychic responses of his characters. Rather than merely recounting how Fay resolves her visions, Palmer uses her as a vehicle for something more unformed, more suggestive: a concept of the realm of nature as part of the unconscious, a concept inclusive of death and destruction as well as the will to live. Like

Mary Shenton in Palmer's short story, "The Big Wind," Fay will not be afraid of the wind again. Leviathan may still be out there, waiting, but Fay is now forewarned and prepared.

As if to reiterate his Easter Sunday point, Palmer wrote another resurrection into *Cyclone* of minor historical character models who died during the actual 1934 storm. In the novel, two girls named Mara and Jessie board the *Gannet* and ask to sail with Halliday and Donolly. Disturbed by the on-coming storm, they have become fearful, "as if the strange omens in sea and sky had touched their imaginations and conjured up terrors new to their experience" (p. 132), and they have decided to leave their uncle's boat. Despite the girl's pleas, however, Halliday and Donolly return them to the lugger, only for it to sink during the cyclone. While in Palmer's novel they are found alive after being washed up on a beach like Donolly, these two female characters are evidently fictionalized versions of Annie and Adelaide Pitt, who with a number of others drowned while attempting to swim ashore from a foundering boat during the historical cyclone.

Other characters also survive the storm of chaos in *Cyclone* and are granted the opportunity to restore their lives because the cyclone reveals other options to them. Uplifted in the aftermath of the storm by "a sense of having shaped something," Tod defeats his monster of uncertainty as he senses that his life will have future direction (p. 195). He realizes that a potential allegory made up of all the "teeming images that had filled his mind during the storm" has taken shape in his head if only he can find the right words, and there may be a possible future for him as a writer (p. 195). The pilot, Randall, also becomes aware of new opportunities. Previously distracted from the moral path by his affair with Halliday's wife, Bee, he takes off in search of the *Gannet*, aware that his sense of morality is restored and that he is in charge of himself again.

Not only individuals emerge from the storm renewed, but so does the port as a whole because, "The spectre of the monster as an 'outsider' enemy gives people cause and symbol to unify, as disaster victims characteristically do" (Hoffman, p. 130). Before the cyclone, people in Palmer's fictional town were lethargic, argumentative, and divided among themselves. Having forgotten what it means to care for their fellow man, they were even ready to evict the unemployed by force. However, the cyclone has been like an external enemy attacking them from the sea. It may symbolize their intangible fears but at the same time, it is a tangible opponent against whom they can rally: a cause in whose name they can unite in defense of the town, their property and their lives. Consequently, the sense of lurking evil in the town dissipates in the storm's aftermath, and a calm settles over a place that was ready to self-destruct, "as though with the passing of the storm some conflict had been resolved, some cord of tension relaxed" (p. 190). The streets of the town have been baptized by the rain and appear cleansed and newly washed. There is a new-found sense of community optimism, support and co-operation as streets are cleared and damage repaired, and there is economic opportunity as people are employed as the cane harvest begins and fishing boats put out to sea. This apocalyptic cyclone has revealed to them that the source of that strength by which they can survive such catastrophes lies within themselves and, just as importantly, lies within the strength of family and community. As the cyclone moves on and a new week dawns, the town and the people in it are resurrected into a new life.

Cyclone reads as a thoughtful, tightly constructed and controlled work, with themes of Edenic fall and recovery, of mythic chaos monsters that challenge order, of apocalypse and revelation, and of death and resurrection, and these are evidently themes upon which Palmer had been reflecting for some time. Although there was a gap between when the historic events occurred between 1932 and 1934, and when Palmer began writing *Cyclone* in 1945, an examination of plot and character elements in his three earlier short stories reveals that Palmer was apparently thinking about and experimenting with some of the themes, situations and characters in the novel prior to its publication.

In these stories, as in the novel, Palmer's major characters experience revelations about their lives during cyclonic events. His short story "Cyclone" begins with similar dreams of shipwreck and omens of bad weather, feelings of dread and of "terrors lurking on the edge of the skyline" as the novel (p. 30), but in this story the roles are reversed. The dreamer of disaster here is the male protagonist, Harry Shirlow, who like Gessler in "Tempest," and Fay Donnolly, is a character with a sixth sense for seeing things and hearing the wind before they happen. Like Brian Donolly, Harry's charter boat business has fallen on hard times and he and Flora are struggling to make ends meet. Harry suspects that his occasional crewman, Gourlay, is trying to seduce his wife, and this is the serpent in this particular Eden that rears its ugly head to gaze at him with "snaky, insinuating eyes" (p. 30). As in his other stories, Palmer uses the close and ominous weather to enhance and incubate tension until there is a sense of "ugly passions stored up in the smothering earth and windless air" (p. 30). When, despite his own misgivings, Shirlow takes Gourlay with him up the coast on his boat, their journey into the storm quickly becomes an epic struggle for survival against mythic beasts in an environment where the sea moves "as if swayed by some tide beyond the world's far edge." Palmer indulges in some zoomorphism here as his beast-like cyclone arrives with roar and a leap, and a "whistle of myriad wings" (p. 31). Shirlow and Gourlay, like Halliday and Donolly, attempt to seek shelter, only for them to be washed overboard as their boat is overwhelmed by the storm. As Shirlow also fights demons of the air to stay alive, he too has an epiphany that fear of the future has been paralyzing him. He has been trying to keep his boat above water, literally and metaphorically, by sheer strength of will and now, as the ship sinks, he is free from that. The conclusion of the short story is thus remarkably similar to the novel: boats are wrecked but both men survive to be reunited with their wives; the cyclone ravages the area north of Cairns while the town is largely unscathed; a lugger is lost with its crew. In Shirlow's case, he learns a lesson that he should have trusted his wife, but they will be able to start again with the insurance money. This cyclone apocalypse, like that of the novel, cleanses the protagonists' world of evil to reveal a place cleansed and renewed.

Palmer was still thinking about chaos monsters stalking the boundaries of a society terrified by the thought of some "wild thing moving across the sea-wastes beyond the still horizon" in his short story "Tempest," written a few months later (p. 30). Here the pilot protagonist, Gessler, scarred and blinded in one eye in a plane crash during the previous cyclone that struck the town, is a more complex character than his *Cyclone* counterpart, Randall. Much like Tom Fury, the lightning-rod sales-man in Ray Bradbury's *Something Wicked This Way Comes*, Gessler is intimately sensitive to changes in the weather: like Gessler, Fury could feel a storm approaching that "like a great beast with terrible teeth could not be denied" (1969, p. 5). Because of their violent encounters with them, Fury and Gessler are both marked harbingers of storms who warn heedless people of their approach.

Unable to reconcile with Gessler's injuries, his former lover Claire has left him to marry the womanizing Harry Monaghan, captain of the trading ship *Kestrel*, which has failed to return to port as the cyclone approaches. When Claire pleads with Gessler to search for him, he suspects Monaghan has been lured into some other harbor by feminine temptation, but he feels sympathy for Claire's plight and eventually agrees to search for him. However, once in the air he begins to doubt free will as the impression grows within him that he is facing some appointment with destiny. When his suspicions that Monaghan is with another woman are confirmed, Gessler becomes mentally blinded by rage and a desire for revenge, and he fails to heed his interior weather warnings as he recklessly takes off into the storm to tell Claire. As the cyclone's increasing power threatens to wrest control of the plane away from him, Gessler experiences an epiphany that while in succumbing to violent emotion he has risked being subsumed into "this idiot leviathan from the outer spaces that had turned earth and air into a meaningless welter of sound and fury," this is not who he really is. Instead, Gessler realizes that he must resist being tempted into a vengeful darkness and so he prays for light, which duly streams down from above to transfigure him. Whether Gessler survives or not, he has found his true destiny in "knowing more deeply what had been saved from destruction" (p. 31). Within the apocalypse, he has found revelation.

The only prototype for the character of Fay Donolly within this trio of cyclone stories is the character of Mary Shenton in Palmer's 1932 story "The Big Wind," published after his return from Green Island and before the previous two stories. Although she does not appear in person until nearly the end of the story, when even then she speaks only a few words, Mary's unseen presence dominates the entire work. It is because of her impending childbirth as a cyclone approaches Cowrie Island, on which she and her husband live, that he has to sail to the mainland in their small boat to bring back the doctor. Like the later characters of Gessler and Shirlow, her husband has ignored all natural warning signs that a storm is imminent, such as frigate birds, heavy surf, and windless air, and consequently he is now suffering fear and guilt for perhaps leaving his voyage too late, even for persuading Mary to live on the island in the first place. Once again, Palmer uses the atmosphere of the tropical environment to build tension: the heat is oppressive, the still air hangs "heavy and dead," and the "very trees seemed to have something ominous in their stillness" (p. 12). Yet, he reflects, they had known the dangers: he and the courageous Mary had heard the stories of previous "big winds" that had uprooted trees and thrown water-tanks through the air. Now, Shenton has had to leave her there while he makes a frantic journey across the intervening stretch of water to find the doctor.

As the cyclone overtakes them on their return journey, Shenton feels terror as he hears the shriek of the monster. Palmer again uses animal imagery to enhance that fear of the non-human: the wind that wants to destroy him leaps and roars; it is a "demonic tumult" like those earlier "big winds" about which Mary had expressed her fears (p. 13). Having taken shelter on an island as the storm passes over them, the two men reach Cowrie Island the next morning, only to discover that the baby was born during the night without difficulty: Mary has faced those fears and emerged triumphant. "I won't be afraid of wind again," she declares defiantly. "Afraid of anything else, either" (p. 13). As it will reveal to Brian Donolly in *Cyclone*, the cyclone as apocalypse reveals to Shenton the folly of hubris. He is a humbler man now who will be more confident in his wife's strength and more receptive to her needs. Because of her experience, Mary will no longer be afraid of the monster. She has faced her inner fears and discovered new strength that has enabled her to bring new life into the world. For both she and her husband, this is a genesis as well as a revelation.

"What tongue does the wind talk?" asks Bradbury's Tom Fury, posing a series of rhetorical questions like those of God to Job. "What nationality is a storm? What country do rains come from?" (p. 7). Like the lightning-rod sales-man, Vance Palmer's characters in his group of inter-connected cyclone stories sense and experience the mystery as well as the terror of these apocalyptic weather events, for the impact of these spiraling storms is more than that of a material disaster. These cyclones act as a revelation of things to come, a catalyst for change; they lay bare the inadequacies of lives while at the same time revealing opportunities by which we can overcome our fears and move forward into the future. Because of their cyclone experiences, Palmer's characters experience epiphanies that reveal their lives have been changed. While these are storms with the power to destroy, they can also create opportunities to rebuild new lives, new worlds. In writing *Cyclone*, Vance Palmer sought in his imagination to understand and cope with the challenges of a North Queensland place that now included memories of catastrophe and chaos, along with those of paradise and peace. In this novel he develops a response and relationship to that tropical place and so reveals an understanding of that *terroir*, for he wrote not only of tragedy but also of resilience and continuity of community during hard times. He wrote of a search to restore balance in time of disruption, of a search for meaning. He wrote of revelation.

FOUR

"Touching the edges of cyclones"

Thea Astley's Cyclones of Revelation

"Disaster comes out of the most sheltered places."—Thea Astley

In Thea Astley's universe, cyclones could also be much more than weather events. She, too, was aware that those paradoxes of destruction and re-creation could exist on a deeply personal level. She perceived an intimate relationship between the personal and the elemental: the cyclone is within as well as without. For Astley, we are all part of a swirling, spiraling, cyclonic universe that embraces the personal as well as the physical landscape. In her novel, *The Acolyte*, she describes the novel's protagonist and narrator, Paul Vesper as, "always touching on the edges of cyclones" (1985, p. 119), and in a 1991 interview with lecturer and literary critic Ray Willbanks she agreed that this applied to a number of her characters. After all, "Just being alive is like living on the edge," she declared, adding that her friend Patrick White had said this, not only in his 1973 novel, *The Eye of the Storm*, but in all his books, in which White had "taught us to look at the essence of things" (p. 28). When Willbanks suggested that she tended to bring her characters out of the eye of their storms to that very edge, Astley agreed by drawing another comparison with Patrick White. While he was taking his characters into the eye, she argued, "I think mine have been misguidedly trying to get right away, out of the entire ambient of the cyclone and, of course, that is not possible, not for any human. The minute you are born you are put into this situation" (p. 30). Astley believed that, like her characters, we are all in "this situation," that is we are all in the cyclone together. In order to survive that kind of intense, life-encompassing experience, she proposed, humanity needed to be aware of their connection by a common spiritual conscience that would enable them to withstand the storm if they came together to work as a group. There is "an unseeable umbilical cord linking all humans," she declared, and so instead of trying to go it alone, we should be reaching out to each other and reasserting commonality from which to gather strength as a community as it developed a spiritual conscience: "You find out about yourself," she advises, "by talking to others" (p. 30).

Astley's characters ignore this potential for connectivity at their peril. The symbolic storm that encloses them can divide them "by its very existence and psychologically oppressing nature" (Matthews, 2008, p. 43), as they endeavor to establish their position and their balance in a universe that often seems to make little sense. In *Girl with a Monkey* (1958), for example, trapped within her storm's eye for twenty-four hours, Elsie retreats to her own inner island where she attempts to distance herself as she watches the storm of Harry's anarchic love approaching her. It is not a storm she can avoid, however, and she fails to control the emotional cyclone that then whirls into chaos around her. Vinnie Lalor in *Descant for Gossips* (1960) shares with Elsie a sense of being on the edge of things and an intense consciousness of self, of being an island in the sea of humanity. Vinny, Moller and Helen all shelter on this island as a storm of malice, rumor, carelessness and squalor masses around them, encircling and eventually destroying them. George Brewster, *The Well Dressed Explorer* (1962), can be seen as a cyclone, laying spiritual and psychological waste to the lives of others around him as well as his own life, although he never sees it. His is the all-consuming insatiability of the cyclonic storm that grows larger until it collapses in on itself. In *A Kindness Cup* (1974), Dorahy the schoolteacher becomes caught up in his own personal cyclone as he becomes obsessed by his mission to finally reveal the truth about the massacre of Aborigines at Mandarana, a quest that had previously failed at the official enquiry that had exonerated whites for black deaths. Returning to a local reunion many years later, Dorahy's obsession drives him on despite the trail of destruction in its wake. His revealed truth raises no cup of kindness for a time long ago but, instead, wreaks havoc after which no-one's lives will be the same again.

Trapped within their whirling personal storms in Astley's Hardyesque vision of an uncaring Nature that defeats efforts to escape one's fate, Astley's characters often seem to be waiting for some revelation that will provide the key to their predicament and enable them to find something with which to fill an empty life. As D.H. Lawrence observes in *Kangaroo*, "You can't face emptiness long. You have to come back and do something to keep from being frightened at your own emptiness and everything else's emptiness. It may be empty. But it's wicked, and it'll kill you if it can. Something comes out of the emptiness to kill you" (1994, p. 204). As Vance Palmer's character Fay Donolly perceived, there is danger in paradise and one can sense—quite powerfully—the spectre of the uncanny in Astley's struggle to come to terms with the danger inherent in Australian space. The uncanny experience … both reality and nightmare, is simultaneously an expression of the sublime and an invitation to terror [Genoni, 2007, p. 40].

In three of Astley's novels, *It's Raining in Mango* (1987), *The Multiple Effects of Rainshadow* (1996) and, in particular, *A Boat Load of Home Folk* (1968), the uncanny experience that is both reality and nightmare is that of the tropical cyclone. For Astley, this elemental force symbolizes the danger that can come out of emptiness, whether personal or geographic, and so is an invitation to terror while at the same time an expression of the imaginary sublime.

In *It's Raining in Mango*, a cyclone makes a brief appearance as an instrument of judgment that destroys the Reeftown bordello, along with sixteen-year-old runaway Nadine Laffey, who has abandoned her home and her baby in a selfish attempt at independence. Yet in the middle of their terror, while the cyclone wreaks retribution on the women, there is a moment of the imaginary sublime. As the rapidly rising storm surge washes the building, the owner and the three working girls out to sea, one of them is still playing the piano. Sylvia's hands are "never more relaxed as they caressed the keyboard and her voice persisted against everything: 'Oh, away,' she sang, 'I'm bound to go, cross the wide Missouri'" (p. 63). Astley's dark sense of humor mitigates a terrible tragedy: four people are about to perish. Yet at least one of those people, Sylvia, demonstrates that while she will accept this judgment by the elements, it will be on her own terms: the sublime experience of music. She may be crossing the river, but it is through the medium of music that her voice persists "against everything." While it may demand her life, the cyclone has also revealed a way in which Sylvia can accept that death.

In *The Multiple Effects of Rainshadow*, it is the destruction of the Aboriginal mission at Hull River in 1918 by a severe tropical cyclone that precipitates the forced transfer of these people to Doebin Island (Astley's fictional name for Palm Island) which, in the book and historically, subsequently became a dumping ground for sick or recalcitrant Aboriginal people and Torres Strait islanders. Astley maintains the connection between the violence of place and weather when another cyclone, with "water that batters and batters in one monstrous waterfall" (p. 40), precedes the tightly-wound Superintendent Brodie's murderous rampage, a rampage that reverberates through the lives and future generations of the characters. As they attempt to contextualize those violent events over time, they are constantly touched by the edge of the cyclone that continues to fill the space of their lives. "You can't hide from the wind," the young Manny Cooktown knowingly predicts, "You close doors on the big wind it get angry, shake your bones, your house bones, body bones, little sticks it think, it knows little people sticks. Flesh fly away like grass in big wind" (p. 2). These cyclones are not just catalysts for events but metaphors of

Four. "Touching the edges of cyclones"

The SS *Tay* ashore after the Mackay cyclone, 1918 (Collection of John Oxley Library, State Library of Queensland).

the destruction and displacement that typifies the nature of life on an island where physical and psychological discontent and violence becomes rife.

Astley's cruise ship passengers in *A Boat Load of Home Folk* also struggle with the dangers of turbulent inner space and outer violent weather when a cyclone maroons them on a Pacific island for 48 hours. During that time, some experience revelation, but others experience a destructive apocalypse. The only Astley novel in which a cyclone plays a central, pivotal role, this is one of the most profound examples of the cyclone trope in Queensland literature. Yet the book has been critically dismissed because of its bleak perception of life. According to her biographer, Karen Lamb, even the London representative for Astley's publisher was "aghast at the awfulness of the new Thea Astley [novel]" because "her view of personality is so anarchistic" (2015, p. 195), and one publisher's reader deemed that it was depressing, unlikeable, and "a study in unhappiness and frustration" (p. 191). Lamb herself considers it the "book by Astley that ought not to have been published," yet her only justification for this broad condemnation seems to be that, like other Astley works, it once again placed doomed marriage and dismal partnerships "centre stage" (p. 191). But, Lamb and the critics before her are missing the point. It is what emerges from such despair that is important in this novel, in which her characters struggle to find their way within a cyclonic universe that strips away personal layers as well as the roofs overhead to reveal that which is hidden. Her use of the cyclone trope in *A Boat Load of Home Folk*, then, is particularly significant.

Astley once said that "literary truth is derived from the parish, and if it is truth it will be universal.... the parish is the heart of the world" (1976 pp. 255, 257), and the book's title characterizes this group of passengers as a parish: a domestic community. Her group is not a "boatload" in the sense of a full ship, but rather a "boat load," as in a load or cargo that is being transported by boat. Nor is this a cargo of "home-folk," as in people from the same hometown, but "home folk" as in people from homes. In other words, this is a cargo of people from homes in parishes consisting of suburbs and country towns. Stevenson is the only one of the group that actually lives on the island, and none of them is indigenous to it. As castaways on this island (and even Stevenson can be seen a castaway from his own home), this group forms a separate, singular, out-of-place community of average Australian townspeople from other communities: in effect, on this island they form their own parish. In her essay "The Idiot Question," in an allusion to suburban caricature characters made famous by the Australian comedian Barry Humphries, Astley proposes that such communities are universal, "that there must also be Upper Mongolian and North Vietnamese Mrs. Everages and Sandy Stones. There have to be" (1970 p. 5). Universal communities, however, also mean universal issues. Everyone, Astley perceived, has to face their own home truths and so, like many of the characters in other Queensland novels featuring cyclones, those in *A Boat Load of Home Folk* must face the ineludible cyclone along with its judgments, penalties and revelations. As the storm strips away the layers of the island's physical structures, it also strips away the layers of Astley's characters to reveal the loneliness, shallowness, absurdity, and unhappiness of their flawed humanity. Some do not survive such an exposure; others emerge changed by it.

In characteristic Astley style, this disaster comes on these "home folk" unexpectedly. After all, "Disaster comes out of the most sheltered places," she commented to Willbanks, revealing her awareness of the "sudden disruption in people's lives, the shock one gets when a situation he's taken for granted does a somersault and he is confronting the other side of it"(2008, p. 32). The way to survive these disruptions, Astley theorized, was to be connected and to be kind. She believed that kindness is "probably what matters more than anything in the world" (p. 35) and that it was kindness and talking to each other that essentially connected mankind, helping us to deal with the disruptions in life. "If you start looking for other people, discovering how they feel," she said, "you'll find out so much about yourself in the process that you won't believe it.... you find out about yourself by talking to others" (p. 30). However, these are traits that few of her self-centered group of cruise passengers possess. In fact, with typical Astley irony, most of them exemplify her argument about community in their efforts to forsake it, even though it is when they venture out alone into the chaos of the storm that they are in the most danger. Instead of recognizing their community, they remain, as Matthews suggests, "islands of intense self-consciousness seeking, in assertive, almost desperate avowals of identity, bastions against encroaching chaos" (2008, p. 43). There are no heroes in this disaster: just flawed and mortal characters trying to survive by guarding their "self," their essence of individual identity, against further damage. Even in the face of punishing opposition, Matthews contends, Astley's characters are convinced that amid all the failure, evil intent and sordidness surrounding them, there is "some last, lucent distillation of the human spirit whose integrity is worth preserving against the coming storm" (p. 53). In fact, he maintains, Astley "experiments both with the kind of individual and the nature of the personal stance that, together, will be most capable of enduring life in the eye of the storm" (p. 46).

Of all the characters in *Boat Load*, it is the island's agent Stevenson who experiences the epiphany that reveals to him that distilled essence of his human spirit within which he finds his integrity. A man "of direct eye and unused by nature to practising duplicity" (1968, p. 71), Stevenson finds that after seven years on the island he is practicing that very art with Marie Latimer. When his wife, Holly, discovers the liaison, she leaves him and returns to Australia with their daughter and son, Timmy, who is sent to boarding school. However, Stevenson finds only temporary sexual fulfillment with Marie, who did not "need men except when the singing of her body became so high and clear it could not be ignored" (p. 72). She is merely using Stevenson and he knows it, and his deep unhappiness manifests itself in a heart attack and chronic internal pain that he seeks to deaden with alcohol. In turn, Marie is aware of her shallowness and inability to find spirituality in love and consequently believes that it is not Stevenson but she who deserves to feel pain (p. 108). Stevenson is conflicted; the sensitive stranger within himself, whom he is attempting to discover and to know, has become obsessed with a woman who has isolated herself because she believes that to show she cares demonstrates weakness. In order to remain with her, he too would have to learn not to care and he does not really want to be that kind of person.

Eventually, Stevenson realizes that his relationship with his wife is about more than himself and physical passion; between him and Holly, there is "a congruence of needs imposed by others that made him feel the relationship shared" (p. 165). In particular, there are the needs imposed by his son, Timmy, with whose loneliness and isolation he empathizes and whose love he does not want to lose. Then, like the Biblical Saul, Stevenson has a vision on a road. While returning down the mountain in his truck during the onset of the cyclone, his son seems to appear in the seat alongside him, urging him repeatedly not to send him back to boarding school. Timmy does not want to live away from home or to be with his father and another woman; he wants to be together with his mother and father as part of a family. Stevenson recalls the model plane he once gave Timmy: although the gift was initially rejected, he would later see the boy hunched over it intently, "stroking the wingspan like a lover" as Timmy comprehends how much the plane symbolizes his father's love for him. Stevenson ultimately realizes that he does not want to continue in a life with Marie Latimer in which he is dying spiritually, as well as physically. She cannot tell him she loves him, and neither of them believes that she will ever actually be his wife, even when she reveals in the aftermath of the storm that she is pregnant. Ultimately, he refuses to succumb to the temptation of death as an easy way out proffered by his medication; instead, he decides to embrace the needs of others and to live, even if that does mean staying in a marriage that could well remain loveless. While Kathleen Seabrook realizes that she is now "miraculously unbound from the rock of twenty years of marriage" (p. 183) as she leaves the island after the storm, Stevenson's new-found sense of duty to his family and of love for his son will bind him to that rock. In making that choice, he perceives integrity within himself worth preserving, in keeping with his belief that "[w]e must concern ourselves [with others]" (p. 83). In doing so, he becomes one of the few characters in *Boat Load* who stands, as Matthews so aptly puts it, "pitiably but unmistakably against the hurricane," strengthened by the vision of his epiphany (Sheridan and Genoni, p. 53).

The same, however, cannot be said for most of the others stranded on the island, for this storm is not just a literal storm trapping them there. It is also a storm of hypocrisy, vanity, stupidity and maliciousness, generated by those who refuse to be part of the group and so who have isolated themselves from their companions and from their own selves. In Astley's world, however, you cannot go it alone; only staying together as a community provides protection from the storm, and yet so many of the characters of *Boat Load* are, in their isolation, living unprotected within their own individual cyclones. Unlike Stevenson, they are "afraid to examine the gyrating circumference of mortality spinning around them because they are afraid of what such an apocalypse might reveal" (Astley, 1965, p. 195). However, cyclones are ineludible: one cannot stop them any more than change their direction. Some damage is inevitable. This inescapable apocalypse reveals the inner lives of these home folk as well as judging their worth. Five of *Boat Load*'s characters, Verna Paradise, Kitty Trumper, Father Lake, and Gerald and Kathleen Seabrook, are already on the edge of cyclones in Astley's preceding novel, *The Slow Natives* (1965), the title of which, Astley suggests in its epigraph, was derived from a joke about elephants stomping on those who do not keep

Four. "Touching the edges of cyclones"   91

moving fast enough. While it is not essential to read *Slow Natives* before reading *Boat Load*, doing so does give some background to character motivation. Astley's suburban and small-town worlds of *Slow Natives* are ones in which "adults talked and corrupted each other, slandered, hated, betrayed, remained pathetically loyal and pretended ... self-containment, assurance..." (p. 16). In *Boat Load*, Astley impels her characters, whose parishes are now removed to an island where they are forced to become slow natives, into intimate and prolonged proximity to each other. These marooned townspeople are overtaken by an apocalypse that not only exposes their underlying corruptible natures but also judges them. In this sense, *Boat Load* can be read as a morality tale in which, "The tropical island represents nature, and nature, in the form of a tropical cyclone, reaps retribution on the whites for their sins" (Lever, 2008, p. 131).

In *Slow Natives,* Iris Leverson asks her husband prophetically: "Think of an island. Think of the most gem-like exotically gleaming island you can.... Who would you most hate to be wrecked with?" (1965, p. 8). For Kathleen and Gerald Seabrook, that person will be each other. They are trying to repair a marriage that has foundered on the reef of Gerald's susceptibility to seduction when they re-appear in *Boat Load*, but it is doomed from the start. Because Gerald has not learned anything from his latest domestic disaster, this voyage is merely a "pseudo-placatory gesture to patch a marital breach" (1968, p. 4). Kathleen, who is tired of the way he uses charm and plausibility to manipulate people, already hates Gerald in any case because of his subtle rejection of her in maliciously refusing to do anything to alleviate her unhappiness with their marriage. He constantly attempts to seduce women to reassure himself of his masculinity, even though success is unfulfilling. His liaisons become, instead, crumbling farces "of stale gesture and promise, unmoistened by the tears of his wife or even of the other women he had used and forgotten" (p. 155). For Gerald, this is all a defense mechanism. Behind the jocular façade, he lives in fear that he might actually be the joke, and so he constantly needs to be reassured that he exists by turning to other people without realizing that his wife, too, longs to be loved. However, as her love for Gerald is rapidly eroding, Kathleen has been indulging in some sexual revenge of her own while considering the ultimate fate of their relationship. Despite being unsure that she has the self-confidence to ultimately divorce him, Kathleen nevertheless decides to leave Gerald, "for my humiliation is too constant and extended." She realizes in her own epiphany that, despite all she has endured, she has made "no ripple at all on the surface of existence and none on him. Victim. All the time victim" (p. 160). Like fellow passenger Kitty Trumper, Kathleen perceives herself as a martyr, as a woman whom Gerald and her occasional lovers never really see, and she vows that in the future she will "avoid the lilt and fall and rhythm that men create in me" (p. 215). Gerald, on the other hand, never sees anyone but himself. Unlike Stevenson, he experiences no epiphany that will unite him with his family, only a solitary desire for revenge as he vows at the end of the novel to continue punishing Kathleen.

Living in a house filled with framed pictures of herself, vain and superstitious Kitty Trumper, "thrower of salt, the avoider of ladders, the reader of astrological forecasts" (1965, p. 88), is a fifty-something former ballerina who never admits to her age. Time and tragic events have, however, taken their inevitable toll. Her forehead furrowed by "barbed wire worries," the Kitty we meet in *Slow Natives* desires to be a saint to atone for her sin of having an abortion during World War II (p. 93). "You love to crucify yourself. You're a born martyr," her friend Verna Paradise accuses, reminding Kitty that even her school nickname was "Alma Martyr" (p. 99). Verna Paradise becomes increasingly frustrated that Kitty Trumper can never forgive herself; her sins never leave her, filling and possessing her life, turning her into a "wary, god-frightened figure … cowering before imagined divine wraths and counting her sins on her fingers" (p. 94). She constantly feels she deserves to be punished, which angers Verna. "It's what you want, isn't it?" she rails at her. "I mean you are really longing to be punished, aren't you, for real or imagined sin? So you can't lose, whatever happens" (p. 93). True to her self-imposed calling, Kitty faithfully and constantly carries her guilt with her, saving her sleeping tablets while contemplating suicide, yet never indulging in that luxury because, like the dedicated martyr she is, she daily resolves that it is nobler to remain alive and endure. Whatever the source of her guilt as a schoolgirl, it is compounded in *Slow Natives* when she turns to her gardener, the virginal teenage Chookie, for physical solace with disastrous consequences. Ultimately unable to surrender to mortal desire, Kitty cries rape and Chookie is forced to flee, only to be killed in a car accident before she can ask his forgiveness. There is more than a touch of dark irony in Kitty's eventual death at the onset of the cyclone in *Boat Load* as the result of an assault by another boy who this time rejects her because of her age and lack of beauty.

On the other hand, Verna Paradise, dressed in clothes as multi-colored as a tropical bird, with her painted face and fingers laden with opals, has played hard to get since the age of sixteen, a game at which she has been much too successful. Now, when she would like to have someone with her, she has no one. Nevertheless, like Kitty, she has always expected that men will be attracted to her. Now, she is bitter that seduction is drifting beyond her ageing grasp. Although each new place in which she arrives, with its unknown people, offers her the chance of finding Mr. Right, by now "She didn't really care if it were Mr. Wrong, although at sixty-two she knew, and her friends told her so, she should have had more sense" (1968, p. 7). With her eyes hidden by large, dark, circular sunglasses, the tall and angular Miss Paradise looks like some predatory insect seeking prey; naturally cruel, she's feigned kindness for years to keep Kitty Trumper as her last and only friend, for "Miss Trumper needed Miss Paradise more than Miss Paradise needed her" (p. 93). But, the cyclone of *Boat Load* strips away the layers of that pretense and destroys the Eden of their relationship.

It was, appropriately, Kitty's curiosity about the existence of hell-fire that triggered their journey to this island and its volcanic inferno. In a moment of sly maliciousness, Verna suggested that they should visit a volcano so that Kitty could look into it and have her first glimpse of the hell-fire she so desires to experience (p. 95). However, once they are on the island together, both women are suddenly aware that they are in fact alone. Verna has a "moment of prescient emptiness" when realizing that for thirty years she has been driven by the need to possess men but now that need has gone, leaving her terrified she will not be able to regain possession of herself. Kitty realizes that she no longer feels completely absorbed by guilt and sin but seems to be left with nothing in their place and because of her own sudden emptiness, loses her will to go on (p. 87). Verna loses her patience and violently rejects her best but last friend, a rejection that leads to Kitty's lonely death. Fleeing Verna, Kitty makes the defining decision to set out on her personal Calvary journey up the mountain, knowing that "until you have done it you will be obsessed" (p. 101). This journey towards her fear is the long-awaited destiny that she must fulfill.

But, when she reaches the crater, Kitty does not find her anticipated pit of fiery hell. Instead, she sees the water of a lagoon, and as the cyclone strikes the island she experiences in the wind and rain an inner turmoil "that matched in its [the lagoon's] surgings the inward gusts of guilt that had been her terrible sea for half a lifetime"(p. 102). As if to wash away that guilt in a form of baptism, Kitty strips naked and immerses herself in the lagoon. Then, at a moment when the storm pauses, like Elizabeth Hunter emerging into the cyclone's eye in Patrick White's *The Eye of the Storm*, when "all else was dissolved by this lustrous moment made visible in the eye of the storm" (1977, p. 410), Kitty has her epiphany. The rain stops, the wind dies away and the trees become still, seemingly watching her, as Hunter too felt watched by the eye, and when Kitty emerges to dry herself in the brief sunlight, she sees she has "no shadow at all" (p. 104). Absolved, she no longer throws a shadow of guilt. Cleansed, she is now unwittingly ready to meet her fate at the hands of a thief on her way down the mountain. Later, Stevenson discovers her dying of shock by the roadside and drives her into the port town already under attack by the cyclone. Although she dies there without the final blessing of Father Lake, she is accepted by the storm and then by the sea that ultimately "beds down the once-lovely Trumper" (p. 218). Too late, Verna discovers she can hate herself as she wishes undone "what was irremediable" (p. 149). Now she is truly alone to assume Kitty's mantle of guilt, while Kitty will remain an integral part of the paradise for which she longed.

Like Vance Palmer, Astley bestows elemental, animistic qualities of the monster on her cyclone, such as when Fay Donnolly envisions the vast, scaly bulk of the wounded, mythic Leviathan within the storm, rearing his "enormous head, dripping with weed and wrack" (Palmer, 1947, p. 159). Astley's cyclone, too, has been pursuing this island all day like some blood-crazed beast of prey until it has finally caught it (1968, p. 145) and then, seizing its quarry, the storm sets about devouring it. This is a contest of elemental gods in which nature defeats a religion that has been artificially imposed on this environment. Traditional religion's surrender is symbolized by the statue of Our Lady of Sion left lying face down in the grass (p. 170), and by the empty ritual of a Mass that merely mollifies faces that have already begun to turn away (p. 218). The island is not the paradise it appears to be superficially; it is as dark and threatening as it is tropical and bright. The active, smoking volcano of Tongoa looms over picture postcard palm trees and beaches, so powerful in its dominance of place that Miss Paradise finds herself repeating its name over and over in "a kind of hieratic rhythm," as if to placate some pagan entity with ritual before she sets foot on the island (p. 6). Even Kitty Trumper believes that there is something within the force of the volcano's presence that attracts her "like God" (p. 91). The trees threaten like "great prongs" and, unheeded, the birds have left the island in advance of the cyclone. The hills stagger back from the heat, the "passion vine jungle" encircles the inhabitants, and even the bar's favorite tune is the Beatles' "Eleanor Rigby," perennially reminding the clientele of all the lonely people. In this desperate place, "We are all waiting for something," Lily the barmaid declares. "Who knows for what?" (p. 115). As they disembark from the ship, the travellers' faces are already like savage gardens, and they will find that this is an Eden in which serpents are alive and well.

In fact, one of the resident island priests, Father Lake, has already met his serpent and been unable to resist the voice of temptation. Under investigation because of his involvement with one of the native boys, Lake is isolated by his struggles with his faith and his sexuality. Afflicted by boredom, alienated from his profession, Lake is now self-destructively intent on leaving the priesthood and an island where the brilliance of the Light of God is outshone by "heat, by everlasting summer, by sea dazzle, by sweat, by the apathy of the congregation … by his own growing despair" (p. 19). According to Lake's bishop, Deladier, such despair is the unforgivable sin, and it is while sinking into this Slough of Despond that pilgrim Lake finally succumbs to temptation in the form of the amoral sixteen-year-old houseboy, Johnny Terope, who epitomizes the potential of paradise to corrupt. Already far too knowing about older people's desires, he becomes Lake's nemesis. In the face of such temptation, Lake is afraid of himself and with good reason. Unable to find anyone to listen to his cries for help, stranded within his cyclone's eye at "the middle of the world, the ripe, seedy, pulpy middle"(p. 27), he seems helpless when confronted with his oncoming destruction upon being discovered in an embrace with Terope. Opportunistically seizing his advantage, Terope writes a letter of complaint to the local Resident that results in Lake being investigated by his church, in the menacing form of the black-voiced, heavily jowled Father Greely. Astley reveals at the end of the novel that Terope is also the thief who fatally terrorizes Kitty Trumper on her return from the volcano, although he is more interested in robbing her than in any sexual attack. Astley implies that is, in fact, Terope's sexual denial of her because he considers her ugly, rather than any physical violence, that ultimately brings on her death from shame and humiliation. It is as if Terope, a figure of moral judgment for Kitty as he is for Lake, arrives from within the cyclone to strip away her last layers of deception, leaving her inner person as naked as her outer body. Kitty dies from exposure to herself as much as from exposure to the elements

Kitty and Lake's sins merge when Lake, still obsessed with self-destruction, refuses to help or offer comfort to the dying Kitty when she is brought back to the bar because he no longer considers himself fit to do so. By the time he admits responsibility for that denial to himself, it is too late; he has refused both the kindness and the duty of absolution, and consequently she has died unconfessed and unshriven (p. 200). Lake is left with, "at the centre of it all, like the red heart of the volcanic core, his own blazoned guilt" for deserting someone in need (p. 212). Yet, in the midst of destruction, the cyclone as apocalypse reveals to Lake that the "wind-purge" of that night has cleansed him of pretense. As he leaves the island, he can now admit to himself his true nature: that he feels "nothing at all, no responsibility of any kind, no moral urgency. That was it, the end, the finish" (p. 208). He, too, has been confronted by the revelations of the cyclone and found wanting.

Ironically, rather than the kindness that Astley suggested should be the motivating force that connects people, it is guilt that serves as the bond between many of the characters of *Boat Load*, most of whom experience some measure of it during the novel and some of whom are still dealing with it at the end. As well as the guilt within Trumper and Lake, for example, Miss Paradise is burdened with guilt by the end of the novel for her bitterness and anger that exiled Kitty to her death; Kathleen Seabrook feels guilt over her internal quandary about whether she will stay with her husband or leave him, and Stevenson experiences such guilt over his affair which has led to his son being sent to boarding school that it is literally eating at him from the inside. It is guilt that binds the group who seeks shelter in Miss Latimer's apartment into a community that survives those storm-wracked hours as they discover in each other a collective strength. Their culminating moment is Verna

Paradise's serving of a meal of cardboard concealed in white sauce. On one hand, this meal is an act of revenge that is meant to expose a man's stupidity: Verna wants to make the foolish Gerald Seabrook "munch folly," which he obligingly does, refusing to admit to his egotist self or to anyone else what he's actually eating (p. 181). On the other hand, Verna as "priestess Paradise" serves a meal that is also an act of communion; it draws the group together in the act of eating and, for a select few, in their secret knowledge of the recipe (p. 182). As a result, some of the group are freed of their guilt and can share types of rebirth, which can happen in communities that have survived traumatic experiences, in which,

> for one dreadful minute, people can feel that their community is destroyed, that they are now naked and alone in a terrifying wilderness of ruins, but then there is a surge of euphoria as people realize that their community has survived.... In celebrating the recovery of the community, they are also celebrating their own rebirth [Erikson, p. 235].

Astley's character Katherine Seabrook, for example, realizes during the storm that she will not now "be won or beaten back" and that she is "miraculously unbound from the rock of twenty years of marriage" (p. 183). On the morning after the cyclone, she awakes in a child-like state, sucking her thumb, rebirthed physically and spiritually. This small community of cyclone survivors discovers strength through common experience that helps them endure the storm, even if in the aftermath some of them still hate each other. This experience changes them all in some way, and so their personal world will not be the same as before. Due to people's post-trauma shared perspectives, "they look out at the world through different lenses. And in that sense they may be said to have experienced not only (a) a changed sense of self and (b) a changed way of relating to others, but (c) a changed world view altogether" (Erikson, p. 241). As a result of their traumatic experience, Astley's cyclone survivors have received revelations of both the end and the beginning.

In *A Boat Load of Home Folk*, the outer storm encompassing Astley's every-day people "was beginning to match the inner one" (Astley, 1968, p. 143). Their cyclones are within as well as without. As these characters attempt to cope with their internal and external violent weather, their perception of themselves, of others, and of the world is changed. Some are touched by the edges of cyclones while others are consumed by them, but no one escapes them. As Astley warns, from the moment of birth we are in the storm. Rather than the pessimistic and depressing novel some have claimed it to be, *A Boat Load of Home Folk* is a profound novel of the human experience in which Thea Astley uses the elemental cyclone as a trope of apocalypse that is both an instrument of destruction and a catalyst of revelation. As such, this novel has a meaningful place within Queensland and international literature that employs tropes of cyclonic storms. Weighed in moral balances by the elemental gods of whirling air, some of Astley's home folk are found wanting; yet in the aftermath of the cyclone, among the ruins, others experience revelations of understanding and enlightenment.

Five

Threading the Eye of the Cyclone

Elizabeth Hunter's Epiphany in Patrick White's The Eye of the Storm

"At the still point of the turning world."—T.S. Eliot

At the center of *The Eye of the Storm*, within the eye of an encircling emotional and spiritual tempest, is the aged and bed-ridden matriarch Elizabeth Hunter who is seeking enlightenment. As she becomes less able to see outward, Hunter's sight turns inward in her attempt to understand the significance of the most meaningful point in her life: an epiphany fifteen years earlier during a Queensland tropical cyclone that ravaged White's fictional Brumby Island. While her daughter, Dorothy, chose to run from this storm, the formidable Hunter remained on the island to meet the gaze of the eye in which she experienced an epiphany that revealed the insignificance of her life and the existence of a power far greater than her own. While on the island, she becomes aware that her life has been significantly favored: she has retained her beauty, her wealth, her sharp mind and her attractiveness to men into late age. Until now, she has taken such attributes for granted, assuming they were due to her own selfish power as a woman. However, while within the eye of the cyclone, she realizes that there is a greater power in the universe that she must accept in order that her life will end at the appropriate time with meaning, and her acceptance of this revelation is symbolized in a communion-like act within the eye when she shares bread with seven black swans. Subsequently, even though Elizabeth Hunter does not appear to change that much superficially, she embarks on a voyage of spiritual discovery about her life that does change her perception about its worth and its significance. Her ultimate reward for this endeavor is that when she does eventually die, she does so with a greater understanding of the meaning of her life and the timing of her death. However, Hunter's journey towards the end of her life is not an easy one, because White believed we needed to suffer in order to find the right path through the labyrinth of our life towards spiritual peace, a labyrinth often symbolized by White with the pattern of the mandala that so appealed to him because he believed life had symmetry (Marr, 1994, p. 412). Hunter suffers as she is stripped of all things material by the cyclonic storm, suffers as the storm of old age ravages the beauty and dignity of which she was once so proud, suffers as she remembers the betrayals and failures of her past, and she suffers as her thankless and loveless children hover like vultures around her bedside waiting for her to die. Only by enduring the inner storm as well as the outer one can she thread her way through the eye of the cyclone to the still center of peace and spiritual awareness.

White invested much of himself in *The Eye of the Storm*, as well as investing his spiritual philosophy. In his memoir *Flaws in the Glass*, White claims the original idea for the novel came to him as a "flash of prescience" after a visit with his elderly mother in London, shortly before her death in 1963 (1981, p. 149). Like Elizabeth Hunter, she was in her eighties, nearly blind and confined to a bed where she was surrounded by a bevy of nurses, and she died sitting on her commode (Marr, 1994, p. 242). Like Hunter's children, Basil and Dorothy, White and his sister had attempted unsuccessfully to persuade their mother to live in a nursing home and to divide her possessions to avoid taxes. His problematic relationship with his mother and the circumstances of her death had a profound impact on White who informed Cynthia Nolan, author, designer and wife of painter Sidney Nolan, that his female protagonist would be, "a great beauty, bitch, charismatic figure, destroyer and affirmer all in one" (p .402). His characterization of Elizabeth Hunter certainly includes those qualities. During the next few years he continued to turn ideas over in his mind for a novel about such a woman, writing in 1966 that "I have an idea for a novel I am going to write one day, about a similar mummy, half senile, but with moments of blinding, brutal perception" (p. 295). By mid–1970, having declared to author and critic Geoffrey Dutton that "I have never known so much about a book before starting to write it," White had almost finished the first draft of his new novel (p. 353). However, with successive drafts, writing such a personal work grew increasingly harder, and he eventually acknowledged that as "Everything becomes more gnarled and inward-looking," this seemed to be the most difficult book he had yet attempted (p. 371). Nevertheless, he kept writing and by the time he was completing the work three years later, he had become aware of its profound significance to his canon.

In answer to a question about his religious philosophy, he once wrote that he had been forced to accept belief in a supernatural power because various "incidents and coincidences" had suggested to him that there was "a design behind the haphazardness." Consequently, he had become "obsessed" by his latest novel "because in it I think I have come closer to giving the final answer" (p. 409). Although White was typically ambivalent about what that answer might be, let alone the original question, he did give clues. White once suggested that in one sense the novel as mandala might represent "the still centre of the actual cyclone," and that in another sense it might be "the state of peace and spiritual awareness which Mrs. Hunter reaches on the island and again before her death" (p. 412). If White does give a "final answer," then, it is that there is a spiritual design: a pattern. He senses that there is a supernatural power forming order from chaos, and we will see in this chapter how he transcended the personal matters which were the origins of his novel to address the universal search for a spiritual path. For Elizabeth Hunter, the peace that she finds within the still eye of the literal cyclone comes to represent the peace and spiritual awareness that it could be possible for her to find at the close of her chaotic life.

White was engaged in his own search during his life. Although raised as a member of the Church of England, he drifted away from it as he "went through youth believing in nothing but my own ego, because I had to rebel against my family and imagine I was an intellectual" (p. 196). Then, one night immediately prior to Christmas, 1951, he fell in the mud of his Castle Hill farmyard while carrying food to some puppies during a storm. As he lay there, blinded by rain and cursing a God in whom he did not believe, he had an epiphany about his mortality and lack of spiritual hope, feeling truly humbled as he suddenly realized that his disbelief "appeared as farcical as my fall." He always believed that this was the turning point in his life, for shortly after this, "faith began to come to me" (1981, p. 144). However, he never did actually return to formal religion, despite some attempts, having decided that because churches destroyed the mystery of God, he "had to evolve symbols of my own through which to worship" (1994, p. 196). He had difficulty coping with the paradox of was it "ever possible to believe entirely in somebody one knows by heart, who is, at the same time, the one it is impossible to know?" (1981, pp. 144–145). This search for answers to fundamental spiritual questions carried over into White's work, and *The Eye of the Storm* "has the fundamental plot of all the books White wrote after falling in the storm at Castle Hill: the erratic, often unconscious search for God" (Marr, 1994, p. 354). Still, the deity for whom White searched remained for him unknown and unknowable, and so he does not seek to reveal the processes of his hidden God. For White, they too were hidden.

Instead, White's chief concern is with flawed human existence and man's spiritual predicament, or what he terms "the relationship between the blundering human being and God." Everyone can make mistakes, he believed, and when we make them there is a Divine Power "who has an influence on human beings if they are willing to be open to him" (White, 1990, p. 24). Like White, his characters struggle within their human limitations to understand their destiny and to comprehend the nature of this hidden deity, but ultimately that deity is beyond their comprehension. White's friend, Thea Astley, who once said that she hoped "so much there is a God" (Sheridan & Genoni, 2008, p. 29), and who was always "interested in the misfit, the outsider, the less than successful" (p. 1), might well have termed that relationship to which White referred as being between the misfit and God. Astley's group of misfit passengers in *A Boat Load of Home Folk* (1968), also have their mortal lives stripped bare by a cyclone and are forced to explore the significance of relationships with each other and with God. Although neither White nor Astley considered him or herself Christian in an orthodox sense, both explored their own kind of faith and wrote about characters who also searched for meaning. However blundering the relationship might be, it did not mean that White thought his God remained remote from humanity. Instead, White believed that there was always potential for moments of dialogue between the individual and God and that one should accept the opportunity for dialogue when God offered it, for it was by engaging in such conversations that the individual could ultimately achieve union with God (Beatson, 1977, p. 9).

Nevertheless, White also accepted that we had to endure some suffering in order to achieve this union because it was only by and through suffering that one could return by grace to the presence of God. White believed that this spiritual journey was a cycle, as Laura Trevelyan explains in his novel *Voss*: "How important it is to understand the three stages. Of God into man. Man. And man returning into God" (1957, p. 411). Despite the obvious reference to incarnation, this cycle was not for White an orthodox Christian pattern overseen by an orthodox god. He admitted that in his books he made use of themes and symbols from various religions in attempting to reach a better understanding, and that range of mythical and cultural references is too wide to confine White to any single belief system (1990, p. 25). Drawing from those broad cultural references, White favored the Eastern mandala, at the center of which is a hidden spiritual presence, as the symbolic cyclic pattern that overlays much of his work. In the mandala, the circle or circles within the square surrounding a spiritual center symbolizes the totality of the self and the unity of the individual with the cosmos. "*A propos* mandalas," he wrote, "I suppose symmetry appeals to me, and life I find symmetrical, when I used think it haphazard, without design" (1994, p. 412). Traditionally, a mandala can be expressed in physical terms (for example, as a structural design) or it can be identified within one's body, or it can be a mental construct within which the individual places themselves as a defense against distraction in order to concentrate on the spiritual presence at the center. The mandala can represent both a macrocosm as an *imago mundi* and a microcosm within one's own body, and the discovery of the right path through it can enable a person to reach what Mircea Eliade terms "the very heart of the real" (1991, p. 54).

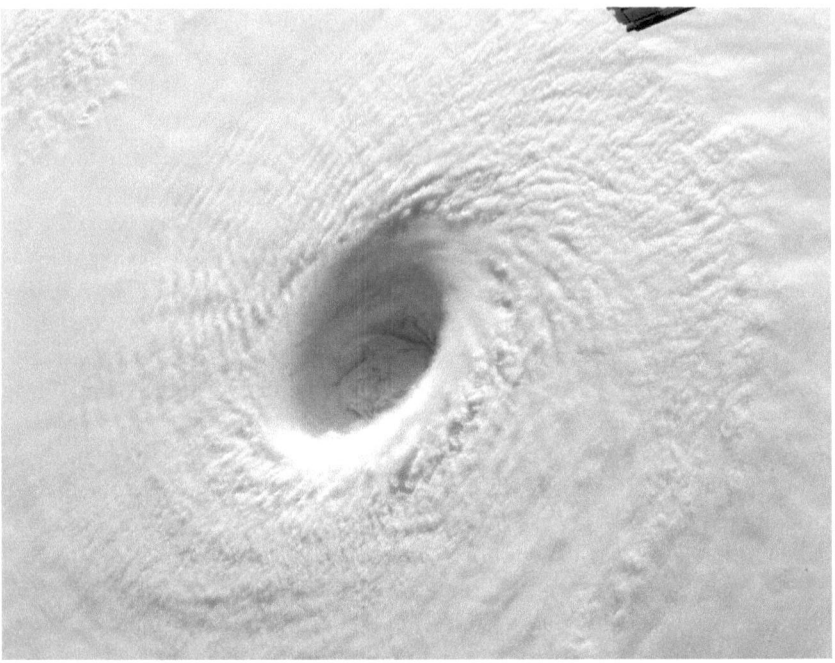

The eye of Typhoon Maysak, estimated to be 30 kilometers in diameter, as it approaches the Philippines, April 2, 2015 (NASA Earth Observatory).

However, the mandala is not the only cultural representation of the cycle of life and the search for meaning. Similar concentric circle representations appear in the cultures of many Native American tribes such as the Hopi people, for example, in which the lines "represent the course a person follows on his 'road of life' as he passes through birth, death, rebirth," according to William Least Heat-Moon (1984, p. 185). The Hopi believe that they are on a journey towards union with the greater universe, an emergence into a realization that life is about more than just the physical self, and the concentric circle pattern is a map of that journey and emergence. "Our religion keeps reminding us that we aren't just wills and thoughts," a young Hopi man explains to Heat-Moon. "We're also sand and wind and thunder. Rain. The seasons. All things" (p. 187). In this way, Heat-Moon observes, such symbols are "a reminder of cosmic patterns that all human beings move in" (p. 185). W.B. Yeats envisioned such patterns as gyres: interpenetrating spirals or cones that whirled around inside one another, representing the constant movement of the human consciousness, either collectively or individually, from one state to another over time, such as from love to hate. He believed that the interpenetrating gyres were "the archetypal pattern which is mirrored and remirrored by all life" (Ellman, 1969, p. 231), maintaining that we should seek balance and harmony at the intersection of the gyres because we all have the propensity for opposites that will pull us away from that center, as he wrote in "The Second Coming":

> Turning and turning in the widening gyre
> The falcon cannot hear the falconer;
> Things fall apart; the centre cannot hold [1971, p. 99].

This center is, according to T.S. Eliot in "Burnt Norton," in *Four Quartets*, "the still point of the turning world," that point at which "past and future are gathered," a point where there is freedom from desire,

> release from action and suffering, release from the inner
> And the outer compulsion, yet surrounded
> By a grace of sense, a white light still and moving [1966, pp. 15–16].

It is to this still point at the eye of the cyclone, at the center of the universal spiral pattern, that White directs his reader's attention.

At the center of White's spiral pattern is the in-dwelling God: the "I" that Beatson defines as the "core of being at the centre of personality which, while being inextricably involved with the temperament and the body, must answer ultimately to the One that lies beyond the material world" (1974, p. 219). For White, that "One" is a God whom he leaves hidden because he is primarily interested in the human struggle rather than in spiritual exegesis. Until Elizabeth Hunter emerges into the eye of the cyclone, she has been too occupied with her material world to notice the spiritual one but suddenly, here in this still point of the circling world, she experiences an epiphany that reveals an aspect of the hidden God to her and how the "I" within her might answer to Him. In this place, she has a dialogue with that spiritual presence during which she realizes her life has a deeper, more spiritual meaning than that which she had previously believed. Her ultimate reward for accepting this revelation will be the union at the time of her death of her in-dwelling "I" with the hidden God. However, the world of being, represented by her children and all their trivial materialism, threatens to intrude on her search and cause her to deviate from her journey, and such a deviation could prevent her arriving at the end of her life journey at the appropriate time. If she does arrive there at the right time, at the spiritual center, her transformation at the moment of her death will eliminate her corporeal matter, releasing her in-dwelling god, her "I," to achieve union with the universal Eye: the hidden God.

It is with this complicated relationship between the human and the spiritual that White is primarily concerned, as his characters struggle "within the limitations of their existence to understand the destiny that God has imposed upon them" (Beatson, 1977, p. 9). Such encounters between human and natural worlds as Hunter's epiphany in the cyclone were significant for White because they presented a chance for spiritual dialogue between the individual and God that maintained the connection between the physical and the divine. White understood that we need to accept the imperfect condition of the world and the emotional and spiritual suffering entailed in living within that imperfect state. "It is impossible to do away with the law of suffering which is the one indispensable condition of our being," White quotes Gandhi in the epigraph to his first novel, *Happy Valley* (2014)*:* "the purer the suffering, the greater is the progress." French philosopher Simone Weil referred to the powers of suffering as "transforming," believing they were as equally indispensable as the powers of joy. In order to hear the universe "as the vibration of the word of God," she wrote, "we have to open the very centre of our soul" to those powers (1973, p. 132), and it this choice of opening her soul that is offered to Hunter in the eye of cyclone. Having experienced an epiphany in the eye of the cyclone that reveals to Hunter her true spiritual condition, or rather lack of it, Hunter accepts that revelation and does open her soul, after which she traverses a personal wilderness in order to find the right path on her journey to the center of the mandala, where she will finally achieve spiritual union with the universe.

Epiphanies are enlightening, illuminating spiritual experiences. The classical Biblical epiphany is that of Saul, the persecutor of followers of Christ, who in Acts 9:3 is travelling to Damascus when a light from heaven suddenly flashes around him and a divine voice questions his motives. It is a life-changing experience for Saul, symbolized by his change of name to Paul. But, epiphanies are not limited to Biblical literature alone. They permeate the early work of James Joyce, for example, which White greatly admired, providing pivotal moments throughout his *Dubliners* stories. In "A Painful Case," James Duffy has an epiphany about the loneliness of a rejected female friend's life after she dies and, consequently, about the loneliness of his own life (1956a, p. 130), and Gabriel Conroy, in "The Dead," has an epiphany about his love for his wife when, "Like a tender fire of stars, moments of their life together, that no one knew of or would ever know of, broke upon and illuminated his memory" (1956b, p. 244). In *Stephen Hero*, Joyce's protagonist defines an epiphany as "a sudden spiritual manifestation … the most delicate and evanescent of moments" that might appear without warning (1960, p. 216). Hero has passed constantly under the Ballast Office clock, until now just "an item in the catalogue of Dublin's street furniture," but suddenly,

> all at once I see it and I know at once what it is: epiphany.… Imagine my glimpses at that clock as the gropings of a spiritual eye which seeks to adjust its vision to an exact focus. The moment the focus is reached the object is epiphanised. It is just in this epiphany that I find the third, the supreme quality of beauty [p. 217].

Like Stephen Hero, Elizabeth Hunter realizes that the spiritual focus of her eye will be brief, and it is in this moment that Hunter becomes, as Joyce puts it, "epiphanised." In that still moment within the Yeatsian gyre, she realizes the nature of her soul.

Within that moment, Hunter stands in the eye of the cyclone, surrounded by light on the waters of life, performing her own Eucharistic act by feeding seven swans floating before her. As a reward for this act, she is granted the gift of knowing the appropriate time for her death, when the universe's eye will once again be focused and concentrated on her. She knows that she is "not hallowed" yet (p. 323), and so she has to wait and earn this gift in the time left to her; she must "learn to re-enter" the spiritual island at the right time (p. 431) because she discovered on that island, she declares to her children, that "nothing will kill me before I am intended to die" (p. 399). When that moment comes, the moment when the eye is focused on her, Hunter knows that it will be only she who can perform "whatever the eye is contemplating for me." She will ultimately have to rely on her strength of will to once again walk "steadily towards the water" in order to experience her final epiphany as she is enfolded by the swans, "no longer filling the void with mock substance" (p. 532). As she undergoes the dissolution of her corporeal self, as "myself is this endlessness," Hunter transcends her life as she is accepted into the universe around her.

Susan Gingell-Beckman argues that the "unity of existence" Hunter seeks to ultimately achieve is represented by the swans of Hunter's epiphanies because they are creatures of the air, of water and of the earth, and as such they "play a seminal role in the growth of Elizabeth's spiritual understanding" (1982/83, p. 318). As black swans, rather than white, they evidently represent to Hunter the union of the spiritual aspect of her life with the corrupt earthly aspect of it, for so closely does she identify with the swans that she eventually subsumes them into the image she has of herself as an imperfect, flawed person, "her flaws too perfectly disguised under appearances: enormous, gaping, at times agonizing flaws" (p. 323), a person who is "a swan herself but black" (White, 1977, p. 322). At the moment of meeting the swans in the eye of the cyclone, Hunter realizes she is but a "flaw at the centre of this jewel of light" (p. 409) that still exists only by grace in the midst of such destruction. That there are exactly seven swans emphasizes the significance of this moment, as seven is the number of perfect order, of the completed cycle and its renewal (Chevalier & Gheerbrant, 1996, p. 860). These swans also appear on the shore of an island where they and Hunter are surrounded by water, which sustains the earth and sustains life. When the swans come to Hunter, she feeds them, sharing bread that the water has provided in a meal with similar symbolic communion elements to the meal Thea Astley's group of cruise ship passengers share while sheltering from the cyclone in *A Boat Load of Home Folk* (1968, p. 182). Having experienced a spiritual epiphany, Hunter is re-born from the water of the storm.

Epiphanies are significant and pivotal events for White and they appear in other novels. In *The Tree of Man*, for example, Stan has an epiphany that reveals to him there is a spiritual One through whom he will find meaning in his life. A White epiphany offers, John Beston suggests,

> the reassurance of a higher state of awareness in an existence that continues after death. It is a two-way process, an interaction between a higher power and the character. It is not just sent as a grace from God: the character has to have attained a certain state in order to be able to open himself or herself to the epiphany [p. 110].

Elizabeth Hunter experiences both of her epiphanies only when she has attained a particular state of preparedness, that "certain state of order" that enables her to be open to the interaction between herself and a higher power. It is during this interaction that she is offered reassurance that her existence will continue in some form after her death that will occur at the appropriate time, the time of her choosing.

Although, as Beston points out, White doesn't use the actual word "epiphany" until 1979 in *The Twyborn Affair*, long after the term had become commonplace in critical discussion about his work and after he'd stopped writing about such ecstatic experiences, he certainly fully appreciated the significance of those experiences. "The novel [Eye of the Storm] that I am working on at present," White wrote to Dr. Clem Semmler in May 1970, "seems to have a more specifically religious content and pattern than the others" (Beatson, 1977, p. 167). It is no surprise, then, that the most significant of those spiritual experiences that he includes in his novels are those of Elizabeth Hunter in the eye of the cyclone and at the time of her dying when her spiritual self finally finds the meaning for which it has sought.

During her epiphany in the eye of the cyclone, Hunter embraces her mortality, perceiving that the jewel in which she is a flaw exists "only by grace" in the eye (p. 409). In his memoir, *Flaws in the Glass*, White remembers "the great gilded mirror, all blotches and dimples and ripples" that hung at one end of the Long Room in the Sussex house in which his family was living when he was fourteen. "I fluctuated in the watery glass," he recalled; "according to the light I retreated into the depths of the aquarium, or trembled in the foreground like a thread of pale-green samphire" (1981, p. 1). White realizes that a perception of self can change according to the light we receive. It was only when the light of divine revelation blinded the Biblical Saul of Damascus, for example, that he finally saw and accepted God's purpose. Likewise, surrounded by light in the eye of the storm, "no longer a body, least of all a woman: the myth of her womanhood … exploded by the storm" (1977, p. 409), Hunter is ready to accept her imperfect condition. The apocalypse of the cyclone reveals to Elizabeth Hunter that humankind is part of a larger spiritual context, and that there are more important matters in the universe than the life of Elizabeth Hunter.

Five. Threading the Eye of the Cyclone

After her epiphany, Elizabeth Hunter maintains her faith in the spiritual presence that she feels was watching her while she was in the cyclone's eye. As a result of her experience, she believes her suffering is part of a plan, that there must be meaning to her life. She "alone had experienced transcendence by virtue of that visit," and like the Dutch sea-captain Dorothy meets on the plane, she has recognized "the sanctity and peace reflected in the eye of the storm" (p. 199). However, Hunter needs to be in a condition of readiness in order to appreciate and understand what will be revealed to her in the cyclone, and various rituals and symbols mark her progression towards that condition on Brumby Island, off the Queensland coast, where Elizabeth and Dorothy have been invited by friends, the Warmings, to share a few days with them at their beach house. Although the island's trees are being logged by timber-cutters, the island is otherwise unoccupied except for its wildlife of sea creatures, birds and the wild horses from which the island derives its name. Dorothy feels intensely out of place here, aware that she has only been invited because the Warmings were so fond of her mother, who is for them "a living breathing object of worship and source of oracular wisdom" (p. 363). But the Warmings have to fly back to the mainland because of a medical emergency, leaving Dorothy and her mother alone with another guest, an ecologist, over whom they compete for the next few days until Dorothy abruptly surrenders and, consumed with hatred for her mother, leaves the island.

Left alone, Hunter begins her unwitting approach towards readiness as she discovers that admitting her flaws to herself produces a rare sense of freedom. She recognizes in herself "her own type of useless, beautiful woman, … a mother whose children had rejected her" (p. 400). She now symbolically releases herself from her confining material bonds by wearing less clothing, walking barefoot, and letting down her habitually controlled hair. Aware her body is still attractive and supple at the age of seventy, she is disturbed for the first time "by the mystery of her strength, of her elect life, … that which stretched ahead of her as far as the horizon and not even her own shadow in view" (p. 401). Her life has been a special life, one not given to everybody and one that does not show any immediate indication of ending. Wandering into the forest, she has an encounter with wood-cutters that has spiritual overtones. Here, Hunter's preparatory progress is marked by more ritual. As she tastes a wood-chip that seems to her like a "transmuted wafer," she sits among men who have become "as reverent as a cloister of nuns" in their respect for her, even though she does not consider herself worthy of it in her developed awareness of her flawed nature (p. 403). When she returns to the Warming's house, she washes and anoints and dresses herself, and thus cleansed and prepared to receive her revelation, she awaits an oncoming apocalypse heralded by the hooves of the brumbies that are, unlike her, "outrunners of life" (p. 406).

As the name Brumby Island suggests, inhabiting this place with Hunter are those archetypal symbols of passion—unridden wild horses "loosen'd by the hands of Love," according to the poet John Wolcot [Peter Pindar] (1835, p. 216). Hunter's wild horses, however, have rarely been set free by love, if ever. Instead, she arrives on the island as a woman who has until now been saddled, ridden and corralled by social constraint, numerous affairs and a physically restrained marriage to her husband. She has preferred to think that this style of living, which has allowed her to still be a hunter of men, has given her freedom, but it has come at a price. She has had to live with a husband who "had got the number of children required by convention from the body he had bought at an inflated price" (p. 400), and in this relationship she was penned within a corral of manners, marriage and materialism of her own making. In contrast to the harnessed Mrs. Hunter, the brumbies stampeding down the island beach are not only symbolic outriders of the storm but they also represent those unbridled passions that she has kept under rein for so long. She settled for the securities of society, wealth, marriage and children while knowing others, such as Lillian Nutley, who rode away over the horizon for love.

According to Hunter's childhood friend, Kate Nutley, her older sister Lillian ran away with a foreign lover, only to be found murdered alongside a river somewhere in China or Siberia, but Hunter refuses to cry for a young woman given over so passionately to love that she died for it. She sees no tragedy here, only the glory of a woman "galloping wildly towards her death on the banks of some great Asiatic river" (p. 23). Currently enduring a childhood she feels to be unbearably shallow and stagnant, Elizabeth "could have slapped her friend for not hearing the thud of hooves, or seeing the magnificence of Lilian's full gallop" (p. 24). From then on, Hunter longs to feel that ultimate passion worth dying for, as much spiritual as sexual, until she finds it in the eye of the cyclone that lets her live.

When the eye of the cyclone arrives, White takes Hunter through further ritual moments. With everything destroyed around her, prepared for death, a humbled Elizabeth serves the fearless swans that accept bread from her hands as an equal. Still, she feels unable to endure further trial by either the storm or her conscience. Plagued by the shambles of her human relationships, Hunter just wants to lie down on the beach and die in the storm until she is jolted from the depths of her own suffering when confronted by the sight of a dead gull impaled on the broken branch of a tree. In her mind, she hears the bird's dying cry, and it is that imagined sound that gives her back her significance, reminding her that there is no escape from suffering, although it is human nature to try. Just when she is in danger of losing her desire to live, and of becoming just another insignificant broken doll that will be buried in the sand with the other debris, her desire to keep living is revived. That bird's death on a tree becomes her salvation and, inspired, she struggles back to the bunker to endure the other side of the cyclone. "Released from her body and all the contingencies" in the cyclone's eye, Hunter is reunited with herself in the aftermath, knowing she has been saved for a purpose rather than being merely saved (p. 413).

Hunter's acceptance of the opportunity for self-discovery is in contrast with the experience of her daughter, Dorothy de Lascabanes, who chose not to remain with her mother on Brumby Island and face the on-coming storm. However, many years later she encounters another storm while flying to Australia to join her brother, Sir Basil Hunter, in deciding their mother's future. Sitting next to her on the plane is a Dutch sea captain, perhaps an allusion to that legendary storm-bound harbinger of fate, the Flying Dutchman, who recounts his experience of once sailing into the eye of a typhoon. For him, that was no chance event. "God had willed us to enter the eye … the still centre of the storm," he recalls (p. 69). There, as in Elizabeth Hunter's experience, hundreds of seagulls resting on the water in an area of remarkable peace and calm surround the Dutchman and his ship. Like the eye of that storm, this Dutchman seems to Dorothy to be the epitome of calm and wisdom, a state which she could have attained years before, like her mother, instead of choosing to flee the island and the on-coming storm in a fit of jealous rage over her mother's attempted seduction of the ecologist. Still consumed by self-doubt and lack of confidence, as she was on that earlier occasion, Dorothy cannot understand the significance of the storm's eye that her potential spiritual guide is attempting to reveal to her now, any more than she could understand the significance of her mother's experience in one. She misses her last opportunity for her own epiphany, saddened that "it might never be given to her to enter the eye of the storm" (p. 69).

Unlike Frank L. Baum's Dorothy Gale, who in *The Wonderful Wizard of Oz* (1900) was transported and enlightened by her encounter with a cyclonic storm, this unenlightened Dorothy continues to wonder, until the time of her mother's death, why Elizabeth was granted her experience in the eye of the storm. Unable to understand the relationship between them, she perceives herself as a martyr to her own cause: a loving daughter who has had to endure a mother so cruel that any attempt to love her is like adoring a jeweled scabbard within which is hidden a sword still sharp enough in spite of age and use to slash off body parts and to impale hearts (p. 71). Only her mother, she considers, is capable "of slicing in half what amounted to a psyche, then expecting the rightful owner to share" (p. 389). That a mother like this could have such a spiritual experience is beyond Dorothy's conception of an appropriately ordered universe, and so she consoles herself by positing that perhaps her mother imagined the whole episode in order to provide herself with her own state of grace (p. 71). Still, Dorothy cannot ignore that it was her choice to escape from Brumby Island, from the "storms of her own imagining" (p. 199), and that in doing so she ran away from her chance of perceiving the truth about herself that her mother has come to understand about herself.

For, in remaining on the island and passing through the eye of the storm, Elizabeth Hunter alone experienced a transcendence that now enables her to recognize the woman beneath the artifice. She acknowledges to herself that as someone whose "love of life often outstripped discretion" (p. 401), she was responsible for encouraging various lovers to the point where affairs were inevitable and barely hidden. Above all, she is ultimately able to admit that her three children have rejected her as a mother. However, Hunter remains a proud and independent woman who admits to herself years after her epiphany that she has not always allowed the understanding she gained in the cyclone's eye to guide her. She does not appear profoundly changed by her experience in terms of attitudes or ethics, but what does change is her *awareness* that there is a wider universe out there, in which she is merely a flaw in a jewel, and this awareness changes her attitude to her life. While she aspires to attain, to understand and experience being such a profoundly changed person, it is a goal that is always difficult for her to reach, being now aware that she is a flawed and mortal person like everyone else. When her nurse, Mary de Santis, declares that "love is a kind of supernatural state to which I must give myself entirely, and be used up, particularly my imperfections till I am nothing," Hunter replies that she knows she is not selfless enough but that she is nevertheless determined to attain that "other love" (p. 157). While on the one hand a place of epiphany for her, Hunter's cyclonic eye also remains that proverbial needle's eye through which it is so difficult to pass. Previously, love for Hunter has been a matter of possession. "I used to long for possessions," she recalls as she reminisces about her poor childhood on the farm to Mary. At first they were dolls and then jewels, and then finally she longed "to possess people who would obey me—and love me of course" (p. 156). After her experience in the cyclone, however, she realizes that possession is no longer relevant, and she symbolically gives away her jewels to various people. Even though it might be ultimately unobtainable, her goal of being able to pass through that eye and be accepted by it is worth seeking.

But, attaining that goal is not easy; the pathway to the center of the spiral is complex. Hunter reflects that although many people insist death must be easy, "it ought to be the highest, the most difficult peak of all: that is its whole point" (p. 184). Indeed, it is only through enduring suffering, both physical and emotional, that Hunter ascends towards that peak. She has been unreachable and occasionally unfaithful to her husband, Alfred, until his approaching death brings her back to him and to her first opportunity to discover the meaning of her life. As her husband is dying, she seeks to be "involved in a mystery so immense and so rarely experienced" into which she will be initiated by the soul that she reveres (p. 198). As she cares for him, Hunter attempts to atone for her sins of not loving him, of leaving their home with the children to live in Sydney, of her affairs with other men, in order to participate in a miraculous transformation with Alfred at the moment of his death as his spirit enters eternity. She believes that at that time she will know the answer to the meaning of her life, but when that moment arrives, Alfred clearly does not have the answer for which she has waited; instead, he dies asking his own question: "*Whyyy?*" (p. 198). For Elizabeth, there is no transformation nor any epiphany about the meaning of her existence, and after Alfred's death she wanders the labyrinth of the house alone, still unable to find the right path. The only answer she encounters is the image of her flawed self in the hall mirror: an aged, ravaged old woman, "eyes strained by staring inward, in the direction of an horizon which still had to be revealed" (White, 1977, p. 198). That horizon, and what is beyond it, will not be revealed to her until her experience in the cyclone on Brumby Island.

Elizabeth Hunter spiritually aspires to find a great love with a "devouring desire for some relationship too rarefied to be probable" (p. 87), but in reality her experience of love has always been fraught with difficulty. As she comments to one of her nurses, "The worst thing about love between human beings, when you're prepared to love them they don't want it; when they do, it's you who can't bear the idea" (p. 11). From early in her life when she was a poor child with few possessions, abandoned by a father who commits suicide (p. 88), Hunter has confused love with possession and a control that extends to her emotions. Even her husband observes that he has never seen her cry unless she wants something (p. 28). Elizabeth simply does not know how to give Alfred the complete devotion that he demands. Feeling hemmed in by the rural landscape as well as the landscape of her mind, she seeks to escape them both by withdrawing from Alfred into her own solitude or into affairs with other men whom she desires to possess along with money and position. People are just like dolls to her that she can own and mistreat, even drown if she so wishes as she drowned the dolls of her friend Kate Nutley in the river near their homes.

Consequently, her children grow up also searching for love, ultimately attempting to find it with each other out of desperation. Her daughter Dorothy longs for someone in whom beauty is united with kindliness, but she is unable to find that person and instead offers her love to a series of maids. Eventually, she is persuaded into an unhappy marriage to a French prince engineered by her mother for the sake of family prestige. Worse still, her mother remains sexually competitive with her, even when Hunter does not really want the man in question, such as the marine ecologist on Brumby Island. While in the eye of the storm, Hunter is forced to acknowledge that her treatment of her son, Basil, has been just as bad. As unable to find love as his sister, Basil has had two unsuccessful marriages, and Hunter must face the possibility that she may be largely responsible for their unfortunate lives from when they were babies. Instead of mother's milk, she imagines, "my baby (surely the most tragic expression?) must have drawn off the pus from everything begrudged withheld to fester inside the breast he was so cruelly offered" (p. 408). This storm explodes the myth of her perfect womanhood, revealing the flawed being within. It strips away the artifice of beauty, the manners and clothes and makeup, to reveal the ageing body beneath, literally baring one of the breasts with which she could not adequately nurse her son.

For Elizabeth, that flawed being with its animal nature becomes symbolized by the skiapod, a legendary half-sea creature, half-human woman. Elizabeth first becomes spellbound by this mythical image when she sees it in a book of French engravings and lithographs while she is caring for Alfred as he is dying. She is attracted to it, not because the creature bears any specific physical resemblance to herself but because of a "spiritual semblance which will sometimes float out of the looking glass of the unconscious" (p. 194), a passage reminiscent of White's autobiographic vision of himself in the mirror of his childhood home. The "spiritual semblance" that Hunter senses at this time is that this creature appears to be, like her, unafraid of and unthreatened by death. It has an indeterminate facial expression that could be one of mystery or simply cunning dishonesty, reflecting Hunter's state of mind that fluctuates between a desire to know the answer to the mystery of death and an awareness of the anguish her husband has endured because of her behavior. The image of the skiapod remains in Hunter's mind, where it is internalized in her dreams. Just before the cyclone strikes Brumby Island, she confides to the ecologist that she often dreams she takes the form of a skiapod, "a kind of shadowy fish, but with a woman's face" (p. 389), and walks on the bed of the sea, sometimes with light flowing around her and at other times as if she is able to play a single beam on objects of interest. He comments that some fish use a light to attract prey. By now, what was originally an indistinct spiritual symbol for Hunter has taken on a more distinct physical form, one so closely integrated with her own self-concept that if its expression looked deceitful, she considers, "you had to forgive, because it was in search of something it would probably never find" (p. 390). The skiapod has come to symbolize more than Hunter the person and her destructive egoism: it symbolizes her search for meaning in which she is as fearless in her waking life as in her dreams, despite being surrounded there by larger fish. Although the ecologist reminds her that a characteristic of some deep-sea fish is their enormous mouth with which they can swallow prey larger than themselves, the stolid and scientifically-fixated professor is unable to appreciate that Hunter is the source of the radiance that attracts others to her, just as he fails to understand that he is currently the prey that the skiapod "equipped with a mouth large enough to swallow an ecologist" is seeking, as Dorothy remembers years later as justification for hating her. Even worse, that seduction was just a game for Hunter to prove the point that even at seventy, she was still a woman who was attractive to men while her younger daughter was not. With no confidence in herself, Dorothy remains just her mother's plaything: her doll (p. 393).

Typically, Elizabeth lays personal claim to her unique and life-changing experience within the cyclone and seeks to possess it, just as she has always wanted to possess everything since she was a little girl. She explains to her nurse, Sister Mary de Santis, that as a vain and gawky little girl dressed in patched clothes and living in a run-down farmhouse, she "used to long for possessions.... I longed to possess people who would obey me—and love me of course" (p. 156). When she grew older, that longing to possess extended to her daughter, who feels that she has just been one of the dolls owned by her mother (p. 393). Elizabeth admits that she has always sought perfection in her children, yet she has planted seeds of self-destruction within them at the same time (pp. 12, 397). She does not see them as part of her, but as "the most forbidding, the least hospitable of islands" (p. 15). In later years, as Hunter becomes increasingly bed-ridden, she substitutes others around her for her failed and lost children but she still persists in treating like dolls that she can control, manipulate, injure and even dress. So, while some part of her might have been spiritually enlightened in the eye of the cyclone, Hunter still struggles to experience a state of mind that she knows exists, but which "was too subtle to enter except by special grace" (p. 15).

If anyone could be said to be undeserving of finding that grace, it would surely be the predatory, selfish, and destructive Elizabeth Hunter because, "Judged by mortal standards of good and evil, she has not deserved salvation; she is, even by her own admission, much less 'worthy' than others around her"(Beatson, p. 225). Yet, she ultimately does find grace at the time of her death. In spite of, or perhaps because of her self-proclaimed fearlessness in swimming with the bigger fish, walking underwater, weathering a cyclone and defying death until she is ready to accept it, Hunter does eventually find that for which she has been searching: acceptance into "the endlessness" of the spiritual universe around her (p. 532). White's novels often advocate that goodness and innocence have their distinct limitations and that redemption can only be found through suffering, through the knowledge of both good and evil. Like the eponymous protagonist in *Voss*, for example, and Hurtle in *The Vivisector* (970), Hunter is, "in her own way, an explorer and an artist, and it is by living out her destiny in all its implications that she reaches the unknown. Only those who can endure the storm at its height can experience the Eye" (Beatson, p. 225). Hunter's endurance of the cyclone, and her epiphany in its eye that is "a precious jewel of a moment, crystallised out of her life, which glows ever after as a pledge of what is possible within a state of grace," opens her eyes to the meaning that she has always sought in her life (Bliss, 1986, p. 138). However, Hunter also understands that she has not always employed methods either ethical or moral, and that she has been greedy in her search for meaning, perhaps too greedy. Because she assumed that she could only gain knowledge of that meaning from other people, in her hunger for that knowledge she has seemed to devour them. Dorothy, for example, readily sees the likeness between her mother's appetite and her dream of being a skiapod with "a mouth large enough to swallow an ecologist" (p. 396). However, Hunter is, if anything, rather a gourmet with a "devouring desire for some relationship too rarefied to be probable" (p. 87): a desire that she has been unable to satisfy until her encounter with the eye of the storm.

As her chosen time of death approaches, Hunter envisions herself back on the beach of the cyclone's eye and the waiting swans. She perceives that now, "I alone must perform whatever the eye is contemplating for me" (p. 532). She must find the strength of will to walk towards the water and into the eye before it is too late, before it moves on and abandons her to chaos. As the water possesses her, it becomes part of her and she part of it. As she releases the "fleshy fist" of her heart with which she has for so long loved and fought and submits to the water, she perceives that she has finally understood the revelation of her epiphany in the eye of the cyclone: that she is just a flaw in the jewel. Because of her understanding, the Eye has granted her this moment. At the time of Hunter's epiphany in the storm, she was re-born from the water but now she is being immersed into the water, signifying a dissolution of her material form into "this endlessness" (p. 532). This is "not a definitive extinction but a temporary re-entry into the indistinct, followed by a new creation" (Eliade, p. 152). As she is granted her special grace, Hunter's sight turns inward and she experiences her second and last epiphany, that state of mind which finally reveals to her the answer to the mystery that eluded her at the time of her husband's death.

According to customary moral standards, though, Hunter should not have received such a gift. While her husband Alfred, a true innocent, suffered through pain, deceit, torture and death, the wife who deceived him about her love and fidelity and who caused that pain demanded and received more from life than most women could hope for. Materialistic, possessive and greedy, she selfishly abandoned her husband and her children, yet she has retained her beauty and her material possessions and the power that comes with them. Having always taken for granted her beauty and a sharp mind that has endured into older age, Hunter is only disturbed for the first time "by the mystery of her strength, of her elect life" while walking alone on Brumby Island the day before the cyclone, in particular about that part of it which still "stretched ahead of her as far as the horizon" (p. 401). As she confesses her faults to herself and accepts blame, Hunter becomes aware that she has not deserved her beauty, wealth and intelligence; her quality of life is a mystery to her. But, her epiphany in the cyclone's eye reveals to Hunter the existence of a spiritual power far greater than the power of possession, and that it is possible to achieve union with that spiritual presence. Such a union will give Hunter the opportunity to achieve that greater love which has evaded her but for which she has always sought. In accepting the existence of this power and thus of her true place in the universe, Hunter will receive the "special grace" that enables her to achieve that state of mind by which she can, in death, transcend her present life.

For the rest of her life after the cyclone, her time in the eye remains "the utmost in experience" for which she can never find words to express (p. 399). Her epiphany there reveals to her a superior spiritual presence that represents itself to her as an omniscient Eye before which she stands with her flaws nakedly visible, and she realizes that only in accepting this as her true condition will she find the peace she seeks. Earlier, Sister de Santis declares that for her, love has always been "a kind of supernatural state to which I must give myself entirely, and be used up, particularly my imperfections, till I am nothing" (p. 157), but surrendering until she is subsumed seems impossible for Hunter, who has always wanted at any cost to be something rather than nothing. Consequently, she has wanted to hold on to both her possessions and herself. "I know I am not selfless enough!" she declares to her nurse, "There is this other love, I know. Haven't I been shown? And I still can't reach it. But I shall! I shall!" (p. 157). Despite her failings, Hunter remains determined to reach that "other love," and at the moment of her death, she maintains her strength of will in order to walk into the water of dissolution while the Eye still sees her. There she surrenders to the enfolding wings of the black swans, no longer to be a "mock substance" but to be one who has accepted the truth of humility, and so she is finally granted grace.

It is through her epiphanies in the midst of apocalypse that Hunter finally attains the love, acceptance and understanding that she has so long desired and sought, despite her flawed humanity. Prepared at first to meet death in the storm, Elizabeth instead meets life there on terms that have nothing to do with status, possessions, or money: elements that she has thought so important up until now. Hunter is a self-made woman, composed from possessions and experience, who has believed implicitly in her dominance and control of everything around her, but the eye of the cyclone reveals that her carefully constructed womanhood is a myth. It breaks down her material assurance and, instead, offers her something more spiritual. In this unique and peculiar place, she is no longer a body or even a woman; she is merely a flaw in a jewel that exists only by grace at the still point of this storm, surrounded by an eyewall whirling around her out beyond the beach. In the cyclone's aftermath, Elizabeth regains her sense of her body and of herself as a woman, but this is now a consciousness that frees her rather than constrains her. This post-cyclone Elizabeth does not bother to cover her breast bared by her torn dress. Now, "nothing mattered beyond her experiencing the eye" (p. 412) and the "great joy she had experienced while released from her body" (p. 413). In accepting that there is a spiritual power greater than herself, Elizabeth Hunter is released from herself.

As reward for her acceptance and the faith that it implies, Elizabeth survives the cyclone. Instead of dying in that storm, she lives on until the appropriate moment for death arrives, a moment that she has to recognize in order to participate in it. In an echo of the Greek *chairos*, the Shakespearean "now" of the appropriate time that is meant to be, that time for her is when the cyclone's eye again approaches, this time in her mind. When it does, she needs to be in a state of readiness: "I have only to learn to re-enter and I shall be accepted," she declares (p. 431). When death arrives at her door one day, as it does for all people, Hunter knows that it will be on the right day at the right time. "Not before my time, … Nothing will kill me before I am intended to die," she declares emphatically to her children (p. 399). When that right time finally does arrive, Hunter experiences a final epiphany in which she returns in her mind to the eye of that apocalyptic cyclone where, ever since her experience on the island, she always knew she would return. There, she must humble herself and be figuratively enfolded by the wings of the swans, before what is left of her life is consumed by the passions and hunger of the human beings around her. At this moment, she alone can participate in "whatever the eye is contemplating for me" (p. 352), which is to achieve union with that Eye. As she slides beneath the water, it rises into her body towards a heart no longer a fist with which to love or fight but a heart that surrenders to humility. Dubious as some of her life choices may have been, Hunter has remained an insatiable seeker after the meaning of her life, courageously willing to yield herself to experience and pay the price for it. Like Laura in *Voss*, Elizabeth Hunter has faith, perhaps not a constant faith but a dynamic one nonetheless, a faith never destroyed by any kind of storm but one constantly questioned and renewed during her life until it is finally rewarded.

Six

Earth Breathing
Susan Hawthorne's Cyclone Within

> I am in with through the cyclone
> which is inside with through me
> —Susan Hawthorne

"The poet's way of articulating the relationship between humankind and environment, person and place, is peculiar because it is experiential, not descriptive," argues the distinguished British academic, biographer and critic Sir Andrew Jonathan Bate in his ecocritical masterpiece, *The Song of the Earth*. "Whereas the biologist, the geographer and the Green activist have narratives of dwelling, a poem may be a revelation of dwelling" (2000, p. 266). A poem can reveal the relationships between people and place, between the world and the humanity that dwell within it through a poetic language that can be a particular kind of expression that "may effect an imaginative reunification of mind and nature," strengthening humankind's ties to place and environment, perpetuating relationships between person and place, body and mind, perception and the word (p. 245). However, Bate points out, a poem can also be like a clearing cut in a forest in that while it is "an opening to the nature of being, a making clear of the nature of dwelling," a clearing is created by felling trees (p. 280). Like cutting an opening in forest that will let in more light, some clarification can only be achieved after chaos.

A cyclone is a chaotic dismantling of order, whether physical or metaphysical, natural or man-made. In *The Georgics,* the Roman poet Virgil implies that "the black whirlwind" which tears up "the heavy crop far and wide from its deepest roots and tossing it on high" is the work of gods such as Jupiter who "in the midnight of storm-clouds, wields his bolts with flashing hand. At that shock," Virgil continues, "shivers the mighty earth; far flee the beasts and o'er all the world crouching terror lays low men's hearts"(1: 317–321, 328–331). Centuries later, and on the other side of the world, Queensland poet Victor Kennedy also contended, in "Man, Building," that the gods have a hand in nature's chaos. He had seen the "vicious wreck" that was the result of the meeting of monsoons and trade winds, he writes, and it was like "titans set to broil/ The whole world with the menace of their blades" (1949, p. 16). Kennedy suggests that these storms are part of nature's cycle: they are created in and of chaos and then return there to be recreated. Nature as woman was wilfully destructive and this wild chaos could only be brought to order by the power of Man, he blithely suggested in the context of the time. The natural will would have to be bent to the will of humankind to prevent disaster (1949, p.18). Decades before Kennedy, the Australian writer "Banjo" Paterson, in his "Ballad of the Calliope" (1902), implies that the survival of the eponymous ship in the catastrophic 1889 cyclone is a triumph of British marine engineering over a destructive natural force that leaped on the unsuspecting ships in the Samoan harbor of Apia like a lion on its prey.

However, poets such as Virgil suggest that order is innate within Nature, rather than needing to be forcibly established; violent weather has meaning and purpose because it brings rain that benefits nature's growth when in Spring "the soil swells and calls for life-giving seed…. Then Heaven, the father almighty, comes down in fruitful showers into the lap of his joyous spouse…. The bountiful land brings forth" (II: 325–332). In his poem, "The Rainbow Serpent," writer and environmental activist Mark O'Connor likewise declares the tropical Wet season is "reward/for blazing hopeless months," always with the promise of more (1990, p. 36). Although it might seem that at times disorder reigns, these poets suggest, it is all for a reason; it is all part of the natural order that will eventually re-establish itself. In fact, Virgil implies, one can make efforts to encourage it to return, to encourage fertility rather than death, creation rather than destruction, by keeping a vigilant "weather eye" on the constellations in the night sky (I: 204) while also observing the behavior of birds, cattle, ants and frogs on the earth (I: 374–380). Nevertheless, despite all that man might do, Virgil reminds his readers they should always be careful to still venerate the gods and to make regular offerings. People should have faith that there is reason and meaning in the universe even if they cannot be seen, he concludes, rather than face the alternative of living in a world of complete random chaos (I: 338).

In her poem cycle, *Earth's Breath* (2009), based on her experience of the March 2006 landfall of Cyclone Larry in North Queensland, Susan Hawthorne searches for reason and meaning in the relationship between person and place when both have been subject to the seemingly random chaos of a violent cyclonic storm. However, like Virgil, she immediately alludes to an order within nature by using the chronological timeline of the storm's arrival and progress as a framework for the progress of her own poem cycle. Beginning with a prologue that embeds the current cyclone within its historic context, she develops her poems within three chronological sections:

"Breathless Calm," in which she investigates the period before the cyclone's arrival; "Earth's Breath," in which she realizes that the storm outside has remained within her; and "Wind's Rasp" in which she seeks to understand the trauma as well as the revelation in the aftermath of the storm. Hawthorne's epiphany as a result of her cyclone experience is that "I am in with through the cyclone/which is inside with through me" (p. 78): that is, the cyclone has affected her on such an intensely personal level that it is now an integral part of who she is. In fact, it may never leave her because the wind "has entered/some inner part of me/and I cannot wrench it out" (p. 77). But, this cyclone event is bigger than one person. Hawthorne draws associations with other peoples and with weather that is political as well as meteorological as cyclonic winds spiral around the globe:

> I am struck by the pain
> In New Orleans and Bangladesh
> Alike, but no one knows the name
> Of the cyclone in Bangladesh
> Only the numbers [pp. 70–71].

Her writing speaks to broad historical, geographical and emotional landscapes as well as to intimate personal spaces, often through meticulous attention to detail in nature that implies an inter-connectedness of environments and a universe in which people recognize the role of nature by establishing a meaningful life within it.

In the course of her poem cycle, Hawthorne's interaction with the cyclone becomes intimate and complete. By the last stanza, the cyclone is now more than in her, as it is in the first stanza: it is *inside* her. It has become an integral part of her; it is *with* her as a constant companion and invasively *through* her. Each different preposition interprets and intensifies the relationship further. By the end of the cycle, Hawthorne insinuates that the storm has become a presence that is part of her psyche, that is *of* her. People who have endured a storm often refer to having been "in" the storm, and the circling, whirling nature of the cyclone's spiral structure

Portrait of Susan Hawthorne (photograph by Naomi McKescher, used with the permission of Susan Hawthorne).

encourages that sense of being enveloped within the storm. The hurricane was a giant of the air, imagined the American Romantic poet William Cullen Bryant, whose,

> ... huge and writhing arms are bent,
> To clasp the zone of the firmament,
> And fold at length, in their dark embrace,
> From mountain to mountain their visible space [1903, p. 117].

Like Bryant, Hawthorne feels caught up within that embrace, so integrated with the storm that together they are "at the heart of things" (p. 78).

In the first lines of "Prologue: South Mission, 1918," Hawthorne perceives that her intimate relationship with the cyclone is part of her relationship with regional place that extends back into history to the Australian Aboriginal people who were here. By positioning her Prologue in a specific place and time, at South Mission Beach in 1918, Hawthorne grounds her group of poems in the temporal reality of actual history. On the night of March 10 that year, a severe cyclone destroyed the Queensland Government's Hull River Aboriginal Settlement at South Mission Beach, established only four years previously, killing a number of people including the Superintendent and his daughter (Holthouse, pp. 98–99). The Queensland government decided not to rebuild the settlement; instead, they created a reserve on Palm Island, some 37 miles off-shore northeast of Townsville. In June, they rounded up the Aboriginal survivors of the disaster, put the men in chains and forcibly relocated them all to Palm Island, separating them from their local lands and family ties to their regions. In their memories, the big wind of the cyclone brought them to this island, where their exile influences the tragic events of Thea Astley's award-winning novel *The Multiple Effects of Rainshadow* (2010) which begins with that 1918 cyclone. Hawthorne argues in her poem that the Aboriginal people had already been dislocated from their ancestral stories when they were first brought to the Settlement and then by the subsequent impact of Western culture. These were stories that might have warned them of the cyclone's approach and saved them "more/than any missionary from foreign lands" (p. ix), and so people perished at this place in this cyclone, she suggests, because they lost their connection with their environment and with their cultural knowledge. Yet, it had not always been that way. Hawthorne recalls E.J. Banfield's (1925) stories of Old Billy who could call up "storms of retribution," suggesting an earlier, closer spiritual affinity of people with country that had enabled this power (p. ix). These stories are reminiscent of the spiritual relationship with country and the storm-calling power of Alexis Wright's Norm Phantom in *Carpentaria,* that we will discuss in more detail in the next chapter, who stirs up the mud and water, "singing up the spirits in the water, boy, to make storms for his enemy" (2006, p. 485).

Six. Earth Breathing

Then, Hawthorne expands the scope of her historic timeframe to point out that "history repeats itself" (p. x). As the Native American author William Least Heat-Moon observes, circles and spirals are "a reminder of cosmic patterns that all human beings move in" (1984, p. 185), and Hawthorne acknowledges ancient symbolic links between the cyclone and the circle. "The nature of a cyclone is to circle/to turn in on itself/like the ouroboros swallowing its tail," she contends (p. x). The Egyptian and Greek symbol of the serpent consuming its tail, representing the eternal cycle of death springing from life and life from death, reached its ultimate form in Norse mythology as Jormungandr (or Midgardsormr), the great serpent that encircles the world, representing the infinite cosmic cycle of creation and destruction (Chevalier & Gheerbrant, 1996, pp. 846–847). Hawthorne connects the ouroboros to other mythic serpents such as the winged serpent and the tempting serpent of the Garden of Eden, seeing them as symbols of "the end in the beginning/the crossing over of time" that subsume the nature of the relationship between herself and the cyclone into the eternal cycle of mankind, "the endless dance" (p. x). Although the immediate event around her is Cyclone Larry, Hawthorne refers in her poem to the "great perturbation of wind and flood/that recurs and recurs" (p. xi): the ever-returning cyclone integral to this place as it is to the Gulf country of Wright's *Carpentaria* and to the various homes of the tropical Australian Aboriginal Rainbow Serpent. In Vance Palmer's novel *Cyclone*, Fay Donolly envisions the cyclone as Leviathan, the serpent from under the sea, "dripping with weed and wrack, from the waste of waters," that in his death agony sweeps cays and reefs with his tail and sparks forked lightning from his tongue. This serpent, always in wait to "turn the known world to an evil waste," dies and is resurrected by the power of apocalyptic dark forces in an eternal cycle (1947, p. 159). Thus the cyclone can represent, like the ouroboros, the infinite cycle of beginning and end, of life from death: the very nature of creation and apocalypse.

As representative of the eternal cycle, Hawthorne's cyclone exists within more than the present geographical place; it is also part of the landscape of the climate-changed future. E.J. Banfield's storm will constantly recur as part of this cycle, writes Hawthorne, but the "greenhouse storms" of the future will contain winds like the "great tempests/of the mythic world" (1925, p. xi). Aristotle declared that it was different winds falling upon each other that caused hurricanes, and that these winds were formed by a vapor, a "dry exhalation," arising from subterranean caverns (*Meteorologica* II.vi.). Hawthorne too hears the breath of the earth as the winds "inhale the breathless cloud" and create the cyclone that causes the sea to "exhale coral sand and turtle death" (p. xi) as part of the universal cycle of destruction and creation, of death and life.

In the first section of *Earth's Breath*, "Breathless Calm," Hawthorne prepares for the physical cyclone but also for the metaphysical one. In "Timescale" she warns that while tourists think they see the real tropics, "only time brings other ways of seeing." After a month of heat and rain, the ground is soggy and mold is growing on clothes. Seasons here do not turn; they swell as they soak up weather and after twenty years in the tropics, you are sure to have experienced a few cyclones. You learn to read the signs of them in the environment around you: despite "a perfect day in front of a mirror sea—/looks can deceive" (p. 2). Heeding Virgil's admonition in *The Georgics* to keep an eye on animal behavior in storm seasons (I: 204), Hawthorne reads the signs in nature of on-coming bad weather, such as the appearance of frigate birds (p. 3). The rain that swamps a rain gauge is answering the call of the "storm bird" (p. 13), also known as the channel-billed cuckoo, while butterflies such as

> The blue-winged sailor
> and the green birdwing
> float in on storms—
> they like a depression [p. 14].

Yet, as Hawthorne suggests in "Warning" and "Feast of the Senses," humankind often ignores such natural warning signs. Although the warnings are given in plenty of time, "people have lives to live/and the dinner was not postponed" (p. 16). Ironically, the people of Silkwood were dancing in the streets the day before the cyclone struck the town during a festival. Perhaps they should have been taking notice of the cattle in the fields that were defensively "standing in a ring/rump out, calves surrounded" (p. 16).

By presenting the Latin species name for each creature as well as the common English name in the titles of poems, Hawthorne reminds the reader that she is no longer referring to the mythic and legendary bestiary but to creatures she encounters in her garden and in her home that are part of her place. Including them in her exploration of the cyclonic event reaffirms Hawthorne's sense of Queensland place while still connecting her to the global place:

> Butterflies circle
> ringing the breezes
> orbiting earth from the Amazon
> to this Pacific coast [p. 15].

These symbols of beauty take flight on winds that eddy around the world in the same universal spiral pattern of the cyclone, warning of coming storms and the chaos of destruction, and Hawthorne sees the same circular pattern revealed in the curve of an olive python curled by her driveway. The python reminds her of the legendary ouroboros that has "swallowed the world" (p. 4), and of the ascending flight of sea eagles spiraling into the air on thermal up-draughts as she follows a similar spiral path while walking to the top of Bicton Hill, near Mission Beach. She can see the universal in the immediate present.

Yet, while the earth inhales and people "run to prepare/for the exhalation" (p. 18), Hawthorne observes that many aspects of the natural life continue as usual: "flowers bloom/leaf and petal/as if life will go on for ever" (p. 18). The air is still, and there is little obvious warning of danger: we talk, she writes, "as if it's the last day/of the world and yet/how can we believe it?"(p. 19). Even after the cyclone, she contends, life will continue on, because nature has survived more

> cyclones than any human
> will endure, its tall trees
> grounded by vines and
> keeled buttressed roots [p. 6].

Hawthorne perceives that "this hill with its layers of life ... will go on being what it is" (p. 6).

Having grounded the cyclone firmly in the history and culture of place, Hawthorne now maps out the impact of it in "Earth's Breath," the second section of her poem cycle. The Earth has inhaled; here it exhales, resuming a breathing cycle as old as time for, she argues, "Breath is an origin story/before breath is non-existence" (p. 22). In the Biblical story of origin, the spirit of God in the form of wind moves across a "black spaciousness beyond comprehension and without meaning" to create the earth, recounts the American writer Jan DeBlieu in her book, *Wind* (1998, p. 12). In that sense, she maintains, God is perceived as wind, as a "divine current that envelops us, swirls through us, and joins us to a great, organic, barely fathomable whole" (p. 13). One Hebrew word, *neshawmaw*, connotes not only a puff of wind or vital breath, she points out, but also "divine inspiration, intellect, ... soul, spirit" (p. 13). It is *neshawmaw* that God breathes into Adam during the Biblical creation story, instilling him with life and intelligence. However, the winds of origin not only bestow life but, as part of the eternal cycle, they also take it away. Another Hebrew word for spirit, or breath or wind, *ruwach*, is the breath of life that God takes back from humanity at the time of the Flood. Ruwach was traditionally the east wind, with the help of which the plague of locusts descended on Egypt and Moses parted the Red Sea. On the other hand, the New Testament Greek equivalent of the Old Testament *ruwach* is *pneuma*, the renewing breath of the Holy Spirit at Pentecost that moves across the face of the people while at the same time moving them inwardly as part of a cycle of spiritual transformation (pp. 13–14).

However, the wind's breath "has spanned millennia," Hawthorne maintains, and its appearance is not limited to only the Jewish origin story (p.

22). Various winds are significant in the myths of many countries. "Breath joins each person to the whole of creation," claims DeBlieu (1998, p. 22), who notes that in the Babylonian creation epic known as the *Enuma Elish*, the four winds assist the storm god Marduk, along with evil winds that he creates such as the hurricane and cyclone, to defeat his grandmother Tiamat in battle. He then divides her into two parts, from which he creates the sky and the earth (1998, p. 21). The *Popol Vuh*, the Quiché Mayan book of creation, records that one of the Mayan gods of creation was Heart of the Sky, Hurricane (1996, p. 65). For the Navajo, too, human beings are created by *nilch'I*, the Holy Wind, which imprints on them the spirals of fingerprints to remind them from where they came and to enable them to hang on to the sky, as the ones on their toes enable them to maintain their grasp on the earth. It placed itself in the spiral whorls of the ears of the First People and taught them to talk, and now their living breath, posture and balance remain gifts from the Wind (DeBlieu, 1998, p. 28).

The wind, then, is part of the cycle of humanity's existence, and in "Earth's Breath" Hawthorne reinforces the cyclone's mythic connections to human culture. "Myths are made of such noise," she writes, likening the storm to the rampages of Heracles and any possibility of calming it to the unlikely appearance of a Delilah "brave enough/to calm Samson with a pair of/ scissors" (p. 22). She personifies Cyclone Larry as a shambling god-creature, "Larrikin Larry" who, with shredder over shoulder,

> larks about turning bark and leaves
> to confetti and in his next breath
> plays graffiti artist, pasting every
> wall door and window [p. 23].

However, the playfulness of this larrikin is deceptive. He can suddenly become a very serious brat indeed, changing direction at will, blundering around, destroying things while he is "bellowing earth's grief" (p. 23). That monstrous noise reverberates through "Cyclone Time," as the darkness "lopes across the void/of sea in tormented uncertainty" as the cyclone strikes. In the middle of the storm while it whirls around her, Hawthorne feels so attuned to it that

> when earth exhales
> we inhale, hold our breath
> as that great turbine of wind
> rolls over us [p. 24].

Yet, as the destruction rages outside, inside her "a strange/equilibrium holds me still/in a state of cosmic acceptance." At her own still point, Hawthorne seems to have found her eye of the storm.

Like Elizabeth Hunter within the eye of her cyclone, Hawthorne experiences an epiphany during her cyclone experience. (In fact, beneath the title of her poem, "Eye of the Storm," Hawthorne has an epigraph taken that Patrick White novel: "All else was dissolved by this lustrous moment made visible in the eye of the storm.") Like Hunter, the eye reveals to Hawthorne that there is more to the universe than her. The cyclone forms around the eye and spirals out from the eye at its heart, and so "the eye patterns the storm" (p. 27). Hawthorne merges the forms and meanings of "eye" and "I," envisioning the eye of the storm as also the universal, panopticon eye, and that she as the personal "I" is within the view of them both. Like Elizabeth Hunter, she realizes that this Eye has the capacity to devour her if she does not accept that it is a greater power than herself: it is "all-seeing" and "all-devouring" (p. 27). It is both a physical storm and a spiritual storm, located in a geographic place "at the southern edge of the storm," and also "at the immaterial edge of self" (p. 27). Hawthorne's epiphany is that even though significant life decisions await, that seemed so important before the cyclone arrived, this storm has reduced life to its basic elements. It strips away the superfluous matters along with the shredded leaves until, like Elizabeth Hunter, Hawthorn realizes that there is a force greater than herself: "the eye, the I, is always central" (p. 28). In the midst of apocalypse, there has been revelation.

In his poem, "Tully Under Cyclone," Ivan Head experiences a similar epiphany. As a cyclone approaches the town, he can see just a single, narrow sliver of green beneath the descending black curtain of the storm, and that vision raises within him emotions associated with the Burkean sublime (2011, p. 126). Whatever could "excite the ideas of pain, and danger, that is to say, whatever is in any sort terrible, or is conversant about terrible objects , or operates in a manner analogous to terror," wrote Burke (1992), "is a source of the sublime" (p. 36), and Head feels drawn toward the beauty of the oncoming storm while at the same time he pulls back from the terror of it. He visualizes this inner struggle as a road sign on which is written the single line—"*mysteriumtremendum et fascinosum*" (p. 126)—a phrase that refers to the simultaneous experience of the tremendous awe-full mystery from which one's instinct is to turn away because the senses are unable to cope, yet to which one is simultaneously attracted because of its allure as a mystery. Like Hawthorne, Head perceives the cyclone as an all-powerful, dreadful and fearful event before which one feels helpless, unable to put it into words. Yet, at the same time, one can experience the *mysterium fascinosum*, an equal sensation of fascination and allurement, even seduction, as the spiraling storm draws the observer in as it moves inexorably closer. Terror has its own attraction; beauty can be perceived within the truly terrible. Together, these conflicting emotions form the great mystery of the sublime experience of the cyclone.

As Hawthorne emerges into the light of the storm's aftermath she, like

Elizabeth Hunter, enters a wasteland of silence where destruction reveals what has previously been concealed:

> mountains we've never seen
> islands we've tried to.
> a beach long hidden [p. 29].

While danger still lurks here in the form of biting ants, broken glass, and fallen trees, this new world is a place of revelation. Here the experience of passing through the cyclone's eyewall has left survivors with mixed emotions, with a "walled eye" that is "half-blind/with fear, the other half/in a state of exhilaration" (p. 31). In a series of wordplays, Hawthorne writes of exhausted survivors having "hit the wall" and that their ability to see through to the end of the storm is impaired when a nearby "glasswall/explodes glazing splinters across/the horizon of our view" (p. 32). This new world is a place of mystery where the relativity of time seems altered as "the clock moves in one time space/our bodies in another, one day by/the clock, years by our bodies" (p. 30). They seem suspended in time here, as "a spindle seems still/while the threads whirr at the edge" (p. 32), as if they are at T.S. Eliot's "still point of the turning world.... where past and future are gathered" (1966, p. 15). Hawthorne and her partner feel momentarily as if they might be the only survivors, who are "left to our solitary epiphanies" (p. 32) about the fragility of their environment.

Surrounded in the days after the cyclone by volatile weather that promotes uncertainty and instability, Hawthorne takes comfort from a sign, "a triangle of hope—/seven frigatebirds flying in formation" (p. 34), reminiscent of the seven black swans that Elizabeth Hunter encounters in the eye of the cyclone in Patrick White's novel. As the sum of the number four, which represents the earth's four compass points, and the number three that symbolizes heaven, "seven is the number of the completed cycle and of its renewal" (Chevalier & Gheerbrant, 1996, p. 860). In placing seven birds in a triangle formation, Hawthorne combines traditions associated with use of the number seven with the three-point triangle symbol of divinity (Chevalier & Gheerbrant, 1996, p. 1034), and so this formation of frigate birds, the traditional harbingers of a cyclone, signifies that an environment made incomplete by the cyclone's damage will once again be restored to completeness.

However, for some time at least, this environment is one of chaos where the usual expectations are confounded and confused:

> traffic lights point to the sky
> bananas are mashed with soil
> a kitchen sink in the grass...
> a boat listing grounded [p. 38].

The substantial structure of the local hotel "is folded like an origami swan" (p. 38), and houses are "pried open ... like a can opened," revealing that they are merely "houses of cards/fragile and limp" (p. 38). While buildings appear at first glance to still be complete, on closer inspection they are now mere facades, adding to the feelings of artificiality and instability generated in the survivors of this new post-cyclonic world where you can no longer trust what you see. In this unreal world, personal tragedies become media clichés like "power-lines kiss the ground," or the use of "war zone" to describe the destroyed landscape that Hawthorne hears spoken by television news reporters. Instead, Hawthorne understands the very real personal tragedy of a "straggling group of porous people" that is symbolized by a child's teddy bear set out to dry or a damaged house wrapped in plastic like an art work, and the "psychic rebellion in some people's faces/as they tell stories of survival and entrapment" (p. 41). The camera pans over

> a landscape of skeletons
> trees in spiral twist, trunks unbarked, vertebrae exposed
> tarsal and metatarsal, twig and branch [p. 41].

It is a damaged landscape, stripped down to a bare skeleton, as exposed as the damaged people within it.

Yet having recognized their "triangle of hope" symbolized in the birds flying above them, Hawthorn and the other survivors begin to re-impose order on this chaos as,

> I climb I walk I carry I sweep
> I mop I wash I wipe I sweep.

As she and the community collect the fragments of their lives, they "rush to close up/against more wind and rain," for sleep only opens "the psyche/to a canticle of pain" (p. 35). The community experience in times like these is important because "it is the community that offers a cushion for pain, the community that offers a context for intimacy, the community that serves as the repository for binding traditions" (Erikson, p. 234). In sharing their experience, particularly through stories, people who have gone through disaster and trauma discover a kinship and commonality of culture that strengthens bonds between them. "Afterwards," Hawthorne writes,

> like new lovers telling stories
> we talk of all the storms we've ever
> witnessed, all the storms
> that have snatched at our lives. Stories make
> sense of the new state of existence
> in the post-cyclonic world [p. 42].

Brought together by catastrophe, they tell stories about other storms that they have survived: her partner's experience of sandstorms in Tunisia, or blizzards on Mt. Kosciusko here in Australia. They find that despite experiencing different storms at different times, there is a common sound that they remember: *"It's the roar of the wind that is the same"* (p. 43).

In the aftermath of disaster, Erikson contends, people feel for a short time that their community has been destroyed irreparably; they feel naked now and alone in a terrifying wilderness of ruins. But then, there is a surge of euphoria as they realize that the community has survived and that they can rebuild and re-establish old ties and networks. In celebrating the recovery of the community, they are also celebrating their own rebirth (1995, p. 235). In rebirthing their tropical community, Hawthorne and her fellow cyclone survivors restore the environment within which that community exists, discovering as they do so that the apocalyptic destruction of the old world allows the recreation of the new. Their "slash and burn" before replanting trees,

> lets in the light, makes forest into life.
> Like the mosaic burners
> fire renews, breaks open seed pods
> …This cyclone
> is the planet's biodynamic gardener [p. 44].

Although their human efforts to restore order are important to them, Hawthorne also realizes that restoration of the post-cyclonic world will occur naturally with "nature imitating people" (p. 44). The storm creates natural compost heaps, and natural regeneration will occur: "where the cyclone/ came past, leaves die, yet some/turn again to life" (p. 45). While the winds did uproot some trees, some were ready to fall and Hawthorne observes that this is nature bringing in light again to the earth.

> As time passes, Hawthorne senses that
> this roaring *is* inside her
> the body speaks
> its unvoiced pain [p. 46].

Her traumatic cyclone experience has become part *of* her, not just something that happened *to* her.

Even while visiting another country, "the cyclone still/fibrillates our minds" (p. 48). Three weeks later, "dreamlife and waking life/crosshatch into fantasy and fearfulness," and she is still waking in the night too shaken and scared to close her eyes, "the scream strangling my breath" (p. 49). Her mood is stormy, too, as the

> wind swells in me with its ravages. A walking
> catastrophe, I am goaded by furious tempests [p. 49].

Four months later, though she may seem outwardly calm, the cyclone has not left her. Without warning, while visiting a gallery to view an art installation, she suddenly experiences

> the earth roaring as if death has come
> the water rages we are mere twigs
> floating, broken by the water's wash
> and the wind—
> the wind is inside me...
> and this—this—cyclone inside [p. 51].

As time passes, Hawthorne blames the cyclone for the mental darkness that surrounds her like a barometric depression. In "Moondark," her life is now "as flat as the moon's/dark." It is the fault of the "rampaging wind" and

> this giant eye for exposing
> all the weaknesses
> all the fractures.

For Hawthorne, these are not just fractures in structures or the earth, but they are also fractures in the soul (p. 55). The cyclone has laid waste both to body and to land; in exposing the land, the cyclone has exposed her inner self. Because the land is so damaged and altered, Hawthorne's body loses the connection with place that was so important and integral to her so before the cyclone, and in her poem "Forest," she likens this loss to the link between the health of the rainforest and that of the cassowary birds that can be broken by a cyclone. Because these flightless birds rely on the fruits of the forest for food and the forest relies on the excretion of the seeds by the bird to regenerate, they are both in danger due to deforestation by a cyclone. Even if they broaden their diet, cassowaries still run the risk of depleting their reserves and dying of starvation (p. 82). Hawthorne is thus reminded of a saying of the local Djiru people, "no forest, no food, no cassowary," from which she derives the tale of the girl and the cassowary in "Forest."

When in this poem the girl first enters the rainforest, the cassowary is her guide because

> the cassowary knows her way through the forest
> She knows all the fruits of the forest
> She is mistress of the forest.

However, when the "big wind" strikes, it destroys the trees and the fruits on them. Although the cassowary shelters the girl and saves her life, they lose their connection with the landscape because of the destruction wreaked by the storm and become lost. Unable to find their way out of the forest or sustain themselves from the dwindling, perishable food resources, they pair ultimately perish. The loss of connection and balance between nature and people, Hawthorne suggests, can be catastrophic (p. 56).

Yet death and life, destruction and re-creation, are part of the eternal, ouroboros-like wheel of natural life. "History repeats itself," Hawthorne declares at the beginning of her poem cycle,

> the end in the beginning
> the crossing over of time
> as a matrix—
> destruction creation
> an endless dance… [p. x].

Because of this endless cycle, then, her connection with place will eventually be restored. As the Australian poet Judith Wright observes in "Cyclone, Aftermath," although a tree felled by a storm may now be "that lovely building debased, that tower pulled down," this is the wisdom of nature that is neither always life nor always death. Rather, it is a constant cycle. Nature is "that wise woman past joy and grief": a cycle of creation and destruction and regeneration (1955, p. 14). So, even though the bare-limbed trees may have surrendered to their fate in Hawthorne's "Candlesticks,"

> …Birds
> come and go, visible
> now on the wind—
> stripped boughs [p. 62].

Life is returning to this cyclone-damaged world as part of that great spiral of nature that ends where it begins.

In the last section of her cycle, "Wind's Rasp," the arms of Hawthorne's spiraling storm broaden and extend as her point of view moves from the personal and local to the universal cyclone. Because "the wind has entered/some inner part of me/and I cannot wrench it out" (p. 77), she feels part of the universal meteorology: Hurricane Katrina in New Orleans, a cyclone in Bangladesh, storm surges that flood the Irrawaddy River. Hawthorne begins to see that a destructive event she once only saw as isolating her from the world is now revealing to her that she is part of humankind. "Each time the wind scrapes people from/the earth's surface I am in it all over again," she writes (p. 72). However, being borne on this world-wind is not without risk: while rising currents of air can lift birds aloft, for example, those same thermals can carelessly cause their death. On a seemingly perfect day, Hawthorne sees "a dying bird/with no call left/shattered by the wind's antics" (p. 64), an image reminiscent of the dead gull that Elizabeth Hunter sees "skewered to the snapped branch of a tree" in Patrick White's novel. Hearing the death cry of that bird in her mind jolts Hunter out of surrendering to the cyclone. It causes her to challenge a power that she had previously assumed was superior by returning to her shelter and ultimately surviving (1977, p. 410). As the death of that bird inspired Hunter to challenge assumptions about her place in the universe, so the death of this bird inspires Hawthorne to ask her own questions, such as:

> How does a pelican know
> when it's safe to fly in

> fly over in solitary silence
> bringing hope? [p. 64].

Her world is no longer her known world. She no longer feels secure.

As we noted earlier, Alexander von Humboldt felt a similar loss of faith that destroyed "the illusion of a whole life" after he experienced an earthquake in South America. With his sense of stability disturbed in the face of "unknown destructive forces," he felt that he could no longer trust the ground on which they stood (1849, p. 212). In the face of similar unknown natural forces, Hawthorn agrees that "[t]he dark hurlings of nature/are terror enough for our reptile brains." In that condition, we can do no more about inevitable meteorological events than the ape in the zoo that "beneath the sun's eclipse/ stood tom-tomming his chest." Consequently, people would rather watch these events on television as distanced observers than be immediate participants in such potentially life-changing moments (p. 65).

In "Storm Warnings," the American poet Adrienne Rich writes about similar personal anxieties of people who feel powerless before forces that they cannot influence or control, such as change, for which she uses the allegory of an oncoming storm. We cannot predict the weather of the heart any more than we can predict the weather outside, she writes. Change is inevitable, yet in the face of such approaching storms, people attempt rituals of preparation as defense. People who live in "troubled regions" draw their curtains, close their shutters and light candles because they have learned to do these things. The "I" of the poem is resigned and fatalistic about the outcome of the approaching storm. Even though they indulge in these motions of preparing, they know rituals will not entirely protect them because they will always hear the whine of the wind as it finds some crack in the boards. Instead, the only true defence will be to find a place of inner calm as the air moves inward "toward a silent core of waiting." We must find our own way of dealing with change, Rich implies, because change is a constant in our lives. We might close the shutters against it, but the wind will still rise (1951, p.1).

Hawthorne, too, is conscious of the importance of understanding the cycle of changes in her life that have been wrought within her by her cyclone experience. In her poem, "Yugantameghaha," the title of which is the Sanskrit word for a gathering of clouds at the end of the "yuga," an era, she looks beyond the spiral of the literal storm into the cycles of time. "We will need to listen again to the myths that have sustained us," she writes (Hawthorne, 2010–11, p. 114). Hawthorne sees the people of the world reacting to climate changes as being in psychic shock, like the moths in the quote from the *Bhagavad Gita* rushing to their ruin "flying right into an inferno" (p. 63). She is aware that some people think we are currently living in the Kali yuga, an epoch of "rattling bones" and "thundering clouds/breaking the world apart" (p. 67). Yet there is still hope, she proposes, employing the metaphor of the

Hercules moth that "climbs every building/rising upwards through 110 floors" as he seeks the light of the moon that "he might escape earth's pull/and melt into the inferno of light" (p. 67). The moth not only accepts that the cycle of change is inevitable in life but it actively seeks for that change to happen as a transforming element which it ultimately transcends.

This powerful and personal experience of the cyclonic storm can forever change you, Hawthorne claims in "Sista Katrina" (p. 69). Her epigraph for this poem about the 2005 New Orleans hurricane is taken from African American author and anthropologist Zora Neal Hurston's novel, *Their Eyes Were Watching God* (1937), in which the articulate and self-reliant Janie Crawford survives the 1928 Okeechobee Hurricane in Florida during her search for love and her own personal identity as a woman. One of the deadliest tropical storms in North Atlantic basin history, the historical hurricane caused a storm surge across Lake Okeechobee that flooded hundreds of square miles and took the lives of some 2,500 people in the Lake region and over 4,000 along the storm's overall path. Having survived a more powerful hurricane, although it was not as fatal, Hawthorne senses a commonality of experience between decades and countries, past and future, "Sister Katrina or Brother Larry" (p. 68): she, too, knows the feeling of "Days when you look at the poles of your home, wondering/where the walls went" (p. 69). At the beginning of the collection, Hawthorne speaks of how the forced disconnection of local Aborigines with country meant that they did not remember to heed the warning signs in their natural environment about the on-coming cyclone that struck Mission Beach in 1918. Now, towards the end of the poem cycle, she returns to that loss of connection with the environment, comparing the Seminole people who vacated the Okeechobee area prior to that hurricane to people who did not leave the New Orleans area at the time of Hurricane Katrina. "What they had known," she writes, "was all/long forgotten" (p. 68). Those who did not heed warnings had culturally forgotten their spiritual connection with the environment, and so they did not leave, and in the aftermath of Katrina, the city is "a place scoured of hope" (p. 68).

However, she points out, compared to the publicity that was given to Hurricane Katrina, the tragedy of the cyclone that struck Bangladesh in 2007 was ignored because in the minds of the world's media, "Bangladesh is basketcase" (p. 70). People care so little about this event in this place that, unlike Katrina, this cyclone does not have a name. Neither do the victims, who are deprived of more than their possessions: "Says one, We are *bhumiheen/ bhumi*–land, *been*–less" (p. 70). They are deprived of their land, of their place to which they were connected, which has been either immersed or washed away, as were those caught up in the floods of the Okeechobee hurricane. Once again, Hawthorne reminds us of the universality of the cyclonic storm experience, no matter where it might be taking place. It is "the same wind rasping through me," she writes in "Irawaddy speechless," referring to the 2008 Nargis cyclone in Burma:

> Each time the wind scrapes people from
> the earth's surface I am in it all over again.
> I cry with the woman whose face is stained
> with tears... [p. 72].

Not only the wind, but it is also the same waves that wash away the houses and, like the mouths of the Irrawaddy drowned in floodwater, so are "the voices of the people strangled." No one knows their story; no one knows how many have died or lived. For Hawthorne, the ecosystem and the human system are equally alive. "It is no accident that time and again earth is compared to the human body," she argues. "Our planet, like us, is a living system—its ecosystems, like our circulatory and endocrine systems, rise and fall responding to the events taking place on its surface and in its interior spaces" (2010–11, p. 105). The waterlogged mouths of the Irrawaddy "can hardly breathe," but like the drowning people, they still "spill breathless words/crying out against the bruising of the land" (p. 73).

In the last poem in the cycle, "Wind mind," Hawthorne finally accedes that she will never again be that person she was before her epiphany in the cyclone. The wind is within her now; it "has entered/some inner part of me" (p. 77). She and the wind are now part of the same living system, breathing the same warm ocean air together, but she is determined not be one of those "drowning in the scouring sea" (p. 77). Unlike Letty in Dorothy Scarborough's *The Wind* (1925), she will not succumb to the wind. Although in her dreams she still longs to find a place where she can shelter from the incessant wind or find a tree to which she can cling so that she will not be blown away, she survives the storm like Hurston's Janie Crawford, accepting that she and the cyclone are now entwined intimately and inextricably. "I am in with through the cyclone/which is inside with through me," she concludes, realizing that "the cyclone which is at the heart of things" has permeated her so that it is at the very center of her existence (p. 78). She is aware that this is a dangerous, edgy existence because, like Thea Astley's characters who were always "touching the edges of cyclones" (Willbanks, 2008, p. 30), Hawthorne senses that she and the cyclone are "at the edge of chaos." Yet, on that edge, she is waltzing with the cyclone like the swirling, orbiting objects in Spanish surrealist painter Remedios Varo's "Still Life Revolving," spiraling simultaneously at the edge or near the center of this universe "in a massive creation of life" (p. 78). At the same time, being one with the wind she can be the wind, such as the cross-hatched whirling wind of Australia's Kimberley region seen in Australian Aboriginal artist Samuel Namunjdja's "Gungara (the spiraling wind)." Then, she is also a poet "defiantly writing herself into creation" as she attempts to understand the whirling winds of chaos within (p. 78). She and the wind are in a close relationship now that she likens to that of the dog asleep with its paw across her partner's shoulder. "Our human experience suggests such metaphors to us," Hawthorne contends, "as we grapple with ways of understanding ourselves and our relationship to the world whether it be earth as body, wind as breath, the great flows of rivers, oceans and lava as tears and blood, grass and trees as hair and limbs" (Hawthorne, 2010–11, p. 106). Such metaphors help us to understand ourselves and our relationship to the place in which we live.

As Bate suggests, the experience of Hawthorne and other writers in the cyclone has opened them to the nature of being, of *who* they are in terms of *where* they are, as revealed in the lines of their poetry. In the new millennium, the function of poets could be, as Bate proposes (p. 282), to remind the next few generations that, as the noise of civilization drowns out earth's own poetry, "it is we who have the power to determine whether the earth will sing or be silent" (p. 282). There is now, he argues about the function of poetry, "an ever greater need to retain a place in the culture, in the work of human imagining, for the song that names the earth." Hawthorne agrees with him. "Poetry has always been the song that is imprinted in human culture," she declares, "and equally importantly the song that we learn from the natural world" (2010–11, p. 101). Hawthorne and other poets have drawn on their experience to articulate the relationship between them and humanity and the environment, between person and place. A successful relationship between person and place is developed from learning to incorporate the paradoxes of order and chaos, of destruction and creation, into that relationship along with the possibilities of re-creation both personal and material that may enhance and prolong one's co-existence with the natural environment of their place.

SEVEN

The Apocalypse and Epiphany of Cyclone in the Land of Alexis Wright's *Carpentaria*

> "...the old people ... will tell you cyclones don't come from nowhere, because there is plenty of business going on when cyclones come onto the country out of the rooftop of the world..."—Alexis Wright

Structurally bracketed by cyclones, Alexis Wright's novel *Carpentaria* is permeated by the spirits of the wind, the rain and the ancestral serpent. This is a story about hope in a land of the imagination in which a prophet emerges from a cyclone to bring warning of the town's hypocrisy and an opportunity for cultures to come together. However, the white townspeople reject the prophet, use him as a scapegoat and exile him, after which a second cyclone destroys the town and strips bare the land. While this cyclone is called up by one of the novel's protagonists to act as judge and executioner, in the true sense of apocalypse it also offers the opportunity to begin again and create anew and in this way, *Carpentaria* country is a place of both end and beginning. While on the one hand, the "little black girls" return from church on Sunday, "look around themselves at the human fall-out and announce matter-of-factly, *Armageddon begins here*" (Wright, 2007a, p. 1), this is also a land where "a child who was no stranger to her people asked if anyone could find hope. The ghosts in the memories of the old folk were listening, and said anyone can find hope in the stories: the big ones and the little ones in between" (p. 12). Because the stories of this land are fundamental to its very existence, "*Carpentaria* does more than present a critique from an Indigenous perspective. The novel also expresses a profound way of rethinking being and knowing about the world," but more than that, this is literature that "*makes a world*" (Daley, 2016, p. 9). This is a world "where legends and ghosts live side by side in the very air" (p. 12); it is a world in which events take place within cyclical patterns, embodying the cyclonic spiral weather systems of Wright's setting: the tropical cyclone coast of the Gulf of Carpentaria.

These patterns are inherent to the Aboriginal concept of time, which is cyclical rather than linear, spatial rather than temporal (Strang, 1997, p. 247). Wright's concept of time in *Carpentaria* is a very different concept to the Western understanding of time as linear and chronological because in Aboriginal time, "there is no linear procession of generation and events, rather a recurring cycle of existence" (p. 248). Daley agrees that "[t]he novel's events are depicted by cyclical (climatic) and generational (remembered) experiences of time rather than by the time ... measured by clock, calendar, and chronology" (2016, p. 9). Wright said that when writing *Carpentaria*, she was consciously striving "to create an authentic form of Indigenous storytelling," and so this cyclic, multi-dimensional narrative is different in form and style from the traditional chronologically linear European mode (2007b, p. 84). The result is a work that has a visual descriptive form that Wright describes as looking

> something like a spinning multi-stranded helix of stories ... forever moving, entwining all stories together, just like a lyrebird is capable of singing several tunes at once. These stories relate to all the leavings and returnings to ancient territory, while carrying the whole human endeavour in search of new dreams [2007b, p. 84].

Wright's *Carpentaria* embodies cyclic patterns of narrative and meaning that are similar to those within other literary works featuring cyclones, such as White's *The Eye of the Storm*, Astley's *A Boat Load of Home Folk* and Hawthorne's poetry cycle *Earth's Breath*. These stories, too, contain "leavings and returnings" and "human endeavour in search of new dreams," imagined using the trope of the cyclone. Wright's cyclones in *Carpentaria* are tropes of the cyclic journeys on which her characters and their place embark. Their place journeys full circle, returned by the final cyclone to its original, naked earth form before the ancestral creative serpent moved through it. Characters such as Norm Phantom and his son Will embark on cyclic voyages of self-discovery, while Elias Smith's body returns to the sea from whence he came. Hope sets out to find her father to bring him home, giving her grandfather Norm hope for her and for the future, hope that stories forgotten can be learned again. When Armageddon arrives in the form of the second cyclone, the ensuing apocalypse cleanses the land of *Carpentaria* to make way for a new world, while Hope takes the knowledge and stories she has learned back out to sea in search of Will on a journey that symbolizes the potential of the future.

"To me," Wright explains, "fiction penetrates more than the surface layers, and probes deep into the inner workings of reality" (2002, p. 13), and *Carpentaria* challenges the reader as Wright penetrates the surface and probes deep into the inner workings of this particular reality from the very opening words of the storyteller: "A nation chants, but we know your story already" (2007a, p. 1). The nation might assume that they have heard this story before, but this version of that story is told by those on the outskirts of the nation as they look in. This is a different story than the one that is "known"; this story is composed of and mingled with scraps of culture: secular and spiritual, Aboriginal and European. Consequently, *Carpentaria* is not an easy novel to approach because its style and its content defy pre-conceptions. Wright herself agreed that potential readers often find her work challenging, and that consequently she has to "work terribly hard to get my work ... understood. We meet white resistance all the way" (Sharrard, 2009, p. 52). Yet, some critics such as Adam Shoemaker have described the book as the "greatest, most inventive and most mesmerizing Indigenous epic ever produced in Australia," and agree that Wright's novel has "genuine significance ... both within the space of Aboriginal fiction and within the wider field of the Australian and postcolonial novel" (Sharrard, p. 52). Much of that significance lies within the way in which the novel speaks both to the past and the present, to the land, the spirit, and the environment.

Alexis Wright (publicity photograph).

Carpentaria is a work within which Wright asserts cultural difference, for in it Wright speaks for herself and her culture in a saga that harks back in its oral form and historical reach to the Norse sagas of traditional European literature (Wright, 2007b). However, it is a work that also speaks to the present because "the orature of the ancient stories of Aboriginal Australia touches modernity in Wright's literature through the formal qualities and protocols of oral storytelling within the novel form" (Daley, p. 14). *Carpentaria* is a story that is, in fact, "about the importance of the story and the ways in which story maintains memory and offers strength, resilience and the future" (Loomes, 2014, p. 125). It is a story of all time and it will take time to tell, and so Wright decided that *Carpentaria* "should be written as a traditional long story of our times" (2007b, p. 80). Every saga needs a storyteller, and Wright consciously presents her story in the voice of an Aboriginal elder (2007b, pp. 89), with all the detours, nuances and deviations from chronological timelines typical of oral story form. As Aboriginal story-teller David Gulpilil comments in the film *Ten Canoes* (2006), a good story grows in its own time while putting down roots and branching out; that time could be days or even weeks, but it is the time that the story takes to unfold, and each story has its own time. While the long story of *Carpentaria,* the big story and the small ones in between, may take time to tell, it is a story that carries all time because Wright is conscious that Indigenous people live with the stories of all times in this country.

It is difficult for us to understand the Australian Aboriginal creative epoch, known as The Dreaming, within Western concepts of linear time with its separation of past and present. For Aboriginal people, the activities of The Dreaming may have occurred at the origin of the world but they are also still present. By participating in ritual and ceremony, it is possible to have a direct relationship with The Dreaming that is accessible by every generation. Because the Aboriginal people's concept of historic time is thus cyclical rather than linear, the Dreaming is an "heroic time which existed in the past and still exists today" (Bourke, p. 67). Wright agrees that "the everyday contemporary Indigenous story world is epic," and that it follows the patterns of the "great ancient sagas that defined the laws, customs and values of our culture." The oral tradition that produced those stories, she argues, "resounds equally as loudly in the new stories of our times" (2007b, p. 80) and it resounds loudly in *Carpentaria.*

The story of *Carpentaria* is a synthesis of Aboriginal and European Christian belief and culture that cannot be contained, as Wright herself maintains, "in a capsule either time or incident specific." She wanted to question those limiting boundaries and create a work that would extend beyond them as it explored "how ancient beliefs sit in the modern world" (2007b, p. 81). Norm Phantom, for example, passes on stories that question those boundaries. He believes in the Bible not only because white people had prospered by believing it but because of his own personal experience. "The sea could part and a man could walk on water," he declares, using as proof a combination of his experience and his memories of the appearance of Elias. "I was walking, if you please, straight out of a world that belonged to marine creatures and what have you swimming about in seawater, who had made enemies of men in the history of Dreamtime"(2007a, p. 510). Phantom has learned deep wisdom, with which he has survived the sea and cyclones, from his own experience and from stories that he has been told, compared to Hope who has no experience, no stories, and thus no wisdom, for she represents a future that is yet to be defined. She has to be taught that wisdom by Norm through stories that she can remember, assimilate, and take with her into the future in her search for Will.

Mozzie Fishman, on the other hand, is less broad-minded. To him, those "eons of indoctrination heaped onto the hapless by bible-bashers were the scourge of the blackfella's earth." For him, these stories are merely "Biblical stories lived in somebody else's desert" (p. 142). His own name epitomizes his identity issues; he is annoyed when people take it for granted that his European name, Fishman, means that he likes fishing or that he can provide fish, stating that "Biblical stories about baskets of fishes and loaves of bread belonged to Jewish people or some other people" (p. 142). He is not interested in the stories of other people; Fishman is interested in the stories of his own people and in teaching them to the younger generation. As one of his group of "disciples," Will Phantom is an apprentice to Fishman's stories in the same way that Hope is an apprentice to Norm Phantom's stories. Following a more conservative, traditional path than Norm, Fishman tells stories that provide knowledge about the rules and guidelines for living as an Australian Aboriginal person. It is important that these are passed down to the next generation, for loss of these stories would mean loss of culture, of history and even, ultimately, of life for these people.

Wright's stories in *Carpentaria* wind in and out of each other in a helix pattern to form a landscape and its history, and the complex characters who inhabit that landscape, and the result of Wright's unique representations of time, plot and myth in *Carpentaria* is "a discourse that displaces whiteness as the dominant paradigm" (Loomes, 2014, p. 125). These are stories from within her culture with which Wright was familiar, told from the point of view of those Indigenous people who live on the outside of European settlement looking in. Much like Western fables, they "are about having a belief system and principles of the right and wrong way to live" (Wright, 2007b, p. 89). Stories like these do not belong to any one society; all cultures hold them in order to perpetuate cultural memory. These stories explain origins and obligations to one another and the environment, and elucidate codes of morality and warn against living beyond them. They point out the importance of learning to live with one another, and they may even provide guidelines for physical survival in dangerous environments or circumstances.

"I want to explore the gift of our true inheritances," declares Wright, "by disallowing memories of times passed to sink into oblivion" (2002, p. 19), and to avoid that oblivion, the stories that bear those memories come with their own obligations of preservation, care, and maintenance that are best fulfilled by telling those stories. Such obligations can become the work of a lifetime, as Samuel Taylor Coleridge's Ancient Mariner discovered who, as penance for killing an innocent albatross, had to wander "like night, from land to land," telling his story of the cursed voyage as a warning to people to heed God and be kind to the fellow inhabitants of this planet (1933, p. 344). In this way, stories can become history and history, argues Alexis Wright, quoting African American writer James Baldwin, "is present in all that we do," because "it is to history that we owe our frames of reference, our identities, and our aspirations" (2007b, p. 83). Without stories, there is no history, and in the words of J.D. Woods, a South Australian journalist writing in 1879 about Australian Aborigines, "Without a history they have no past" (Loomes, 2014, p. 179). The stories keep memory alive and so, "The story has to go on," Mozzie Fishman instructs his young men. "Nothing must stop our stories, understand?" (Wright, 2007a, p. 429). However, while history might be in the stories, Wright's *Carpentaria* is not a mere re-telling of documented historic events; instead, the past pervades this narrative in the form of memory in all its unreliability and malleability. This is memory rich and poor, inherited and paid for, stolen and found, painful and sweet. This is the memory of children and old people, the living and the dead, the corporeal and the spirit. Here, Wright's spiral helix of interweaving stories forms landscape and a history of people within that place. These stories are a saga of apocalypse and hope in the ancient tradition of heroes caught up in situations larger than themselves.

In the tradition of sagas such as the Babylonian *Enuma Elish* and the Mayan *Popol Vuh*, Wright begins *Carpentaria* with a creation story, an evocative account of the Gulf of Carpentaria country being formed by the Aboriginal sacred serpent, which as

> a creature larger than storm clouds, came down from the stars, laden with its own creative enormity.... Picture the creative serpent, scoring deep into—scouring through— the slippery underground of the mudflats, leaving in its wake the thunder of tunnels collapsing to form deep sunken valleys.... The water filled the swirling tracks to form the mighty bending rivers spread across the vast plains of the Gulf country.... They say its being is porous: it permeates everything. It is all around in the atmosphere and is attached to the lives of the river people like skin [pp. 1–2].

However, this is more than just a creation narrative; this is a cultural story of beginning and being that immediately evokes a region permeated with the spiritual and the animate: a sentient region that lives and breathes. Aboriginal spirit-beings formed country during the Dreaming, as well as people and their belief system. These are the stories of the origin of Australian Aboriginal world.

In the beginning, there was only featureless terrain, water, the elements, and various spirits. It was a world waiting to be awakened, and that wakening was carried out by the deities, characters and beings of the Dreaming, including the Rainbow Serpents. These beings made and left various physical reminders of themselves as they continued on their way. A rocky peak could be a kangaroo-man sitting upright, or off-shore islands might be sisters trapped by rising tides or they may have risen up into the sky to become a constellation. A river might be the track of a serpent that could now be sleeping underground or can be seen in the sky as a rainbow. The entire landscape through which an Australian Aboriginal person moves is humanized and spiritualized in a way that can be read and told, assimilated and understood. The Dreaming-event is at the same time Dream-place and thus it is "country": the environment that is experienced by Aboriginal people as place in which the events of the Dreaming happened and are still happening. "For Aboriginal people, the land is a conscious entity that generates and responds to their actions," explains Strang, "creating life with them, nurturing them, grieving with them and sometimes dying with them" (1997, p. 252). In the more personal words of Aboriginal man Eddie Kneebone, "Aboriginal spirituality is the belief and the feeling within yourself that allows you to become part of the whole environment around you—not the built environment but the natural environment.... Birth, life and death are all part of it, and you welcome each" (Mudrooroo, p. 34). For an Australian Aboriginal person, the environment is a living place. All that occurs in it and has occurred in it is part of it.

Here, history is measured not in time but in space. In *Carpentaria*, the winding river "takes in breaths of a size that is difficult to comprehend" (Wright, 2007a, p. 2). Its tides, ebbing and flowing across a land that is "sometimes under-water and sometimes bone-dry," in which "the cyclones linger and regroup," are like the rhythmic breathing of the giant spirit serpent lying beneath the river and the land (p. 3). This living environment exists as much in the spiritual plane as the physical; it is that of the Dreaming and of the present. There is no separation or alienation of the Australian Aboriginal people from an environment with which they share a spirituality that is "an affirmation of the spirit of humanity and of the earth" (Mudrooroo, p. 54). Their stories of the Dreaming are more than a historic mythology: they are a living part of the consciousness by which this environment is mapped and, as such, these stories assist in constructing the Aboriginal sense of self. As anthropologists Ronald and Catherine Berndt explain, "No Aboriginal myth was told without reference to the land, or to a specific stretch of country where the incidents it narrates were believed to have taken place.... The land and all within it was irrevocably tied up with the content of myth or story, just as were (and are) the people themselves" (1989, p. 5). This is not a passive land to which things are done; this is a participating land with an active role to play and the stories of this land, regarded as equally relevant to people of the past, present, and future, are regarded as a powerful literary device by which to portray that role. Although they are now becoming a canon of written literature, we must not forget that these were originally stories passed down through generations by being spoken, sung, or rendered through some form of art (such as rock or bark paintings or string figures), or as told through the mediums of religious ritual, ceremony, and visions. The spirit-beings who strode, or flew, or swam across the land and through the lives of the people were brought to life in the story by the storyteller's voice and actions and so were active participants in their own mythologies.

The giant snake known as the Rainbow Serpent is an integral part of Australian Aboriginal mythology as a creator spirit-being, often seen as being under the ground (as in *Carpentaria*) and often connected to or associated with water (Mudrooroo, p. 53). In the Cooktown region, for example, the Serpent was responsible for creating the bed of the Endeavour River on his way to the coast (Tulo, 1986, pp. 1–3). At Cairns, the Rainbow Serpent was Buda:dji, the giant carpet python that lived on Double Island and formed the Barron River Gorge when he travelled inland to present nautilus shells to the people (Moses and Dixon, 1991, p. 43). The tracks commemorating the Serpent's journeys, sites and actions are among the many Dreaming paths, or "song-lines," sung by the Indigenous people across the continent that form a grid of links between often widely dispersed clan groups and by which one could navigate between them (Clarke, 2003, p. 21). In one form or another, spirit-beings were in the land from the beginning, playing a part in the shaping of geographic landforms, the people inhabiting them and their law, and they are still here. "The serpent sovereignty threaded through *Carpentaria*," argues Daley, "is depicted as not 'simply of the past,' but as a living and continuing authority of everyday-to-metaphysical matters for a particular and emplaced group in the present" (2016, p. 9), and this thread connecting the physical and the metaphysical, the object and animate spirituality, weaves throughout the novel. Wright herself sensed that connection to the Dreaming prior to writing *Carpentaria* while standing on the banks of the Gregory River in the Gulf country. "What I saw," she recalled, "was the mighty flow of an ancestral river … flowing with so much force I felt it would never stop, and it would keep on flowing, just as it had flowed by generations of my ancestors, … It was like an animal, very much alive, not destroyed, that was stronger than all of us" (2007b, p. 79). Consequently, the river, the serpent and the weather associated with it have fundamental roles in her novel.

Across the sub-tropical north of the continent in particular, the ancestral Serpent is often associated with water, rain, floods and storms. According to Ronald and Catherine Berndt, the connection between snakes and storms "is expressed more vigorously and consistently" in the Dreaming in North Queensland and the Gulf region because of the nature of the local weather patterns (1989, p. 124). Throughout this area, the Serpent in its various manifestations can be a law-giver with rain and flood-making powers, and is associated with fertility, tidal movements, spring and water-hole replenishment. In North Queensland, the Serpent is actively linked with the taipan and other dangerous snakes because of its involvement with destructive cyclones, storms and floods (1989, p. 124). It is also linked to the large rock or carpet python that lives among the rocks and crevices (or your garage, sundeck or ceiling) and can grow to around four meters and weigh 10kg, strengthening the analogy of the serpent with an earth creator (Mudrooroo, p. 53). The Rainbow

Seven. The Apocalypse and Epiphany of Cyclone

Serpent for the Djabugay people of the Cairns region in North Queensland, for example, is a carpet python that lived on Double Island as the incarnation of the storm season (Moses & Dixon, 43). On the west side of Cape York, in an area of the Gulf country swept by the Wet season's cyclones, heavy rains, floods, and tidal surges, the Rainbow Serpent is Taipan, regarded by the Aboriginal people with awe and respect as the maker of floods, cyclones, lightning, and thunder. After the storms, you can then see the colored form of the serpent in the sky. The brown to black, red-flecked coastal taipan snake, the name of which is derived from the local Wik-munkan language, possesses the third most toxic land venom in the world from which, until anti-venom was developed in 1955, you died from coagulation of the blood within a few hours of being bitten. Regarded by the local indigenous people as the controller of life and death through the blood supply, the Taipan spirit-being is a master of healing who inspires the "clever man" of the clan (McConnel, 1957, p. 111).

Their story of Taipan is that he was once a healer who could make lightning and thunder by throwing a red flint knife tied to the end of a long string into a tree, producing a flash. When he pulled it quickly back to him through the air, the movement caused the growling noise of thunder. He would do this to settle quarrels between people, frightening them into behaving (p. 112). Although he had three wives (all snakes), he had only one son. That son eventually coveted his cousin, the black water-snake wife of Wala, the blue-tongued lizard, and they ran away together. However, the vengeful Wala tracked them down and killed Taipan's son, draining his blood and removing his heart. These he took them back to Taipan who drenched the land with the blood, leaving the red land spoiled and the people now mortal with blood coursing through them. He took some of the blood and rubbed it over his daughters and sisters, creating menstruation, and then his sisters took that blood with them into the sky to become the red color in the rainbow. In the dry season, they stay underwater in streams and waterholes (billabongs), while Taipan lies underground, but in the Wet the sisters climb back into the sky to join their brother in the rainbow as the color blue (p. 115).

On the one hand, this is a multi-faceted story of the creation of storms, land, and the blood supply (and thus mortality) of people, transfused from the heart of Taipan's son. On the other hand, this is a story of conflict between individual desires and social controls: this couple may have eloped in the name of love, but one of them has to die for it because they broke the law. When Wala kills Taipan's son, he is defending the honor of aggrieved husbands. When Taipan spoils the ground and the women with blood to punish his niece for breaking the social law, he ordains the future suffering of women but he is upholding that social code. Stories such as this have a social function to perform in Aboriginal society. They allow the listener to see themselves, as if reflected in a mirror, in an ordered relationship with their community and with their environment. In these stories, the listener recognizes familiar landmarks that remind them of and direct them toward common moral, social or legal goals. At the same time, while listening to the story they experience the emotions that bind them together with their community. We, in our society, use disaster stories in much the same way. When we tell and re-tell stories of how we survived cyclones, wind and rain, or bushfires and flood, they too are stories that are actually educating people, teaching lessons about survival techniques such as evacuation, safe house construction, preparedness, and communication. These are stories through which people experience and realize needs and emotions that are common to their community and that bind them together.

As we have explored earlier, great serpents of power such as the Rainbow Serpent are not limited to Australia but are part of an international mythological trope. There are other storied serpents embedded within cultures everywhere, such as the Biblical Leviathan that appears in Palmer's *Cyclone* (1947), the ancient Egyptian and Greek ouroboros that appears in Susan Hawthorne's *Earth's Breath* poetry cycle, the Chinese celestial serpent-dragon, the Indian serpent Ananta that is coiled around the base of the World Axis, and the Norse serpent Midgardorm that is older than the gods and causes tides when it drinks and storms when it belches (Chevalier & Gheerbrant, 1996, p. 846). Then there is the South American plumed Serpent-Bird, Quetzalcoatl, that D.H. Lawrence describes as the "Serpent of the earth … snake that lies in the fire at the heart of the world." Only his living keeps the earth alive, and if he dies, "we should all perish" (1987, p. 196). Characteristically, these great serpents have power over the four elements of wind, water, earth, and fire, and in *Carpentaria* Alexis Wright uses the strength of these elements to invoke a knowledge and a mythology as old as time itself that resists European attempts to know, claim and control the Gulf of Carpentaria area. Her novel seethes with an elemental, apocalyptic fury of storms, lightning, dust, rain, fire and flood that invokes the mythical and spiritual. The largest man-made site in the region, the Gurfurritt mine, is finally destroyed by a fire that rages "like a monster cut loose from another world…. roaring like a fiery serpent, looking over to us with wild eyes, pausing, looking around, as if deciding what to do next" (2007a, p. 410). This is a fire encouraged by a mysterious wind that "sprang up from the hills themselves," although there had been no wind for days (p. 411). "The idea of the novel," Wright tells us, "was to build a story place where the spiritual, real and imagined worlds exist side by side" (2007b, p. 85), where it would be as if "the land was telling a story about itself as much as the narrator is telling stories to the land" (p. 87). In this country, the natural elements and the mythical elements are together part of this story that the land is telling about itself and its people.

Wright saw this land of *Carpentaria* as "the land of the untouched: an

Indigenous sovereignty of the imagination," about which such an epic story could be told that might grow the land and through which the future might be envisioned, a story that reaches forward into the future as much as it reaches back through the layers of time and history (p. 94). Into this land and story appears a man who emerges from a cyclone onto the shore near the Gulf town of Desperance, into a country where storms are "like second nature to these people" (2007a, p. 86). In this storm, however, a once-in-a-century cyclone named Leda, this man of the sea "who was a wizard of many oceans" loses his identity when his memories are taken from him by "thieving sea monsters" (p. 43). He then makes the mistake of cursing the sea as he pursues his memories across it, and such disrespect for the spirits has to be punished by them, and while they return his memories of sailing and fishing, they do not give him back his memory of his identity (p. 166). Like the mythological Leda birthing Helen of Troy, Cyclone Leda births a man with no name and no memory, a *tabula rasa* on whom the people of Desperance seize the opportunity to impose their own wishes and desires.

There are signs that this birth has significance: at the very moment his memory is stolen, miracles occur. Lightning rises *upward* from sacred locations under the sea to travel in a straight line south until it strikes a tree growing in the middle of Desperance to the sound of thunder, after which all the clocks stop at eleven minutes after midnight (p. 44). In effect, chronological time or durational time in a Western European sense stops for everyone in the town at the same instant, and it stops to mark this man's transformation in a cyclone from human being into a spiritual messenger. This is no longer the time of the calendar and the clock; the time of this story will develop and grow in its own time and occupy its own space. The people of Desperance feel that something is about to happen. The air is charged with static electricity; the people and their surroundings, including the water, are turned red by churned-up dust as if one of the Egyptian plagues prophesied by Moses has arrived.

Then a stranger with long white hair and beard materializes in the distance along the shore, walking across the shallows of sand and mudflats towards the town, appearing to be walking on the very water. As he approaches, heralded by children, various people in the watching crowd perceive him differently. While some see him as a seasoned fisherman cast up from some foreign land, to others he resembles a "perfect human pearl" (p. 50). To yet another group, he is Jonah: the archetypal unwilling prophet whose name is a sailor's byword for a person who brings bad luck to a ship and its crew. Their perceptions also differ along racial lines. To the local Indigenous people, he is a magical being possibly affiliated with the Dreaming because the theft of his memory evidently appeased the cyclone, which has skirted the town instead of laying waste to it. However, to the white population of Desperance, this man also has spiritual significance. He too exemplifies their origin story because, like them, he is a stranger appearing from out of nowhere on some foreign shore, just as "their original forebear, a ghostly white man or woman, simply turned up one day" (p. 57). They also wonder if this mysterious stranger will be able to provide answers to their mysteries, such as why the Lord's hand has delivered them drought, rot, termites and plagues, and why the fish always seem to gather somewhere the fisherman are not. They hope that "God had given Elias to the town" (p. 76), and that their prayers will be answered, so they place "the richness of prophecy squarely on this man's shoulders" (p. 69). This man quickly becomes Everyman for the town, no matter what their ethnic affiliation, and now anyone's wishes might come true but, as yet, he has no name.

It is Captain Nicoli Finn, another man who appeared in Desperance from nowhere, who christens him with the name of a prophet-as-saint. Finn has become a kind of guardian of the white population and the closest that they have had to a prophet until now, and he quickly proceeds to imbue this stranger with similar qualities. Accepted by the town as the only person there who can deal with the unexpected, Finn is appropriately the first to see the stranger, claiming later that he looked "almost spiritual" as he approached to the sound of an organ playing Handel's *Messiah* (p. 67). When questioned as to his identity, the stranger replies that he does not know who he is, identifying himself only as "I," an echo of the Christ-like "I am" (p. 75). The townspeople make the logical leap of faith and declare he is a savior, at which Finn passes on the prophet's mantle by announcing the stranger's name to be Elias Smith, transforming him into "the anointed one"(p. 76), the new guardian of Desperance. "It was the beginning of the story of the day," sums up Wright's narrator,

> the spirits of the seas and storms mixed their business and sent Elias from out of oblivion into Desperance for a good reason. This was the story about Elias Smith which was later put alongside the Dreamtime by the keepers of the Law to explain what happened once upon a time [p. 54].

As far as the Aboriginal people are concerned, Elias is part of their story.

However, as a man who cannot remember who he was, Elias has moments when he questions the validity of this new, unique, status as a celestial being but, in doing so, he questions the belief of the townsfolk in their uniqueness, that their town is unlike any other in Australia, and so naturally they resist his uncertainty. "You either are or you are not, and you are," they inform him, again echoing the "I am" of the Biblical Christ-figure who, like Elias, emerged into this world with nothing (p. 78). As a man with no memory, Elias is in stark contrast to Norm and Will Phantom and Mozzie Fishman, who are always carrying with them the wealth of their ancestral memory that stretches back into a past time of thousands of years. Instead, Elias is a man without a past, without tradition, without wealth, some times without even belief in himself. Eventually, his life turns full cycle towards another cultural tradition when he becomes the town scapegoat. Having been judged guilty by the town of a multiplicity of crimes he could not possibly have committed, Elias is subsequently exiled back into the wilderness of the sea from where he came, there to be murdered by mine security personnel. Like a crucified Christ or apostle Peter, however, while his death might be the end of his physical existence, Elias' spiritual influence lives on in the lives of Norm and Will Phantom.

Here Wright is mixing "business," as she mixes the implications of the Christian tradition with Indigenous lore. Elias is another version of the name Elijah, the name of the Biblical prophet who heard the "still, small voice of God" (1 Kings 19), and the parallels in *Carpentaria* are clear. In the Bible, God speaks to Elijah from out of the whirlwind, during the time of King Ahab and Queen Jezebel, and he becomes a prophet of drought (1 Kings 17), as well as a prophet of rain (1 Kings 18), while he resists the will of the king in order to restore tradition. Likewise, Elias Smith emerges from out of the cyclone, the water and the wind, into a landscape of drought in which the people are waiting for rain. Deprived of the knowledge of his real origin, Elias creates his own tradition with an origin story that he was blasted into the night sea from out of a bolt of lightning, entering the atmosphere so fast his memory was left behind. To the Aboriginal Pricklebush people, Elias is a "man of ancient ways" (p. 77) with whom they sit at night to count stars. They adopt him because they sense something spiritual about him, as does Norm Phantom who is aware that Elias knows the sacred place of the groper fish far out in the waters of the Gulf. He is sure that Elias can communicate with them because Norm has been out there with Elias when he has called them up from the deep to their boat (p. 236). Within the stories of both cultures in Desperance, then, Elias Smith becomes a prophetic symbol of hope.

As a character, Smith sits within a wilderness prophet trope in Australian literature. The poet A. D. Hope wrote that he was glad to turn away from contemporary thought on the coast, that he likened to a dense, forbidding jungle, towards the more open expanse of the Australian interior in search of the "desert of the human mind,/Hoping if still from the deserts the prophets come" (1991, p. 222), and one of the most memorable examples of that trope is Patrick White's explorer in *Voss* (1957), who also makes a pilgrimage into the redemptive desert: one of spiritual exploration by suffering man seeking salvation in the wilderness. In many ways, Elias is reminiscent of another of these prophet figures: Michael Random, the stranger found wandering outside the desert town of Tourmaline in Randolph Stow's novel of the same name. Although Random emerges from the desert, like Elias he seems to have come from the sea. "Something about him always recalled to me the sea, the coast," recalls the narrator of *Tourmaline*, The Law; "there was so much hope in the look of him"(1983, p. 37). In the same way as the people of Desperance react to Elias Smith, the people of Tourmaline use Random as a blank slate on which to write their hopes and desires, so much so, suggests the character of Tom, that perhaps he is actually inspired by Tourmaline rather than by any God because, "You [Tourmaline] thought you needed him. You convinced him he was what was wanted" (p. 185). Also at first unable to remember who he is, Random later claims to be a water diviner and thus to be able to save Tourmaline, a town that has not seen water for years. Like Desperance, Tourmaline is situated where "there is no stretch of land on earth more ancient than this" (1983, p. 7), where the local Aboriginal people believe that the Dreaming spirit-being moved through the country, creating rocks and hills, caves and waterholes as it passed by. When it became tired, it went down into the ground, creating a spring from which the water once rose to fill Lake Tourmaline, but the spring has ceased flowing and the lake has dried up, deserting Tourmaline just as Wright's river has deserted Desperance.

Just as the people of Desperance attach their hope to Elias, the people of Tourmaline pin their hopes on the diviner, Michael Random with such optimism "that there seemed to be a hazy feeling that the drought might break with the diviner's coming, and the millionaires go yachting on Lake Tourmaline" (p. 36). But, both these potentially inspirational prophet-figures prove to be flawed. Random, the water diviner, believes God has saved him and sent him to Tourmaline for a purpose. He has come from Hell, he claims, and God has spoken to him in the wilderness (p. 113). In a sense, Random has also been washed ashore here from the sea of the desert, after a failed suicide bid, and his life is also saved by a town that gives him a purpose. "We made you," The Law declares; "And not for your use. For ours" (p. 192). Random's purpose is to save the town just as Elias' purpose is to save the town by looking after the invisible protective net that surrounds it. However, unlike Elias, Random's eventual exile is because he commits a real sin, rather than an imagined one: he deceives the town that has taken him in and so he loses their trust and faith as they finally see that he does not really care about them at all: he just cares about himself (p. 192). Like the protagonist of Dorothy Scarborough's *The Wind*, who finally surrenders and runs out into the storm, fleeing across the prairies "like a leaf blown in a gale, borne along by the force of the wind that was at last to have its way with her" (1979, p. 337), Random too finally runs into the wind and the desert. A flood of red dust borne on the wind then overwhelms Tourmaline, like the apocalyptic flood of water that removes Desperance from the face of the earth, sparing only The Law who knows that although terrors will ensue, there will be "wonders too, as in the past. Terrors and wonders, as always" (1983, p. 221). Like the English philosopher Burke, he understands that to truly appreciate the wonders, we need to understand the terror.

Like many a prophet, Elias eventually discovers that he can quickly become the subject of people's anger when they lose faith in him. Having been made caretaker of the town's sacred and invisible defense net, "made of prayers and god-fearing devotion," that is drawn over the town during the Wet season from November to March to protect it from cyclones (Wright, 2007a, p. 82), Elias is accused by the town of arson when a spate of mysterious fires occur that culminate in the complete destruction of the Shire office building, along with the Queen's portrait within it. The Biblical prophet Elijah called down fire from heaven as a sign of God's power; Elias Smith, too, is accused of bringing down fire on Desperance and destroying the town records, ironically rendering amnesiac the town that had sheltered him as a man with no memory. His reply is to point out to them, with a prophet's unappreciated candor, just how ridiculous they are. Consequently, the town exiles Elias into the wilderness of the sea from where he had come, after which he is never seen again alive. Norm Phantom, who does not interfere at the time because he doesn't want to upset white people, makes the personal sacrifice of giving up fishing to honor the memory of his friend. Instead, he becomes a marine taxidermist, and so in his own way he restores an appearance of life to the dead. He perceives that in destroying his legendary self, he will create a memorial to Elias that will force people to remember the time it happened and the reason for it.

It is Norm's exiled son, Will, who with his mentor, father-in-law and spiritual leader Mozzie Fishman discovers Elias' body mysteriously sitting in his small green boat, *Choice*, in a remote lagoon. Will recognizes him immediately, "accepting the gift of Elias' spirit," who had been waiting, he sees, to pass memories on to him that he had forgotten since the time of Elias' departure. Mozzie, too, recognizes that this re-discovery of Elias is "a message given to him from the spirit world" (p. 149). Like the Biblical prophet Elijah, who as a reward for his virtuous life is taken up by God in a fiery chariot in a whirlwind and so escapes death (2 Kings 2), Elias' body and boat were also taken up in a whirlwind (created by a helicopter) to this lagoon. After finding the body, Will moves it to a sacred cave, from where he eventually brings it to Norm's workshop in which live the spirits that help him create his painted fish. Even after his death, Elias continues to influence events; figuratively translated, he achieves an immortality as a spiritual influence.

When Norm discovers Elias' body, he believes that Elias has returned because he wants to be taken back out into the Gulf to the sacred home of the groper fish, a deep hole of great spiritual significance, "where the congregations of the great gropers journeying from the sky to the sea were gathered," waiting for Elias to arrive there before travelling on to the sea of stars at the end of the season (p. 236). The Queensland groper (or giant grouper), that can be over two meters in length and up to 400kg in weight, is a sacred Dreaming fish to the Aboriginal people of the Gulf: to kill one is to invite its spirit into your dreams and very bad luck into your life. These huge fish are Norm's friends and fellow fishing partners in *Carpentaria*, rounding up the reef fish for him as well as leading him up rivers to the prawn beds when he is fishing at night. Returning Elias to them is a significant recognition by Norm of Elias' spiritual status and so, guided by the map in his mind, Norm and the body and spirit of Elias embark on a great spiritual journey out across the Gulf to a sacred place in a world that is "the realm of mischievous winds" and which belongs "to the spirits of fishes, women and sea creatures" (p. 240). As a seaman, Elias always navigated by the brightest star in the constellation, Pisces Austrinus, known as Fomalhaut, derived from the Arabic *fam al-hut* meaning "mouth of the Southern fish" or "mouth of the whale." Norm also knows this significant star: to him, it is the groper that swims from the sea up into the sky every night, returning every morning down the sky to his home beneath the water (p. 515). Norm is returning Elias to his spiritual home, the sea from where he came, and to the home of Elias' spiritual animal: a reef abyss containing caves where both Europeans and Indigenous people agree the groper fish have lived for centuries (p. 250).

Norm is guided to this place by a vast shoal of gropers that then form a circle around the boat and wait until he sends Elias' body into the depths, where it is received into the "giant arms of water" (p. 253). Although he had arrived for a purpose connected with death, Norm now feels alive having finally returned Elias to his spiritual home. He has a vision of the groper rising from the sea to swim "through the ocean of air, to ascend into the sky world of the Milky Way" and understands that Elias has gone with them back to his own country where he will "be like a star" that will guide him (p. 258). Elias' spirit becomes a catalyst for Norm's epiphany: he now sees the web of the sea currents and the stars above forming the map that will guide him home. For the rest of the novel, even though Norm can no longer directly communicate with Elias, he always senses Elias' spirit watching over him.

Like Patrick White's Elizabeth Hunter, Norm finds himself at the center of a still point. Birds surround him out there in the Gulf, as they surrounded Hunter in her storm's eye, and beyond them on the horizon is the approaching cloud-bank of the Wet season storms. For the rest of Hunter's life, she was influenced by her spiritual experience in the eye of that storm and Norm, too, perceives he is entering "a spiritual country forbidden to all men" (p. 268). Before the rise in sea level approximately 10,000 years ago, an event still within the oral history memory of Australian Aboriginal people, the Gulf was a freshwater lake around which people lived, and as Norm sails over "place upon place where people once lived in the sea," he understands that he is

Seven. *The Apocalypse and Epiphany of Cyclone* 151

being shown spiritual secrets and that "what he saw he knew should never have been seen again" (p. 268). At that center of life in the ocean, surrounded by gulls and fish during a spiritual ritual of death and homecoming, as he survives temptations of suicide and a violent storm, Norm has another epiphany that after years of being dead inside, of being among dead fish instead of the living, he has now seen life in death. Isolated for so many years by pain, anger and loneliness, Norm Phantom now sees a path home on his mental map that will reunite, relocate and re-establish him with his family, his people and with the land.

At the very end of the Old Testament, in the last verse of Malachi, Elijah is identified as the prophet who will herald "the great and terrible day of the Lord" who will "turn the hearts of fathers to their children and the hearts of children to their fathers" (4:5). In *Carpentaria*, Elias is the man who appears from one cyclone as a herald of another and who turns Norm's heart to his children, for it is on his physical and spiritual return journey from burying Elias that Norm discovers his daughter-in-law, Hope, and her son Bala. With the help of the spirits of ancestors and of the bush country, Norm rescues Bala from a cyclonic storm and flooding tidal surge and this, Norm finally acknowledges, "was the solace of Elias: how he used his death to help an ignorant old man find his grandson, to rekindle hope in his own joyless soul" (p. 307). Elias' prophet's mantle has been passed on to Norm, for it is he who brings the "great and terrible day" of judgment upon Desperance by calling on his spiritual power to create, in one of the sacred "cyclone-making" places, the great cyclone that destroys the town.

"Cyclones don't come from nowhere," says the old Queen of the Pricklebush whom Will meets while sheltering under the roof of the pub from the cyclone that's destroying Desperance,

> because there is plenty of business going on when cyclones come onto the country out of the rooftop of the world, like what is going on outside now from the most powerful creation spirits, who come down out of the skies like a tempest when they start looking for Lawbreakers [pp. 478–9].

In *Carpentaria* country, cyclones have significant spiritual function and bear portent beyond their literal entity. Norm's son Will sees not just "the tremendous fury of the winds gathering up the seas," but also "clouds carrying the enormous bodies of spiritual beings belonging to other worlds.... the sound of the great spiritual ancestors roaring..." (p. 401). He hears

> the spirit waves being rolled in by the ancestral seawater creatures of the currents, and conspiring with the spirits of the sky and winds to crash into the land ... the underground serpent living in the underground river that was kilometres wide, responded with hostile growls. This was the old war of the ancestors making cyclones grow to use against one another [p. 470].

He understands that the cyclone is part of the story of this great creation site that is his homeland, "where predetermined knowledge dwelled from a world full of memories, told, retold, thousand upon a thousand times from the voices of all times" (p. 460). This event he is trying to survive has nothing to do with mortal man. This is an apocalyptic storm that is here to change everything.

Will knows a cyclone is said to always show people the way home, and that the giant cyclonic waterspouts of the ancient serpent pluck the lost souls of the drowned from the floor of the sea and bring them to shore (p. 475), and so when he seeks shelter under the roof of the Desperance pub, he is not surprised to find that he is sharing that confined space with spirits who are also seeking refuge, including the old Queen of the Pricklebush. Surrounded by spirits of Aboriginal old people and of fishermen lost at sea, she reminds Will that as a child he saw a creation spirit in the form of a cyclone follow a Lawbreaker up a river until it found him hiding in a town and killed him there. Cyclones have purpose, her words imply; cyclones are instruments of judgment, and in fact this cyclone has actually been brought into existence for that reason. This cyclone has been "sung" with a creation ceremony in a sacred place and then directed along the path of sea currents to Desperance as judgment and "payback" by Norm Phantom, the man who knows all the sacred storm-making places and who can "fly through storms like an angel"(p. 486).

However, in the true meaning of apocalypse, this is not just a time of destruction but also of the revelation of new possibilities. Will knows he is "being prepared for change…. This was the root of ultimate trust, he thought, the knowledge of intuition, of understanding the vibrations of subtle movement in the environment" (pp. 460–61). In his mind, he sees the waters of the sea "circulating in huge masses hundreds of kilometres wide and as many fathoms deep," sensing "a mysterious change of great magnitude … taking place in the wetted atmosphere" (p. 460). He realizes

> how history could be obliterated when the Gods moved the country. He saw history rolled, reshaped, undone and mauled as the great creators of the natural world engineered the bounty of everything man had ever done in this part of the world into something more of their own making [p. 492].

One of those "great creators of the natural world" is, of course, the Rainbow Serpent with which Wright begins her novel.

While trapped by the cyclone in the roof of the pub, Will has a vision in which he sees that Hope, the mother of his son Bala, is still alive. Wright's constant puns on and allusions to "hope" throughout the novel leave little doubt that her choice of this name was deliberate, and it is significant that these references become more positive as the novel progresses. Will sees her

Seven. The Apocalypse and Epiphany of Cyclone   153

in his vision apparently walking on the water, and this epiphany renews his hope that he will ultimately survive the cyclone and find her again. Wright seems to suggest that Hope may be a successor to Elias, who was also first seen apparently walking on water, and when Norm and Bala discover Hope wandering along a beach, she has emerged from the sea with no memory of what happened to her, just like Elias. In Norm's opinion, miracles do not happen to anyone unless God has given them a miracle key such as the one given to Elias (p. 514). Not understanding Hope's significance at this point, Norm is puzzled by her apparent miraculous survival because he believes that she is disqualified because of her bloodline from being given that key. However, during his voyage with Hope and Bala in search of Will, Norm comes to understand that ultimately Hope will be the only one who can find Will and restore the next generation of the family. She cannot guide Norm to Will because she is afraid of the sea, yet only by travelling across the sea will Hope find him. This cannot be Norm's journey; he cannot do it for her or even with her. It will have to be her journey during which Hope will have to face her own fears.

When Norm and Bala reach the original site of Desperance, the apocalyptic cyclonic flood has wiped the land clean of all traces of humanity. There will be a need for hope as a new cycle begins, and so Norm is not surprised when Hope leaves him and Bala there to set off in the boat to continue her search for Will alone, a search on which she will be guided by her own map. Only then does Norm realize that he has started to believe in her: the man who lost hope has finally found Hope. As Norm's journey-cycle through sadness and revenge culminates in spiritual awakening and renewal sung by the voices of frogs awakened by the rain from the apocalyptic cyclone, another cycle of hope begins for him, his people and their country.

"All times are important to us," says Wright. "No time has ended and all worlds are possible" (2002, p. 20). In seeking to address such an epic story arc and period, Wright creates literature in her narratively complex *Carpentaria* that contributes to making a world at the same time as it enters the already existing world of Aboriginal Australia, a world that speaks in voices of myth and story and time. This is a world that Ronald and Catherine Berndt have described as a land "resonant with sound and presence—a land that is certainly not a passive or negative component" (1989, p. 426). It is country that constitutes "a primary force," that "speaks unequivocally, underlining what people imply is its concern for the affairs of human beings—even though it and what it contains act independently of them" (p. 426). It is, in the Berndt's words, a "speaking land" with a mythology that holds up a mirror in which can be seen not only the actions of mythological beings but in which we can also identify ourselves (p. 427). This land with a voice is in sharp contrast to what W.E.H. Stanner termed "the great Australian silence": the attitude of white Australians to the history of Aboriginal presence (1991, p. 27). Instead, *Carpentaria* voices within the Western novel form an Aboriginal view of the world, using the cyclic patterns inherent in the physical and spiritual elements of the place of the novel, the Gulf country, and this view challenges Western assumptions of the human sense of itself in the natural environment. These patterns are embodied in the cyclones with which Wright begins and ends the cycle of her story. In entering one world, Wright envisages another world made spiritually animate through interconnecting human and non-human forces and so, while embedded in a particular region and place, the novel challenges attitudes to inhabiting that place and to what it means to be in and part of that place. Her cyclones, while apocalyptic instruments of weather, are also spiritual voices and messengers of spirits. They have purpose, like all the natural elements of this country, and this purpose is to not only punish and destroy but also to transform. The cyclones destroy the old, but they reveal the new. Cyclone Leda transforms Elias from person to prophet, but his transformation continues after the death of his physical body into that of a spirit guide and influence so powerful that it becomes part of the astronomy of the region. Will meets the spirits within the later cyclone, enabling his own spirit to be renewed after a suitable forty days and nights in the wilderness of the sea. Normal Phantom, a man with the (anything but normal) power to create cyclones, is guided by a cyclone to find Hope and Bala, a storm of such spiritual and physical power and dimensions that it ultimately alters the entire landscape. Thus the landscape of the old world is stripped and cleansed in order that a new life can be re-created in a renewed land under which the Serpent sleeps, where the frogs have assembled to sing fertility into a new world and a new time.

Eight

The Word Becomes the Cyclone
Revelations of the Literary Storm

"A culture's most cherished places are not necessarily visible to the eye—spots on the land one can point to. They are made visible in drama—in narrative, song, and performance. It is precisely what is invisible in the land that makes what is merely empty space to one person a place to another…. The land gets inside us"—(Barry Lopez, 1986, p. 278)

"I live in a land of great wind, and it defines me."—(Jan DeBlieu, 1998, p. 269)

The Cyclone as Trope of Place

Tropical cyclones are an integral and historical part of tropical place, such as North Queensland. These catastrophic rotating storms are ineludible: although meteorologists can now predict a cyclone's path with increasing accuracy, along with its likely time of landfall and its increases and reductions in strength, cyclones as weather systems cannot be controlled, diverted, nor destroyed. You cannot physically escape a cyclonic storm system unless you leave the area, although you can certainly attempt to protect yourself from the effects of the storm. However, people living on islands have limited possibilities for evacuation or the weather system could be so large that distance itself becomes an issue. For example, the 2011 Cyclone Yasi system encompassed almost the entire Queensland coastline, approximately the distance from Miami to New York City (That's right; in Australia, that is just one state). To avoid it, you had to be in another part of the country! So, if we wish to live meaningfully in the tropics, we need to discover how to co-exist with chaotic weather events such as cyclones, and we can imaginatively respond to them as the monsters that regularly invade our life in order that we can contextualize them within our life. As Edmund Burke suggests, the very awe and terror engendered by such events as cyclones may prompt and heighten imaginative responses to them, and we have explored here a range of such responses to tropical cyclones in Queensland poetry and prose that employ the cyclone as trope of a regional society's literary search for a meaningful context for chaotic and catastrophic nature events. These searches are significant because, "disaster is, by definition, that which cannot be comprehended exactly" (Voss in Coen, 2013, p. 3). Studying the meaning of disaster as expressed in the writing of it, then, can reveal to us enable us how we might comprehend, accept, and incorporate the chaos of nature catastrophes into our relationship with place.

Literary tropes play significant roles in imaginary response because, "To connect the literature of a place with the actual place that gave rise to the literature," argues Lawrence Buell, "can deepen not only one's sense of the book itself but one's sense of what it means to be in communion with place" (Cranston & Zeller, 2007, p. 14). A relationship between person and place emerges from a continual process of exchange through the porous boundaries between society and the environment. In much the same way as many of the physical elements in a wine-growing habitat, such as weather, geology, drainage, soil quality and composition, interact with chemical and mineral compounds during the growing process in a mysterious alchemy known as

A ruined house at Tully Heads after Cyclone Yasi, 2011. The large boulders have been lifted into the house and yard from the nearby stone seawall by the force of the wind (photograph used with the permission of Jonathan Nott).

terroir to produce recognizably regional wine, so imagination interacts with the characteristics of a region in the development of pictorial art and literature that express the qualities and meaning of that region. "We are the cross-hatched winds of/Gungara the spiralling wind/from the Kimberleys, we are a poet/defiantly writing herself into creation," writes Susan Hawthorne about that interaction between place, imagination and creative artist (2009, p. 78). Art and literature are both derived from and contribute to the physical and imagined, literal and literary place in which society exists, described by geologist and *terroir* authority James E. Wilson as the "additional dimension" of the habitat that is "beyond the measurable ecosystem." He proposes that it is, "the spiritual aspect [of it] that recognizes the joys, the heartbreaks, the pride, the sweat, and the frustrations of its history" (2001, p. 141). Thus relationships between people and place can extend far beyond and much deeper than earth, rock and tree.

They can extend, in fact, to the weather of that place for weather is "written into our landscape" (Harris, 2015, p. 9): it is part of *terroir*. Weather is mutually constituted with people into their intimate, interactive perception of place, and so while the weather may seem to be mainly concerned with inanimate elements such as clouds, sun, rain, atmosphere and wind, it nonetheless affects human beliefs, actions and behavior. Just as people shape place, weather is also able to shape place and thus, by implication, shape the people inhabiting that place. As we draw the air and the wind into our bodies as we breathe, it becomes an integral part of us. We become enwinded; we develop a "wind mind" as our environment influences our very perception of ourselves (Hawthorne, 2009, p. 78). After surviving Cyclone Yasi, Kate Campbell-Lloyd referred to the noise of cyclones being "etched" into her very DNA, aware that her self-perception would be forever changed by that experience (2011, p. 85). The weather is written into us as it is written into our place, and in our quest to find meaning in place as we establish our relationship with it, we need to be open to the revelations of weather. They may be revelations about the moral and spiritual dimensions of weather, such as those perceived by John Milton in *Paradise Lost*, Patrick White in *The Eye of the Storm*, and Alexis Wright in *Carpentaria*, revelations of historical and cultural allegory such as those of Virginia Woolf in *Orlando* and Vance Palmer in *Cyclone*, or insight into personal doubts and fears such as occurs in Thea Astley's *A Boat Load of Home Folk*. Perhaps we are all living on the edges of cyclones, as Astley suggested, where weather could isolate people if they do not find strength in the connections of community that would help them survive potential catastrophe.

Having formed at sea, cyclones initially impact coastal place. They have impacted the North Queensland coast for millennia, becoming integral to that region's cultural identity, and this coast is part of the Australian littoral. Coastal culture, in which the coast is a place of encounter of not only land with sea, but also of people with nature, culture, history and, of course, the weather, is a significant element of the Australian national identity. These encounters are even more significant in the present age because, having largely rejected the interior of the country demographically, Australians prefer to cluster along that littoral that has now, Philip Drew argues, replaced the interior "as the chief spatial and symbolic focus in our culture" (1994, p. 3). The coast has become the buffer between the hostile wilderness of the sea and the hostile wilderness of the country's interior, behind which Australians huddle, "surrounded by ocean and ambushed from behind by the desert" (Winton, 1993, p. 21). Fighting "a war of mystery on two fronts" (p. 21), Australians understand their relationship to the coast as little as they understand their relationship to the interior. The coast, after all, is neither stable nor predictable; it is a fluid place of interaction between land and sea. It is a place that threatens as much as it welcomes, with such potential dangers as sharks, jellyfish, tidal rips, and tropical cyclones that can materialize from the sea onto the coast, bringing chaos that emphasizes to people the fragility of their human claim to the littoral and their ultimate inability to impose order on nature. Cyclones may well be part of regional *terroir*, but they are a reminder that elements of that *terroir* remain beyond the control of humanity. It is because these catastrophic weather events insinuate the terror of disruption into our perceived ordered relationship with place that we seek for a means by which we can contextualize the cyclone and its consequences. Perhaps, then, we can in some way restore that order or, at the very least, restore our relationship with our *terroir*.

The Cyclone as Trope

Cyclones as nature catastrophes are woven into the tapestry of place. They have happened in the past, they happen in the present, and they will continue to occur as part of place future. While we may not ever fully explain the randomness and chaos of these events, studying their significance to the relationship of people with place as expressed in the language and literature of place may help us to contextualize nature catastrophes, so that their significance in that relationship can be better understood. "Behind the symbol," proposes Hoffman, "lies a logic that clarifies the event and gives it cause. Once ordered and given reason, a calamity can be given context, content, emotion, and meaning" (2002, p. 114). As nature catastrophes such as cyclones that have impacted on regional culture become part of that culture, telling stories of them enables us to contextualize the catastrophe and to give it meaning. As we attempt to relate to this changed place, we are constantly restoring our sense of *terroir* as we give these events "context, content, emotion, and meaning" appropriate to the place. In this way, the trope of the catastrophe becomes more than a mere representation of the event. As we seek a revelation about the mystery of the catastrophe, as we seek to know the why, the stories and the tropes that may contain these revelations become part of our cultural search for meaning, which is in turn part of our cultural response to the catastrophe.

In using the tropical cyclone in Queensland literature as a trope of apocalypse, of destruction, epiphany, and renewal, writers have sought to explore, expand and reiterate their relationship with and response to a concept of place that is *terroir* inclusive of catastrophe. Although the modern usage of the term apocalypse tends to relate to the destructive event, the original Greek origins of the word have a broader meaning that includes the concept of revelation. In other words, the destruction caused by such an event may have a purpose: that of revealing the possibility of the new that could be recreated from the ruins of the old, for example, or the possibility of a second chance that may enable change. These possibilities can emerge as the extraneous personal, material or irrelevant aspects of life are stripped away. As revelatory apocalypse, the cyclone can be a personal catalyst for epiphany, and for review and renewal of relationship with place, whether for the individual or the community. Consequently, the writer as themselves, or through their characters, re-examines their relationship with tropical place, suggesting to the reader that they, too, might re-examine their own relationship.

Having described Paul Vesper, the protagonist and narrator of her novel *The Acolyte*, as "always touching on the edges of cyclones" (1985, 119), Astley later observed that many of her characters were doing that because "just being alive is like living on the edge." In fact, she conceded, "Everybody's living on a cyclonic edge." Whereas her friend Patrick White took his characters into the eye of the storm, she explained, hers were "misguidedly trying to get away, out of the entire ambient of the cyclone and, of course, that is not possible, not for any human. The minute you are born you are put into this situation" (Willbanks, 2008, p. 30). Astley saw each of us as living within their personal cyclone, and in her 1968 novel, *A Boat Load of Home Folk* (1968), a group of people stranded on a South Pacific island by a cyclone discover that, indeed, they are unable to escape the cyclone within or the storm outside. Trapped by the external storm, they have no choice but to face their inner tempests, confronting secrets and personal torments. As the storm whirling on the outside strips away the layers of the island buildings, so it also strips away the layers of the group's characters to reveal the loneliness, shallowness, absurdity and unhappiness beneath, uncovering their flawed humanity. Some do not survive such exposure, while others emerge changed by it.

The cyclone that maroons this group of cruise ship passengers is not just a literal storm trapping them there: it is also a storm of hypocrisy, vanity, stupidity and maliciousness generated by various members of the group. More importantly, though, it is an *apocalyptic* storm: one that is a revelation of personal truths and of truths about their interaction with each other. Except for Stevenson, who is prepared to accept what the cyclone reveals and act on it, most of Astley's passengers are "afraid to examine the gyrating circumference of mortality spinning around them because they are afraid of what such an apocalypse might reveal" (Astley, 1965, p. 195). However, cyclones cannot stop them any more than one can change their direction. Some damage is subsequently inevitable. Impelled by the cyclone into prolonged and intimate contact with each other, unable to escape cyclones that rage internally as well as externally as the storm strips away their layers of ego, Astley's characters are overtaken by an apocalypse that not only exposes their underlying corruptible natures but also judges them. They are, indeed, living on the edges of cyclones.

For Susan Hawthorne, and other Queensland poets, the experience of the cyclone as apocalypse has opened them to the nature of being, of who they are in terms of where they are in relationship to place. Arguing that poetry has always been the song that we learn from the natural world imprinted into human culture, Hawthorne draws from her experience in Cyclone Larry to articulate the relationship between herself, humanity, and the environment: between person and place. As revealed in *Earth's Breath*, her cyclone experience speaks of the successful relationship between person and place that can be developed from learning to incorporate into it those paradoxes of order and chaos, of destruction and creation, along with the possibilities of both personal and material re-creation that may enhance and prolong one's co-existence with the natural environment of their place, as they spiral together, "at the edge and at the centre of the/universe in a massive creation of life" (2009, p. 78). Here, Hawthorne connotes the internal cyclone as well as the external, suggesting that we are all part of the same elemental universe in which such storms may impact intimately on our physical and personal landscape, stripping away our outer personal layers as well as the roofs above us, revealing what has previously been hidden, changing us. Cyclone and person exist within the spiral helix of the universe, simultaneously at the center and at the edge.

The Queensland cyclone is part of the tropical person and tropical place, imagined and literal. It is an integral part of the change, renewal and recovery expressed by Pamela Galeano in "After Yasi,"

> I was tired of the monsoon
> Exhausted by the monsoon
> Grey with the monsoon
>
> Today I feel a change
> A cool change

> A dry change
> Blue arches over me
> New greens kiss my eyes
> Yellow light floods my body
> Flirting birdwings brush my skin
> And my soul sings [2011, p. 111].

Galeano imaginatively expresses her physical and mental post-cyclone recovery as a change in colors in her environment that elevates her mood. Here, imaginative literature acts as a medium through which, as a poet, Galeano expresses her recovery from disaster: the new light without enables her to see within. Thus, this study of cyclone literature reveals that the great spinning wheel of the cyclone represents more than just weather; it speaks of the cycle of life itself that literature seeks to illuminate.

The Cyclone as Cultural Mythos and Story

Through such illumination, the literary cyclone trope reaffirms people's cohesive status within their relationship with cultural place. In repeating the stories of nature catastrophes, people reaffirm their relationships between the storm and themselves, between place and culture, integrating events into their lives and in the process reconstructing that part of their lives that might have been destroyed. Stories enable people to place themselves within a universe that has shape and sense, to know their relationship to it and that their lives have meaning within it, even though that universe may contain uncontrollable elements. Stories are not only about place but *of* place; they not only form place but are formed *by* the place. Tropical cyclones that impact Queensland are formed by the place, that is they are a product of local meteorological conditions, but they also form the place in people's minds as they are experienced or read about or recounted. Whether expressed orally or in poetry or prose, these stories become more than intersections of words and things, of words and cyclones: the words become the things, become the cyclones, and so speak of the *habitus* and the *terroir*. The stories are not just a matter of the relationship between reality and language; they are about the broader concept of the relationship between person and place.

The more often that stories of cyclones are repeated, then, the more the cyclone becomes inculcated into personal and regional relationship with that weather event. As these stories are repeated from person to person, generation to generation, their events and characters and locations, even lessons they may be teaching, become integrated into the perception of the regional *terroir*. As stories develop as products of the region, they reinforce people's identification with the region. "Place has a more lasting identity than we have," proposes American short story writer and novelist Eudora Welty, "and we unswervingly tend to attach ourselves to identity" (1956, p. 251). In telling stories about cyclones and the impact of those cyclones on lives and landscape, those who write about Queensland cyclones are, in a way, forming the cyclone itself. That is, they are forming a perception of the cyclone and that perception is one that will give meaning to this otherwise chaotic, meaningless event. In offering this meaning, they are offering to people a way in which they can incorporate this event into their lives and so be able to retain their identity with their place. Having encountered uncontrollable weather events that have rendered order and meaning disordered and meaningless, writers of the cyclone are systematically reordering place and thereby allowing those who inhabit it to discover and retain meaning of their *terroir*.

In this way, stories of nature catastrophes such as cyclones are important because they enable people to relate to the weather event as part of the sense of place that is imagined in the mind, as well as externally seen and experienced. The literature, and the stories of which it consists, impacts on the regional imaginary in a way that is specific and unique to the culture of the region. The stories enable us to understand the event, to incorporate chaos into our lives, and so people can integrate nature catastrophes into their sense of place: their *terroir*. Through the discourse of literature, both writer and reader are forming perceptions of cultural identity.

Catastrophe stories have always been part of the cultural heritage of humankind for these very reasons. Wind, air and storms have associations with the Christian God and with other gods in other cultures, and writers have used them in literature as instruments of divine judgment and retribution, or as instruments of revelation and renewal. Daniel Defoe, for example, when writing of the great storm that struck Britain in November 1703, linked that storm with the one God had employed to dry up the Flood as well as the one with which God would render destruction on the wicked at Judgement Day. The wind, Defoe considered, "is more expressive and adapted to his [God's] Immediate Power," and so it is "more frequently made use of as the Executioner of his Judgements in the World, and extraordinary Events are brought to pass by it" (2005, p. 17). As a constant historical, geographic and meteorological presence, wind and cyclonic storms have cultural associations with various geographic and climate areas of the planet and so have gathered various names, but whether cyclone, hurricane, typhoon, or tornado, whether a wind called *zonda*, *mistral* or *Mariah*, they are all elements of the air around us. They are an integral part of geographic and of cultural place, incorporated in literature since classical and Biblical times.

Literature "is conscious mythology," Northrop Frye argues, and as society develops, "its mythical stories become structural principles of storytelling" (1970, p. 295), and various mythic archetypes appear in cyclone stories as

Eight. The Word Becomes the Cyclone

structural principles. In *Cyclone* (1947), for example, Vance Palmer uses the mythical, serpentine sea monster Leviathan as a trope for his cyclone, symbolizing the archetypal qualities of both serpent and weather event as well as those connotations of danger and fear of the unknown associated with it. The mythos of the serpent-monster becomes a structural principle of Palmer's storytelling here: the shape of the natural event becomes that of the misshapen and mythic unnatural. "The serpent is one of the most important archetypes of the human soul," writes the French philosopher Gaston Bachelard in *Earth and Reveries of Repose* (2011b, p. 192), so significant that even "serpent" as a word "listens to itself speaking" (2011b, p. 199). He argues that literary images of the serpent, such as allegories, go beyond mere descriptions of the serpent's form and movement to "make the serpent such an eloquent being," and consequently, "we never stop telling stories about serpents" (p. 199). Indeed, serpents pervade Palmer's *Cyclone*, as both literal and allegorical threats to Fay Donolly's family. Caught up in their own personal storms, the Donollys have descended into a chaos within which Fay struggles to maintain order and protect her family. A physical serpent invades the Donolly's own small Eden, into which Fay brings death when she orders its execution. However, the serpent continues to haunt her as an allegory for her mounting stress, culminating in her dream of the serpent-as-cyclone-monster, Leviathan, that could take her husband from her but over which she triumphs. This is the wounded and angry serpent from beneath her sea of trouble, her "waste of waters," with the power to destroy everything if she but surrenders to it. It is the monster that is always in wait to "turn the known world to an evil waste," periodically resurrected by the power of apocalyptic dark forces (1947, p. 159). But in the end, Fay triumphs over the monster in a novel that is ultimately about resurrection and victory over dark forces, symbolized by Palmer's deliberate timing of events for Easter Sunday. Palmer's apocalyptic cyclone reveals a way ahead for his protagonists, and as the clouds clear from potential dark tragedy at the end of his novel, the aeroplane returning with Fay's resurrected husband descends from the sky over the town like an angel bringing new life.

However, Palmer's novel is not the only one of the group of literature presented here to associate the serpent with the cyclone. In Susan Hawthorne's poetry cycle *Earth's Breath*, Hawthorne acknowledges ancient symbolic links between the cyclone, the serpent and the circle. "The nature of a cyclone is to circle/to turn in on itself/like the ouroboros swallowing its tail," she contends (2009, p. x). The Egyptian and Greek symbol of the serpent consuming its tail, representing the infinite cosmic cycle of creation and destruction, also appears in Norse mythology as Jormungandr (or Midgardsormr), the great serpent that encircles the world. Hawthorne connects the ouroboros to other mythic serpents such as the winged serpent and the tempting serpent of the

Garden of Eden that are also symbols of "the end in the beginning/the crossing over of time" that subsume the nature of the relationship between herself and the cyclone into the eternal cycle of mankind, "the endless dance" (2009, p. x). Extending the scope of the cyclone trope, Hawthorne refers to the "great perturbation of wind and flood/that recurs and recurs" (2009, p. xi) that is the ever-returning cyclone integral to this place. For Hawthorne the cyclone represents, like the ouroboros, the infinite cycle of beginning and end, of life from death, that is the very nature of apocalypse itself.

In the same sense of epic tradition, Alexis Wright begins *Carpentaria* (2007) with the creation story of the sacred ancestral serpent forming the regional place, a story of beginning and being evoking a region that, like the serpent, seems to live and breathe. It is country that is conscious and sentient, that not only generates action but also responds to it. Even the ebb and flow of the river's tides are likened to the breathing of the great serpent beneath it. Giant snakes are an integral part of Australian Aboriginal mythology as the Rainbow Serpent; tracks commemorating their journeys, sites and actions are among the many mythic paths sung across the continent. They were always associated with the region, playing a part in the shaping of topography and the people inhabiting it, and serpents are still there as a form of living serpent sovereignty connecting the physical and the metaphysical, the geology and the animate. Consequently, the river, the serpent and the weather associated with it have fundamental roles in her novel.

As well as being part of the land, the ancestral Serpent in Alexis Wright's *Carpentaria* is also associated with the storms of the tropical north of Queensland and, indeed, of the entire tropical region of Australia. Throughout this region, the ancestral Serpent in its various manifestations can be a law-giver with powers associated with cyclones, rain and flood-making, tidal movement and fertility. As such, the Aboriginal mythical serpent is one of the group of great world mythical serpents of power that include those just mentioned, along with the Indian serpent Ananta that is coiled around the base of the World Axis, the Chinese celestial serpent-dragon, and the South American plumed Serpent-Bird associated with rain and clouds. In *Carpentaria*, Wright uses the strength of the four elements, wind, water, earth and fire, that are often controlled by the mythical serpents to not just invoke a knowledge older than the current Australian nation, but to resist European attempts to know, claim and control the Gulf area. The largest man-made site in Wright's fictional region, the Gurfurritt mine, is finally destroyed by a fire that rages like a monster and roars like a fiery serpent. Wright wanted to "build a story place where the spiritual, real and imagined worlds exist side by side" (2007b, p. 85). She wanted to create story that reached into the future as much as it drew from history in which mythical archetypal elements, as well as natural elements, are all part of that story. Wright imagines new ways for readers to develop an appreciation of the deeply spiritual place and of the weather that is an integral part of that place. In her imagined place there is "plenty of business" concerning cyclones that bring prophets and then apocalypse. The landscape is destroyed but also renewed. Stories bring hope.

The other great archetype that threads through these stories to ground them in the culture of place is the shapes of the cyclone: the spiral and the circle. In Patrick White's novel, *The Eye of the Storm* (1977), the circle represents for White, on the one hand, the cyclic spiritual journey through suffering towards being accepted into the presence of God. The symbolic circular pattern, at the center of which is a hidden spiritual presence, overlays much of White's work, and as a type of that pattern White favored the Eastern mandala: the circle (or circles) within the square surrounding a spiritual center that symbolizes the totality of the self and the unity of the individual with the cosmos and through which one must discover the right path to that spiritual center in order to achieve union with it. However, the mandala is not the only cultural representation of the cycle of life and the search for meaning; a number of other cultures express their journey towards achieving a spiritual bond with their place as circular or concentric circle pattern designs. Poets such as W.B. Yeats and T.S. Eliot also wrote about the search for balance and harmony in terms of circular patterns at the center of which one would find meaning. When the wealthy, ego-centric Elizabeth Hunter of White's novel crawls out from the cellar on Brumby Island where she has sought shelter from a cyclone, she finds herself in the stillness of the cyclone's eye, surrounded by birds. Her experience there, though brief, is one of grace and peace but also one of an immense symbolic significance, which she seeks to understand during the remainder of her life. The eye becomes her core of reality, her true reason for existence at the very center of her outer layers of appearance. It is Hunter's meaning in a world that increasingly becomes meaningless to her.

At the center of White's spiral pattern is the in-dwelling god: "the 'I' that must answer ultimately to the One that lies beyond the material world" (1977, p. 219). For White, that "One" is a God that he leaves hidden because he is primarily interested in the human struggle rather than in spiritual exegesis. Until Elizabeth Hunter emerges into the eye of the cyclone, she has been too occupied with her material world to notice the spiritual one but suddenly, here in this still point of the circling world, she experiences an epiphany that reveals the hidden God to her and how the "I" within her might answer to Him. There she has a dialogue with that spiritual presence during which she realizes her life has a deeper, more spiritual meaning than that which she had previously believed. Her ultimate reward for accepting this revelation will be the union at the time of her death of her in-dwelling "I" with the hidden God. Although the world of being, represented by her children and all their trivial materialism, threatens to intrude on her search and cause her to deviate from her journey, she ultimately arrives at the end of her life prepared for her transformation at the moment of her death that will eliminate her corporeal matter, releasing her in-dwelling god, her "I," to achieve union with the universal Eye: the hidden God. Accepted into an apocalyptic meteorological inner circle, the eye of a cyclone, where she has an epiphany that reveals to her the potential relationship she could have with her spiritual place, Hunter is ultimately able to accept her death, at the time of which she transcends into that place and becomes one with it. Not until the end of her life does she ultimately discover her truth and is granted dispensation by the watchful universe as she experiences, at the moment of her death, a final revelation of that beach on which she stood in the eye of the cyclone. In this work, White has used the patterns of circle and mandala, here associated with the cyclone and the cyclone's eye, to express the potential and development of relationship between person and spiritual place.

The Cyclone as Trope of People and Spiritual Place

There is an underlying bond between story, person and place, a relationship succinctly summed up by Welty as, "You and me, here." Fiction, she argues, "is all bound up in the local" and it "depends for its life on place. Location is the cross-roads of circumstance, the proving ground of 'What happened? Who's here? Who's coming?'"(1956, p. 251). In writing about cyclonic storms, writers of the tropics are putting into words *terroir* as well as their terror, forming and re-affirming a sense of *terra* that includes the spiritual and the imaginative as well as the physical, finding the sublime within the storm.

So close can be our spiritual relationship to place that the ancient Romans believed each place had its own spirit, the *genius loci*, which gave identity to that place through presence and action. Later writers such as Shakespeare made much of that tradition and like Ariel and Puck the cyclone as spirit of North Queensland place manipulates and impacts on place and, in doing so, imbues it with identity. The cyclone experience can be a deeply spiritual one, as Patrick White's Elizabeth Hunter discovers. Like her, we seek to engage with and to understand our relationship with place by contextualizing the landscape as it is to us. After all, each of us is primarily the point from which landscape is perceived and experienced and so becomes our ego-centered place. Thus our sense of place is deeply personal, truly understood only when we perceive in our mind the spirit within place that is of place. As Irish writer Seamus Heaney explains,

> There are two ways in which place is known and cherished, two ways which may be complementary but which are just as likely to be antipathetic. One is lived, illiterate

and unconscious, the other learned, literate and conscious. In the literary sensibility, both are likely to co-exist in a conscious and unconscious tension [1964, p. 131].

This tension, he goes on, becomes resolved in the imagination, in what he calls the "country of the mind." It is this "feeling, assenting, equable marriage between the geographical country and the country of the mind," he writes, "that constitutes the sense of place in its richest possible manifestations ... or, better still, our sensing of place"(1964, p. 132). In reading the stories of place, we experience that place in our imagination, resolving in our country of the mind the tension between what we unconsciously understand of place and that which we consciously learn and appreciate through literate sensibility.

As one of the major elements within the literary sensibility of Queensland place, the cyclone is part of the North Queensland "country of the mind," part of our sense of the relationship between person and place. Heaney wrote of the English Lake District that it "was not inanimate geography but active nature, humanized and humanizing" (1964, p. 145); neither is the North Queensland landscape inanimate geography but likewise a *terroir* of active nature, "humanized and humanizing." As the cyclone shapes the local stories, so it shapes that regional "country of the mind." As Kim Callander perceived so personally after Cyclone Yasi, the cyclone inside of us can be as much a part of our *terroir* as the one outside (2011, p. 123). Yet, it can also be a shared, common personal experience. As Barbara Bender observes in her introduction to *Contested Landscapes* (2001), people's sense of place "extends out from the locale and from the present encounter and is contingent upon a larger temporal and spatial field of relationships.... The familiar topography gives way to the unfamiliar, one landscape nests within another like Chinese boxes—except that the boxes are permeable" (2001, p. 6). Even though a place might be individually understood as "our" place, each of us exists within a larger community that co-exists with other communities, and so our perception of individual place nests within the broader community perception of place. In a very real sense, our place is also their place. Similarly, our personal experience of the cyclone has much in common with the shared community experience of it, and as this is revealed in our stories and our literature of the cyclone, our community is strengthened by that mutual understanding and recognition. Our cyclone is their cyclone.

For us to understand and engage with our communities, we need to contextualize them within the landscape of those larger worlds, for our individual landscape is primarily ego-centered. We perceive the communal landscape from our point of view across a personal landscape that is not only literal but that can exist temporally, engaging with the past or future, or out into space, or under the earth and water. It may exist in the mythological sense of Australian Aboriginal peoples, who live within their landscape of creation myths and songlines that locates them simultaneously within literal and spiritual topographies. Landscape is never inert as we "engage with it, re-work it, appropriate and contest it. It is part of the way in which identities are created and disputed" (Bender, 1995, p. 3), and as we engage, we position ourselves within our landscape in order to render it meaningful. We endow cyclones with names, for example, not merely for identification but to enable us to incorporate them into the landscape of the familiar. By naming, charactering, and gendering cyclones, we attempt to maintain an order on elements of our landscape that threaten to become random and chaotic. Naming according to a historic, recorded system enables people to form patterns of experience that may help them contextualize and cope with the weather catastrophe and its effects.

Being able to cope with the tropical cyclone and incorporate it into your cycle of life is important for those who live within regions affected by them. Cyclones are random, chaotic events neither controllable nor avoidable; they exist because of certain arbitrary combinations of sea temperature and air circulation. The arrival of the cyclone and the consequent damage and death that may be caused by it is not anybody's fault, such as because someone did not do their job properly or committed a sin, and this makes that destruction and those fatalities harder for us to understand and contextualize for there is no one to blame. Endowing the weather event with a name, however, does enable us to form patterns of experience by which we may be able to make some sense of the phenomenon. We search for explanations within the context of such patterns, whether they relate to gods or fate, to cope with and survive such violent, elemental and unexplainable natural events as cyclones that cause extreme changes to our otherwise ordered, rational world.

However, while for some of us there must be a reason, for others there never will be one, precisely because the cyclone is a force of untamed, primordial nature, a meteorological pulse that contradicts linear time and order. Cyclones typically demonstrate that natural elements should be accepted as part of daily life, for the spiral of the cyclonic storm is the universal spiral seen in a galaxy, a DNA helix and the whorl of a seashell. As the cyclone is experienced across literary and literal geographical landscapes, a regional consciousness is engendered by this common circulation of elements, and in this way the cyclone becomes a key constituent of a socio-ecological relation that roots North Queenslanders to their land and to the tropical region. Thus, the cyclone can be a trope of deeper, universal meanings, as it is in Alexis Wright's 2007 novel, *Carpentaria*.

The two cyclones that bracket Wright's work are part of an "imagined, hopeful and alternative landscape of literature" (Archer-Lean, Carson &

Eight. The Word Becomes the Cyclone

Hamilton's Bakery in the aftermath of the Mackay cyclone, 1918 (Collection of John Oxley Library, State Library of Queensland).

Hawkes, 2013, p. 30) within which Wright shapes the possibility of a new future for that landscape's inhabitants, while she imagines new ways for readers to develop an appreciation of this deeply spiritual place. This entire environment has been formed by the ancestral serpent whose being continues to permeate not only place but people, yet this has become a place of hopelessness in which the people's last hope is story. "Anyone can find hope in the stories," the elders remember, "the big stories and the little ones in between" (2007a, p. 12). After the apocalypse of the second cyclone, there is hope of a new landscape, of a promise symbolized by earlier, seemingly miraculous events: thousands of seagulls hovering in the sky before a storm, atmospheric conditions that cause all the clocks in the town of Desperance to stop, and the Messianic vision of Elias Smith seeming to walk across water towards the townspeople after the cyclone.

In Wright's novel, Elias Smith is a tabula rasa, a blank slate on whom people will write their stories of hope, of loss and of storms to come. As the old Aboriginal people say, "Cyclones don't come from nowhere, because there is plenty of business going on when cyclones come onto the country out of the rooftop of the world" (2007a, p. 479), and in this landscape there is indeed "plenty of business" concerning cyclones. As the final cyclonic flood surge obliterates the town of Desperance, Will Phantom realizes how history could be obliterated when the Gods move the country. He saw history rolled, reshaped, undone and mauled as the great creators of the natural world engineered the bounty of everything man had ever done in this part of the world into something more of their own making [p. 492].

As a true instrument of apocalypse, Wright's final cyclone destroys the landscape but also rebuilds and renews it. At the novel's end, there is "so much song wafting off the watery land, singing the country afresh" (p. 519), as Will and his son walk into their new home. In Wright's story, the environment is given sentience through an animal embodiment both literal and spiritual that permeates everything, including human life and, in this way, *Carpentaria* imagines new ways of understanding relationships with the physical, natural landscape. This cyclone is a spiritual as well as a physical experience that brings together the conscious with the unconscious in the landscape of the mind.

The Cyclone as Universal Trope

The metaphorics and aesthetics of tropical cyclones permeate Queensland literature. The cyclonic storm in Queensland literature reverberates with contexts of theme and setting, of plot and place, of tropes and tropics that encompass the complicated and symbiotic relations between society, nature, landscape, place and space. The cyclonic storm is a literary trope of both personal and collective awareness, of revelation within the stillness and spirituality of the cyclone's eye that enables the individual to emerge from the experience transformed. To transcend the tropical cyclone experience, one needs to be open to the epiphany of the revelation as these violent storms strip away the historic human over-growth, leaving room to re-build and for new life to grow. Cyclones can in this way narrate resilience in the face of nature's disasters and allegorize the power of cultural consciousness to strengthen and unify communities and regions. Individuals and communities who have been alienated, weakened, or seemingly destroyed can be drawn closer by cyclonic events, discovering in the aftermath that which had previously been hidden, discovering hope and opportunity where previously were despond and despair. Such events and the stories of them can challenge previous human experience, thereby providing opportunity to move forward and rebuild, opportunity for the emergence of the new.

While we have been concerned here with the implications of cyclonic events in Queensland, we do of course recognize that cyclonic storms occur in many regions, and so the search for the meaning of them through literature is a search in which many are engaged around the globe. Such stories of catastrophe within these regions and their symbols and metaphors, writes anthropologist Susanna Hoffman (2002), "reflect the mental processes of a collective people and the fruits of both creative impulse and sense-making reasoning" (p. 113).

As tropical regions continue to develop, so will the challenges of living within them. Some challenges, like the weather, may not be issues humankind can solve, but rather will be challenges with which we must learn to live, and one of the ways in which we can learn is through a shared literary experience. In living within the community of the tropical region, we not only accept the cyclonic storm as an integral part of life, but we should also be prepared to heed the epiphanies and revelations of cyclones as expressed in the literature of the tropical region. We can better understand and enable our developing tropical world by embracing new worlds revealed by the literary storm, as we broaden our perception through revelations about the relationship between the individual, society, and the tropical biosphere, between weather, person, and place.

Appendix A: Fiction and Poetry Written and/or Set in Queensland Featuring Cyclones

Novels

Astley, Thea (1968). *A Boat Load of Home Folk*. Sydney, NSW: Angus & Robertson.
Astley, Thea (1987). *It's Raining in Mango: Pictures from the Family Album*. Ringwood, Vic.: Viking.
Astley, Thea (2010). *The Multiple Effects of Rainshadow*. Camberwell, Vic.: Penguin Books.
Baillie, Allan (1997). *Wreck!* Ringwood, Vic: Puffin/Penguin Books.
Buirchell, Anthony (2015). *Daintree Reflections: Living in Crocodile Country, North Queensland*. Fremantle: Vivid Publishing.
D'Ath, Justin (2005). *Crocodile Attack*. Camberwell, Vic.: Penguin Books.
Hatfield, William (1948). *Barrier Reef Days*. Melbourne: Oxford University Press.
Orr, Wendy (1999). *Nim's Island*. St Leonards, NSW: Allan & Unwin.
Palmer, Vance (1947). *Cyclone*. Sydney, NSW: Angus & Robertson.
Townsend, Ian (2008). *The Devil's Eye*. Sydney: HarperCollins Publishers.
Weston, Kate Helen (1914). *The Prelude*. London: Holden & Hardingham. [This is the earliest known Australian novel in which a cyclone features prominently in the plot].
White, Patrick (1977). *Eye of the Storm*. Sydney: Penguin.
Wright, Alexis (2007). *Carpentaria*. Artarmon, NSW: Giramondo.

Short Stories

Bedford, Randolph (1912, January 20). Sigma, the Cyclone. *The Australasian*, pp. 46–47.
"Bulloo" (1904, December 10). Wyreema. *The Queenslander*, pp. 52ff.
Caldwell, Norman (1938, September 22). Survivor's Graphic Story of Fatal Wreck. *Referee*, p. 20.
Caldwell, Norman (1939, February 9). The Eternal Triangle: Romance on fishing boat and the sequel. *The Referee*, p. 19.

Carleton, Stephen James (1994, Autumn). Heinz's Women. *Westerly*, No. 1, pp. 56–60.
Charlton, Royd (1959, April 29). Test of Time. *The Australian Women's Weekly*, p. 24.
Forrest, Mabel (1930, November 15). Cyclone. *The Australasian*, p. 46.
Halcro, Hugh (1896, December 23). Little Sigma: A Cyclone Story. *North Queensland Register Christmas Number*, pp. 10–11.
Hill, Deidre (1967, December 6). The Storm's Eye. *The Australian Women's Weekly*, pp. 71–73.
Knight, Esther (2008). Monsoon Two. In *Raining on the Sun*, Cairns, Qld: Tropical Writers of Far North Queensland.
Larner, S.G. (2014, April 30). Chasing the Storm. *SQ Mag: International Speculative Fiction EZine*. Edition 14. Accessed 9 July 2014. http://sqmag.com/2014/04/30/edition-14-chasing-the-storm-by-s-g-larner/.
Moncrieff, R.A. (1969, October 1). The Lark and the Eagle. *The Australian Women's Weekly*, pp. 91–92.
Palmer, V. (1932, November 2). The Big Wind. *The Sydney Mail*, pp. 12–13.
Palmer, V. (1936, March 4). Cyclone. *The Bulletin*, pp. 30–31.
Palmer, V. (1936, September 9). Tempest. *The Bulletin*, pp. 30–31.
Porteous, R S ("Standby"). (1945). Cyclone. In: *Little Known of These Waters*, Sydney, NSW: Dymock's Book Arcade Ltd.
Porteous, R S ("Standby"). (1955). Quite a Blow. In: *Close to the Wind and Other Stories*, Sydney, NSW: Angus and Robertson.
Porteous, R S ("Standby"). (1963). The Hard Way. In: *Salvage and Other Stories*, Sydney, NSW: George G Harrap & Co. Ltd.
Reid, Frank (1931, November 4). Three Pearl Isle. *Townsville Daily Bulletin*, p. 4.
Timms, E.V. (1938, August 27). Woman on Board. *The Australian Women's Weekly*, pp. 8–9.
Traherne, Meredith (1982, June 16). Cry of the Wild Wind. *The Australian Women's Weekly*, pp. 57–62.
Woodhouse, Jena (2006). Voices in the Wind, *Hecate*, 32: 1, p. 77.
Woolsey, Sybil (1969, October 15). The White Kitten. *The Australian Women's Weekly*, p. 86.

Poetry

Callander, Kim (2012). The Cyclone of Our Time. In *Cyclone Yasi: Our Stories* (p. 123). Cardwell, Queensland: 3E Innovative on behalf of Cardwell and District Historical Society.
Campbell-Lloyd, Kate (2012). Cyclones. In *Cyclone Yasi: Our Stories* (pp. 84–5). Cardwell, Queensland: 3E Innovative on behalf of Cardwell and District Historical Society.
Crist, Alice Guerin (1927). The Way of the Bush. In *When Rody Came to Ironbark, and Other Verses* (pp. 78–80). Sydney: Cornstalk Publishing Company.
Delaney, David J. (2008). True North Queenslander. In *Raining on the Sun* (p. 40). Cairns, Qld: Tropical Writers of Far North Queensland.
Dillon, P J (1893, December 23). Christmas Memories. *Freeman's Journal* (Sydney). p. 17.

Galeano, Pamela (2012). After Yasi. In *Cyclone Yasi: Our Stories* (p. 111). Cardwell, Queensland: 3E Innovative on behalf of Cardwell and District Historical Society.
Hawthorne, Susan (2009). *Earth's Breath*. North Melbourne, Vic: Spinifex Press.
Head, Ivan (2011). Tully Under Cyclone. *Quadrant*, 55: 5, p. 126.
J.S.W. (1870, January 21). In The Deep Bosom of the Ocean Buried. *Illawarra Mercury*, p.4. [This is the earliest known poem referring to a cyclone in an Australian newspaper or journal].
Kennedy, Victor (1949). Man, Building. In *Cyclone: Selected Poems of Victor Kennedy* (pp. 16-18). Hawthorn: Hawthorn Press.
McNamara, Noela (2008). A Mother's Fear. In *Raining on the Sun* (p. 99). Cairns, Australia: Tropical Writers of Far North Queensland.
Menehira, Hazel (2008). Cyclic Dance. In *Raining on the Sun* (p. 119). Cairns, Australia: Tropical Writers of Far North Queensland.
O'Connor, Mark (1990). The Rainbow Serpent. In *Fire-Stick Dreaming: Selected Poems 1972-90* (pp. 34-38). Sydney: Hale & Iremonger.
The Owl (1897, February 10). What's Up With That Wragge? *Sunday Times* (Sydney), p. 7.
Patterson, Andrew Barton "Banjo" (1902). The Ballad of the *Calliope*. In *Rio Grande's Last Race and Other Verses* (pp. 96-101). Melbourne: Angus & Robertson.
Scott, W.N. (1972). The Innisfail Song. In *Brother and Brother* (p. 53). Milton, Queensland: Jacaranda Press.
Stable, Prof. J.J., and Kirkwood, A.E.M. (n.d.). *A Book of Queensland Verse*, Brisbane: Queensland Book Depot.
Vallis, Val (1961). Forecast. In *Dark Wind Blowing* (p. 41), Brisbane: Jacaranda Press.
W.M. (1897, December 4). Ithiel, Jakan, Wragge & Co. *The Queenslander*, p. 1076.
Wright, Judith (1955). Cyclone and Aftermath. In *Two Fires* (pp. 13-14). Sydney, NSW: Angus and Robertson.

Appendix B: Selected International Novels and Poetry Works Featuring Cyclonic Storms

Novels

Bradbury, Ray (1969). *Something Wicked This Way Comes*. London: Corgi/Transworld.
Close, Robert (1972). *Love Me Sailor*. London: White Lion Publishers.
Conrad, Joseph (1975). *The Nigger of the Narcissus/Typhoon/and Other Stories*. Harmondsworth, Middlesex, UK: Penguin Books.
Greenleaf, Sue (1901). *Wed by Mighty Waves*. Chicago: Laird & Lee.
Hamilton, Elizabeth Verner (1988). *Storm Center*. Charleston, S.C.: Tradd Street Press.
Hayes, Courtenay (1924). *On the Fringe of the Cyclone: A Tale for Adventurous Youth*. London: Frederick Warne & Co.
Hearn, Lafcadio (1889). *Chita: A Memory of Last Island*. New York: Harper and Brothers Publishers.
Hersey, John (1967). *Under the Eye of the Storm*. New York: Borzoi/Alfred A Knopf.
Heyward, DuBose and Dorothy (1925). *Porgy*. New York: Grosset & Dunlap.
Hughes, Richard (1938). *In Hazard*. London: Chatto & Windus.
Hughes, Richard (1971). *High Wind in Jamaica*. London: Chatto & Windus.
Hurston, Nora Zeale (1986). *Their Eyes Were Watching God*. London: Virago.
Kingston, William H.G. (1876). *Twice Lost*. London: Thomas Nelson & Sons.
Lowell, Joan (1929). *The Cradle of the Deep*. New York: Simon & Schuster.
McCauley, Diana (2012). *Huracan*. Leeds, UK: Peepal Tree Press.
Melville, Herman (1967). *Moby Dick; Or, the Whale*. (Harrison Hayford and Hershel Parker, Eds.). New York: W.W. Norton & Company.
Murray, John F. (1969). *The Devil Walks on Water*. Boston: Little Brown & Co.
Satterthwait, Elizabeth Carpenter (1898). *A Son of the Carolinas: A Story of the Hurricane Upon the Sea Islands*. Philadelphia, Pa: Henry Altemus Co.
Scarborough, Dorothy. *The Wind*. Austin, Texas: University of Texas Press. (Reprint of the 1925 edition published by Harper, New York, with a Foreword by Sylvia Ann Grider).

Smiley, Nora K., and White, Louise V. (1954). *Hurricane Road: A Novel of a Railroad That Went to Sea*. St. Petersburg, Fla.: Great Outdoors.
Stewart, George R. (1941). *Storm*. New York: Random House.
Woolf, Virginia (1993). *Orlando*. London: Penguin Books.

Poetry

Brathwaite, Edward Kamau (1990). *Shar: Hurricane Poem*. Mona: Savacou Publications.
Bryant, William Cullen (1855). The Hurricane. In *Poems, Volume 1* (pp. 270–273). New York: D. Appleton & Co.
Cader, Teresa (2009). History of Hurricanes. In *History of Hurricanes* (pp. 3–5). Evanston, Ill.: TriQuarterly Books/ Northwestern University Press.
Coleridge, Samuel Taylor (1933). The Rime of The Ancient Mariner. In W. MacNeile Dixon and H.J.C. Grierson (Eds.), *The English Parnassus: An Anthology Chiefly of Longer Poems* (pp. 330–345). London: Oxford at the Clarendon Press.
Crane, Hart (1946). The Hurricane. In Waldo Frank (Ed.), *The Collected Poems of Hart Crane* (pp. 124–125). New York: Liveright Publishing.
Cruz, Victor Hernandez (2001). The Problem with Hurricanes. In *Maraca: New and Selected Poems, 1965–2000* (p. 148). Minneapolis, Minnesota: Coffee House Press.
Finch, Anne (1999). Upon the Hurricane. In David Fairer & Christine Gerrard (Eds.), *Eighteenth Century Poetry: The Annotated Anthology* (pp. 26–33). Oxford, UK: Blackwell.
Harte, Bret (1871). St. Thomas: A Geographical Survey 1868. In *East and West* (pp. 105-8). London: John Camden Hotten.
Hayne, Hamilton (1900). A Cyclone at Sea. In Edmund Clarence Stedman (Ed.), *An American Anthology, 1787–1900* (p. 613). Boston: Houghton, Mifflin & Co.
Nicholls, Grace (2010). Hurricane Hits England. In *I Have Crossed an Ocean* (p. 85). Hexham, UK: Bloodaxe.
Rich, Adrienne (1951). Storm Warnings. In *A Change of World* (p. 1). New York: AMS Press.

Bibliography

Literature

Novels

Astley, Thea (1960). *Descant for Gossips*. Sydney: Angus & Robertson.
Astley, Thea (1962). *The Well Dressed Explorer*. Sydney: Angus & Robertson.
Astley, Thea (1965). *The Slow Natives*. Sydney: Angus & Robertson.
Astley, Thea (1968). *A Boat Load of Home Folk*. Sydney: Angus & Robertson.
Astley, Thea (1974). *A Kindness Cup*. Melbourne: Thomas Nelson.
Astley, Thea (1985). *The Acolyte*. Sydney: Angus & Robertson.
Astley, Thea (1987). *Girl With a Monkey*. Ringwood, Australia: Penguin. [First published in 1958].
Astley, Thea (1987). *It's Raining in Mango: Pictures from the Family Album*. Ringwood, Australia: Viking.
Astley, Thea (1993a). Inventing the Weather [Novella]. In *Vanishing Points* (pp. 123-234). Port Melbourne: Minerva/Reed Books.
Astley, Thea (1993b). The Genteel Poverty Bus Company [Novella]. In *Vanishing Points* (pp. 1-122). Port Melbourne: Minerva/Reed Books.
Astley, Thea (2010). *The Multiple Effects of Rainshadow*. Camberwell, Australia: Penguin Books.
Baillie, Allan (1997). *Wreck!* Ringwood, Australia: Puffin/Penguin Books.
Baum, Frank L. (1900). *The Wonderful Wizard of Oz*. New York: George M. Hill Company.
Bradbury, Ray (1969). *Something Wicked This Way Comes*. London: Corgi/Transworld.
Close, Robert (1972). *Love Me Sailor*. London: White Lion Publishers.
Condon, Matthew (1995). *A Night at the Pink Poodle*. Milsons Point, Australia: Random House.
Conrad, Joseph (1971). *Heart of Darkness* (Robert Kimbrough, Ed.). (2nd Ed.). New York: W.W. Norton & Co. [Serialised 1899, first published 1902].
Conrad, Joseph (1975). *The Nigger of the Narcissus, Typhoon, and other Stories*. Harmondsworth, Middlesex, UK: Penguin Books. [First published 1903].
Eco, Umberto (1984). *The Name of the Rose*. New York: Warner Books.
Hatfield, William (1948). *Barrier Reef Days*. Melbourne: Oxford University Press.
Hughes, Richard (1971). *High Wind in Jamaica*. London: Chatto &Windus.
Hurston, Nora Zeale (1986). *Their Eyes Were Watching God*. London: Virago. [First published 1937].
Lawrence, D.H. (1987). *The Plumed Serpent (Quetzalcoatl)*. (L.D. Clark, Ed.). Cambridge, UK: Cambridge University Press. [First published 1926].
Lawrence, D.H. (1994). *Kangaroo*. Cambridge, U.K: Cambridge University Press. [First published 1923].

McCauley, Diana (2012). *Huracan*. Leeds, UK: Peepal Tree Press.
Melville, Herman (1967). *Moby Dick; or, The Whale* (Hershel Parker &Harrison Hayford, Eds.). New York: W.W. Norton & Company. [First published 1851].
Orr, Wendy (1999). *Nim's Island*. St Leonards, Australia: Allan & Unwin.
Palmer, Vance (1947). *Cyclone*. Sydney: Angus & Robertson.
Palmer, Vance (1957). *The Rainbow Bird and Other Stories*. Sydney: Angus & Robertson.
Proust, Marcel (2003). *À la Recherché du Temps Perdu* [In Search of Lost Time] (Christopher Prendergast, Ed.). London: Penguin Classics. [First published 1913-27].
Scarborough, Dorothy (1979). *The Wind*. Austin: University of Texas Press. [Reprint of the 1925 edition published by Harper, New York, with a Foreword by Sylvia Ann Grider].
Stewart, George R. (1947). *Storm*. New York: Modern Library/Random House.
Stow, Randolph (1983). *Tourmaline*. Sydney: Angus and Robertson.
Townsend, Ian (2008). *The Devil's Eye*. Sydney: HarperCollins Publishers.
Weston, Kate Helen (1914). *The Prelude*. London: Holden & Hardingham.
White, Patrick (1957). *Voss*. London: Eyre and Spottiswoode.
White, Patrick (1966). *The Solid Mandala*. London: Eyre & Spottiswoode.
White, Patrick (1977). *Eye of the Storm*. Sydney: Penguin.
White, Patrick (2014). *Happy Valley*. Melbourne: Text Publishing.
Woolf, Virginia (1993). *Orlando*. London: Penguin Books.
Wright, Alexis (2007a). *Carpentaria*. Artarmon, Australia: Giramondo.

Poetry

Amess, J. (2007). 'Cause of Larry!!! In Peace M., Garner G., Portelli, K., Provians L. (Eds.), *Cyclone Larry: Tales of Survival* (p. 44). Innisfail, Qld: Mothers Helping Others Inc.
Astley, Thea (2017). *Thea Astley: Selected Poems*. (Cheryl Taylor, Ed.). St Lucia, Qld: University of Queensland Press.
Ball, C. (2011). A New Beginning. In Cardwell and District Historical Society Inc. (Eds.), *Cyclone Yasi: Our Stories* (p. 9). Cardwell, Qld: 3E Innovative.
Brathwaite, Edward Kamau (1990). *Shar: Hurricane Poem*. Mona, Jamaica: Savacou Publications.
Bryant, William Cullen (1855). The Hurricane. *Poems, Volume 1* (pp. 270-273). New York: D. Appleton & Co.
Bufi, B. (2007). Innisfail, My Poor Innisfail. In TBS Committee (Eds.), *Taken By Storm: Cyclone Larry 20/3/2006* (p. 15). Innisfail, Queensland.
Bufi, B. (2011). Yasi—An Ill Wind. In Cardwell and District Historical Society, Inc. (Eds.), *Cyclone Yasi: Our Stories* (p. 27). Cardwell, Qld: 3E Innovative.
Cader, Teresa (2009). History of Hurricanes. *History of Hurricanes* (pp. 3-5). Evanston, IL: TriQuarterly Books/Northwestern University Press.
Callander, Kim (2011). The Cyclone of Our Time. In Cardwell and District Historical Society Inc. (Eds.), *Cyclone Yasi: Our Stories* (p. 123). Cardwell, Queensland: 3E Innovative.
Campbell-Lloyd, Kate (2011). Cyclones. In Cardwell and District Historical Society, Inc. (Eds.), *Cyclone Yasi: Our Stories* (pp. 84-5). Cardwell, Queensland: 3E Innovative.
Clifford, M. (2012). Yasi Tried. In Lawson B. (Ed.), *The True Spirit of Cyclone Yasi* (p. 104). Townsville, Qld: Life Love Laughter Inc.
Coleridge, Samuel Taylor (1933). The Rime of the Ancient Mariner. In W. MacNeile Dixon & H.J.C. Grierson (Eds.), *The English Parnassus: An Anthology Chiefly of Longer Poems* (pp. 330-345). London: Oxford at the Clarendon Press.
Crane, Hart (1946). The Hurricane. In Waldo Frank (Ed.), *The Collected Poems of Hart Crane* (pp. 124-125). New York: Liveright Publishing.

Crist, Alice Guerin (1927).The Way of the Bush. *When Rody Came to Ironbark, and other verses* (pp. 78–80). Sydney: Cornstalk Publishing Company.
Cristaudo, S. (2007). Cyclone Larry. In Peace M., Garner G., Portelli K., Provians L. (Eds.), *Cyclone Larry: Tales of Survival* (p. 84). Innisfail, Qld: Mothers Helping Others Inc.
Delaney, David J. (2008). True North Queenslander. In *Raining on the Sun* (p. 40). Cairns, Australia: Tropical Writers of Far North Queensland.
Dillon, P.J. (1893, December 23). Christmas Memories. *Freeman's Journal* [Sydney], p. 17.
Eliot. T.S. (1966). Burnt Norton. *Four Quartets* (pp. 15–16). London: Faber & Faber.
Finch, Anne (1999). Upon the Hurricane. In David Fairer & Christine Gerrard (Eds.), *Eighteenth Century Poetry: The Annotated Anthology* (pp. 26–33). Oxford, UK: Blackwell. [Poem originally published 1713.]
Galeano, Pamela (2011). After Yasi. In Cardwell and District Historical Society, Inc. (Eds.), *Cyclone Yasi: Our Stories* (p. 111). Cardwell, Queensland: 3E Innovative.
Hawthorne, Susan (2009). *Earth's Breath*. North Melbourne: Spinifex Press.
Hayne, William Hamilton (1900). A Cyclone at Sea. In Edmund Clarence Stedman (Ed.), *An American Anthology, 1787–1900* (p. 613). Boston, MA: Houghton, Mifflin & Co.
Head, Ivan (2011). Tully Under Cyclone. *Quadrant*, 55: 5, p. 126.
Hope, A.D. (1991). Australia. In Leonie Kramer (Ed.), *My Country: Australian Poetry & Short Stories, Two Hundred Years Vol. II* (p. 222). Willoughby, NSW: Ure Smith Press.
Kennedy, Victor (1949). Man, Building. *Cyclone: Selected Poems of Victor Kennedy* (pp. 16–18). Hawthorn, UK: Hawthorn Press.
Milton, John (1951). *Paradise Lost, and Selected Poetry and Prose* (Northrop Frye, Ed.). San Francisco, CA: Rinehart Press. [First published 1667.]
O'Connor, Mark (1990). The Rainbow Serpent. *Fire-Stick Dreaming: Selected Poems 1972–90* (pp. 34–38). Sydney: Hale & Iremonger.
Patterson, Andrew Barton "Banjo" (1902). The Ballad of the *Calliope. Rio Grande's Last Race and Other Verses* (pp. 96–101). Melbourne: Angus & Robertson.
Rich, Adrienne (1951). Storm Warnings. *A Change of World* (p. 1). New York: AMS Press.
Scott, W.N. (1972). The Innisfail Song. *Brother and Brother* (p. 53). Milton, Australia: Jacaranda Press.
Singh, Gurpreeth (2007). Cyclone Larry. In Peace, M., Garner, G., Portelli, K., and Provians, L. (Eds.), *Cyclone Larry: Tales of Survival* (p. 67). Innisfail, Qld: Mothers Helping Others Inc.
Stable, Prof. J.J., & Kirkwood, A.E.M. (n.d.). *A Book of Queensland Verse*, Brisbane, Australia: Queensland Book Depot.
Students Good Counsel Primary School (2007). The Cyclone Larry Rap. In Peace, M., Garner, G., Portelli, K., and Provians, L. (Eds.), *Cyclone Larry: Tales of Survival* (p. 32). Innisfail, Qld: Mothers Helping Others Inc.
Vaughan, L.J. (2012). Tropical Cyclone Yasi. In Lawson, B. (Ed.), *The True Spirit of Cyclone Yasi* (pp. 54–5). Townsville, Qld: Life Love Laughter Inc.
Virgil (2006). *The Georgics* (Peter Fallon, Trans.). Oxford: Oxford University Press.
Wolcot, John (aka Peter Pindar) (1835). Ode to Lais. *The Works of Peter Pindar, Esq.* (p. 216). Pennsylvania: M. Wallis Woodward & Co.
Wright, Judith (1955). Cyclone and Aftermath. *Two Fires* (pp. 13–14). Sydney: Angus and Robertson.
Yeats, W.B. (1971). The Second Coming. In Jeffares, A. Norman (Ed.), *W.B. Yeats: Selected Poetry* (pp. 99–100). London: Macmillan.

Plays

Shakespeare, William (1975a). King Lear. In Alfred Harbage (Ed.), *William Shakespeare: The Complete Works* (pp. 1060–1106). New York: The Viking Press.

Shakespeare, William (1975b). The Tempest. In Alfred Harbage and Northrop Frye (Eds.), *William Shakespeare: The Complete Works* (pp. 1369–1395). New York: Viking Press.

Short Stories

Becke, Louis (2005). *By Reef and Palm*. Rowville, Australia: The Five Mile Press. [Originally published 1894].
Bedford, Randolph (1912, February 10). Sigma, the Cyclone. *Evening Post* (NZ), p. 9.
"Bulloo" (1904, December 10). Wyreema. *The Queenslander Christmas Supplement*, p. 52. [First installment of a serial concluding June 3, 1905, p. 46.]
Charlton, Royd (1959, April 29). Test of Time. *The Australian Women's Weekly*, p. 24.
Forrest, Mabel (1930, November 15). Cyclone. *The Australasian*, p. 46.
Halcro, Hugh (1896, December 23). Little Sigma: A Cyclone Story. *North Queensland Register Christmas Number*, pp. 10–11.
Hill, Deidre (1967, December 6). The Storm's Eye. *The Australian Women's Weekly*, pp. 71–73.
Hospital, Janet Turner (1995a). Litany for the Homeland. In *Collected Stories 1970–1995* (pp. 410–422). St Lucia, Australia: University of Queensland Press.
Hospital, Janet Turner (1995b). The Second Coming of Come-by-Chance. In *Collected Stories 1970–1995* (pp. 211–221). St Lucia, Australia: University of Queensland Press.
Hospital, Janet Turner (1995c). You Gave Me Hyacinths. In *Collected Stories 1970–1995* (pp. 15–22). St Lucia, Australia: University of Queensland Press.
Hospital, Janet Turner (2011). Moon River: A Memoir. In *Forecast: Turbulence* (pp. 209–229). Sydney: Fourth Estate/HarperCollins Australia.
Joyce, James (1956a). A Painful Case. In *Dubliners* (pp. 119–131). London: Jonathan Cape.
Joyce, James (1956b). The Dead. In *Dubliners* (pp. 199–256). London: Jonathan Cape.
Joyce, James (1956c). *Dubliners*. London: Jonathan Cape.
Knight, Esther (2008). Monsoon Two. In Tropical Writers of Far North Queensland (Eds.), *Raining on the Sun* (pp. 37–39). Cairns, Qld: Tropical Writers of Far North Queensland.
Larner, S.G. (2014). Chasing the Storm. *S Q Mag: International Speculative Fiction eZine*, Edition 14. Retrieved from http://sqmag.com/2014/04/30/edition-14-chasing-the-storm-by-s-g-larner/
Palmer, Vance (1932, November 2). The Big Wind. *The Sydney Mail*, pp. 12–13.
Palmer, Vance (1936a, March 4). Cyclone. *The Bulletin*, pp. 30–31.
Palmer, Vance (1936b, September 9). Tempest. *The Bulletin*, pp. 30–31.
Plath, Sylvia (1979). Ocean 1212-W. In *Johnny Panic and the Bible of Dreams, and Other Prose Writings* (pp. 117–124). London: Faber & Faber.
Porteous, R.S. "Standby" (1945). Cyclone. In *Little Known of These Waters* (pp. 86–110). Sydney, UK: Dymock's Book Arcade.
Porteous, R.S. "Standby" (1955). Quite a Blow. In *Close to the Wind and Other Stories* (pp. 9–21). Sydney: Angus & Robertson.
Porteous, R.S. "Standby" (1963). The Hard Way. In *Salvage and Other Stories* (pp. 169–181). Sydney: George G. Harrap & Co..
Reid, Frank (1931, November 4). Three Pearl Isle. *Townsville Daily Bulletin*, p. 4.
Traherne, Meredith (1982, June 16). Cry of the Wild Wind. *The Australian Women's Weekly*, pp. 57–62.
Woodhouse, Jena (2006). Voices in the Wind. *Hecate*. 32:1, p. 77.

Non-Fiction, Memoir and Critical Works

Books

Agnew, John (1993). Representing Space: Space, Scale and Culture in Social Science. In James Duncan and David Ley (Eds.), *Place/Culture/Representation* (pp. 251–271). London: Routledge.

Anderson, Mark (2011). *Disaster Writing: The Cultural Politics of Catastrophe in Latin America.* Charlottesville: University of Virginia Press.

Archer-Lean, Clare, Carson, Susan J., and Hawkes, Lesley (2013). Fiction as a Form of Change: A Paper Overview of a Literature Panel Discussion. In Susan Davis (Ed.), *Future Nature Future Cultures* (pp. 29–36). Noosa, Australia: Noosa Biosphere Limited and Central Queensland University.

Aristotle (1978). *Meteorologica.* (H.D.P. Lee, Trans.). In G.P. Goold (Ed.), *Aristotle in Twenty-Three Volumes.* (Loeb Classical Library Vol. VII). London: William Heinemann.

Astley, Thea (2008). Why I Write. In Susan Sheridan and Paul Genoni (Eds.), *Thea Astley's Fictional Worlds* (p. 1). Newcastle upon Tyne, UK: Cambridge Scholars Publishing.

Atkinson, R.L. (1984). *Bush Tales and Memoirs.* Mareeba, Australia: Pinevale Publications.

Bachelard, Gaston (2011a). *Air and Dreams: An Essay on the Imagination of Movement* (Edith R. Farrell and C. Frederick Farrell, Trans.). Dallas, TX: Dallas Institute Publications/Dallas Institute of Humanities and Culture. [Originally published 1943, Paris, as *L'airet les songes, essai sur l'imagination du movement.*]

Bachelard, Gaston (2011b). *Earth and Reveries of Repose: An Essay on Images of Interiority* (Mary McAllester Jones, Trans.). Dallas, TX: Dallas Institute Publications/Dallas Institute of Humanities and Culture. [Originally published 1948, Paris, as *La Terre et les rêveries du repos: essai sur les images de l'intimité.*]

Banfield, E.J. (1925). *Last Leaves from Dunk Island.* Sydney: Angus and Robertson.

Bate, Jonathan (2000). *The Song of the Earth.* London: Picador/Macmillan.

Beatson, P.R. (1977). *The Eye in the Mandala: Patrick White, A Vision of Man and God.* Sydney: A.H. and A.W. Reed.

Bender, Barbara, and Winer, Margot (Eds.) (2001). *Contested Landscapes: Movement, Exile and Place.* Oxford, UK: Berg.

Bender, Barbara (Ed.) (1995). *Landscape: Politics and Perspective.* Oxford, UK: Berg.

Berger, James (1999). *After the End: Representations of Post-Apocalypse.* Minneapolis: University of Minnesota Press.

Berndt, Ronald M., and Berndt, Catherine H. (1989). *The Speaking Land: Myth and Story in Aboriginal Australia.* Ringwood, Australia: Penguin Books.

Bjorksten, Ingmar (1976). *Patrick White: A General Introduction.* St. Lucia, Australia: University of Queensland Press.

Blackbourn. D. (2007). *The Conquest of Nature: Water, Landscape and the Making of Modern Germany.* W.W. Norton and Co.

Blanchot, Maurice (1995). *L'Ecriture du Désastre* [The Writing of the Disaster] (Ann Smock, Trans.). Lincoln: University of Nebraska Press.

Bliss, Carolyn (1986). *Patrick White's Fiction: The Paradox of Fortunate Failure.* London: Macmillan.

Bourke, Colin, Bourke, Eleanor, and Edwards, Bill (1994). *Aboriginal Australia: An Introductory Reader in Aboriginal Studies.* St. Lucia, Australia: University of Queensland Press.

Bradley, John (with Yanyuwa families) (2010). *Singing Saltwater Country: Journey to the Songlines of Carpentaria.* Crows Nest, Australia: Allen & Unwin.

Britten, R.J. (1978). *Around the Cassowary Rock: Adventures on a Queensland River*. Brisbane, Australia: Rigby.
Bryant, E.A., Walsh, G., and Abbott, D. (2007). Cosmogenic Megatsunami in the Australia Region: Are They Supported by Aboriginal and Mairo Legends? In L. Piccardi and W.B. Masse (Eds.), *Myth and Geology* (pp. 273, 2007, 203–214). London: London Geological Society, Special Publications.
Bryde, Charles, and Bryde, Jack (1998). *From Charthouse to Bush Hut, or The Test of Fortitude*. Mareeba, Australia: Watson Ferguson & Co. [First pub. 1920, revised 1950 and 1977.]
Buckridge, Patrick, and McKay, Belinda (2007). *By The Book: A Literary History of Queensland*. St Lucia, Australia: University of Queensland Press.
Burke, Edmund (1992). *A Philosophical Enquiry into the Origin of Our Ideas of the Sublime and Beautiful*. (A. Phillips, Ed.). Oxford, UK: Oxford University Press. [First pub. 1757.]
Callahan, David (2009). *Rainforest Narratives: The Work of Janet Turner Hospital*. St Lucia, Australia: University of Queensland Press.
Cardwell and District Historical Society (Eds.) (2011). *Cyclone Yasi: Our Stories*. Cardwell, Qld: 3E Innovative.
Casey, Edward S. (1993). *Getting Back into Place: Toward a Renewed Understanding of the Place-World*. Indianapolis: Indiana University Press.
Chevalier, Jean, and Gheerbrant, Alain (Eds.) (1996). *The Penguin Dictionary of Symbols* (John Buchanan-Brown, Trans.). London: Penguin Books.
Clark, Philip (2003). *Where the Ancestors Walked: Australia as an Aboriginal Landscape*. Crows Nest. NSW: Allan and Unwin.
Coen, Deborah R. (2013). *The Earthquake Observers: Disaster Science from Lisbon to Richter*. Chicago, IL: University of Chicago Press.
Collet, Anne, McDougall, Russell, and Thomas, Sue (Eds.) (2017).*Tracking the Literature of Tropical Weather: Typhoons, Hurricanes and Cyclones*. Cham, Switzerland: Palgrave Macmillan/Springer International Publishing.
Condon, Matthew (Ed.) (2011). *Fear, Faith & Hope: Remembering the Long, Wet Summer of 2010–2011*. St Lucia, Australia: University of Queensland Press.
Cowan, James (1992). *The Elements of the Aboriginal Tradition*. Longmead, UK: Element Books.
Cranston, C.A., and Zeller, Robert (2007). *The Littoral Zone: Australian Contexts and Their Writers*. Nature, Culture and Literature (Vol. 4). Amsterdam, Netherlands: Editions Rodopi.
Creswell, Tim (2015). *Place: An Introduction*. (2nd Ed.). Chichester, UK: Wiley Blackwell.
Cunningham, Sophie (2014). *Warning: The Story of Cyclone Tracy*. Melbourne: Text.
DeBlieu, Jan (1998).*Wind: How the Flow of Air Has Shaped Life, Myth and the Land*. New York: Houghton Mifflin Company.
Deckard, Sharae (2016). The Political Ecology of Storms in Caribbean Literature. In Chris Campbell and Michael Niblett (Eds.), *The Caribbean: Aesthetics, World-Ecology, Politics*. Oxford, UK: Oxford University Press, pp. 25–45.
Defoe, Daniel (2005). *The Storm* (Richard Hamblyn, Ed.). London: Penguin. [First pub. 1704.]
Dening, G. (1980). *Islands and Beaches: Discourse on a Silent Land, Marquesas 1774–1880*. Melbourne: Melbourne University Press.
Devanny, Jean (1944). *By Tropic Sea and Jungle: Adventures in North Queensland*. Sydney: Angus & Robertson.
Devanny, Jean (1951). *Travels in North Queensland*. London: Jarrods Publishers.
Dixon, R.M.W., and Koch, G. (1996). *Dyirbal Song Poetry: The Oral Literature of an Australian Rainforest People*. St Lucia, Australia: University of Queensland Press.

Dixon, R.M.W. (Ed. and compiled). (1991). *Words of Our Country: Stories, Place Names and Vocabulary in Yidiny, the Aboriginal Language of the Cairns-Yarrabah Region.* St Lucia, Australia: University of Queensland Press.
Drew, Philip (1994). *The Coast Dwellers: Australians Living on the Edge.* Ringwood, Australia: Penguin.
Eliade, Mircea (1991). *Images and Symbols: Studies in Religious Symbolism.* Princeton, NJ: Mythos/Princeton University Press.
Eliot, Alexander (1994). *The Global Myths: Exploring Primitive, Pagan, Sacred, and Scientific Mythologies.* New York: Truman Tally Books/Meridian/Penguin.
Elkin, A.P. (1990). Steps into the Dreamtime. *Meanjin*, No. 2. In Jenny Lee, Philip Mead and Gerald Murnane (Eds.), *The Temperament of Generations: Fifty Years of Writing in Meanjin* (pp. 9–12). Melbourne: Melbourne University Press. [First published 1943.]
Ellman, Richard (1968). *The Identity of Yeats.* London: Faber.
Ellman, Richard (1969). *Yeats: The Man and the Masks.* London: Faber.
Emanuel, Kerry (2005). *Divine Wind: The History and Science of Hurricanes.* New York: Oxford University Press.
Erikson, Kai (1995). *A New Species of Trouble: The Human Experience of Modern Disasters.* New York: W.W. Norton & Co.
Foucault, Michel (1978). *The Archaeology of Knowledge* (A.M. Sheridan Smith, Trans.). London: Tavistock Publications.
Frost, Cheryl (1978). Literature in North Queensland: Characteristics and Content. In *Lectures on North Queensland History* (Third Series), Ch. 6 (pp. 131–156). Townsville, Australia: James Cook University History Department.
Frye, Northrop (1970). *The Stubborn Structure: Essays on Criticism and Society.* Ithaca, NY: Cornell University Press.
Frye, Northrop (1982). *The Great Code: The Bible and Literature.* London: Routledge & Kegan Paul.
Genoni, Paul (2004). *Subverting the Empire: Explorers and Exploration in Australian Fiction.* Altona, Australia: Common Ground Publishing.
Gibson, Ross (2002). *Seven Versions of an Australian Badland.* St. Lucia, Australia: University of Queensland Press.
Gordon, Jane Anna, and Gordon, Lewis R. (2009). *Of Divine Warning: Reading Disaster in the Modern Age.* Boulder, Colorado: Paradigm Publishers.
Gordon, Tulo (1986). *Milbi: Aboriginal Tales from Queensland's Endeavour River.* Canberra: Australian National University Press.
Hadgraft, Cecil (1959). *Queensland and Its Writers.* Brisbane, Australia: UQP.
Harris, Alexandra (2015). *Weatherland: Writers and Artists Under English Skies.* London: Thames & Hudson.
Heaney, Seamus (1964). *Preoccupations: Selected Prose 1968–1978.* London: Faber & Faber.
Heat-Moon, William L. (1984). *Blue Highways: A Journey into America.* London: Picador/Pan Books.
Henry, C.J. (1967). *GirrooGurrll: The First Surveyor, and Other Aboriginal legends.* Fortitude Valley, Brisbane, Australia: W.R. Smith & Paterson P/L.
Heseltine, Harry (1970). *Vance Palmer.* St Lucia, Australia: UQP.
Hoffman, Susanna M. (2002). The Monster and the Mother: The Symbolism of Disaster. In Susanna M. Hoffman, and Anthony Oliver-Smith (Eds.), *Catastrophe & Culture: The Anthropology of Disaster* (pp. 113–141). Santa Fe, NM: School of American Research Press.
Holthouse, H. (1977). *Cyclone.* Melbourne: Rigby.
Hosking, Susan, Hosking, Rick, Pannell, Rebecca, and Bierbaum, Nena (Eds.) (2009).

Something Rich and Strange: Sea Changes, Beaches and the Littoral in the Antipodes. Kent Town, Australia: Wakefield Press.

Houston, James M. (1978). The Concepts of "Place" and "Land" in the Judaeo-Christian Tradition. In David Ley and Marvyn Samples (Eds.), *Humanistic Geography: Prospects and Problems* (pp. 224–237). London: Croom Helm.

Hudson, W.H. (1923). *A Hind in Richmond Park.* London: J.M. Dent & Sons.

Hulley, Charles F. (1999). *The Rainbow Serpent.* Sydney: New Holland Publishers.

Huntsman, Leone (2001). *Sand in Our Souls: The Beach in Australian History.* Melbourne: Melbourne University Press.

Ingold, Tim (2011). *Being Alive: Essays on Movement, Knowledge and Description.* Abingdon, UK: Routledge.

Jackson, John Brinkerhoff (1980). *The Necessity for Ruins and Other Topics.* Amherst, MA: University of Massachusetts Press.

Jones, R., and Meehan, B. (1997). Balmarrk wana: Big Winds of Arnhem Land. In Eric K. Webb (Ed.). *Windows on Meteorology: Australian Perspective.* Collingwood, Victoria: CSIRO Publishing, pp. 14–19.

Joyce, James (1960). *Stephen Hero: Part of the first draft of 'A Portrait of the Artist as a Young Man.* (Theodore Spencer, Ed.). London: Jonathan Cape.

Ketterer, David (1974). *New Worlds for Old: The Apocalyptic Imagination, Science Fiction, and American Literature.* Bloomington, IN: Indiana University Press.

Kincaid, Jamaica (2000). *A Small Place.* New York: Farrar, Straus, and Giroux.

King, David, and Cottrell, Alison (Eds.) (2007). *Communities Living With Hazards.* Townsville and Cairns, Australia: Centre for Disaster Studies, James Cook University.

Lamb, Karen (2015). *Thea Astley: Inventing Her Own Weather.* St Lucia, Australia: University of Queensland Press.

Larson, Erik (2000). *Isaac's Storm: The Drowning of Galveston, 8 September 1900.* London: Fourth Estate.

Laudine, Catherine (2009). *Aboriginal Environmental Knowledge: Rational Reverence.* Farnham, Surrey, UK: Ashgate Publishing.

Lawson, B. (2012). *The True Spirit of Cyclone Yasi.* Townsville, Qld: Life Love Laughter Inc.

Lever, S. (2008). Changing Times, Changing Stories. In Susan Sheridan and Paul Genoni (Eds.), *Thea Astley's Fictional Worlds* (pp. 126–134). Newcastle upon Tyne, UK: Cambridge Scholars Publishing.

Locke, John (1984). *An Essay Concerning Human Understanding* (Peter H. Nidditch, Ed.). Oxford, UK: Clarendon Press/Oxford University Press.

Longshore, David (2008). *Encyclopedia of Hurricanes, Typhoons, and Cyclones.* New York: Checkmark Books.

Lopez, Barry (1986). *Artic Dreams: Imagination and Desire in a Northern Landscape.* London: Macmillan.

Love, Rosaleen (2000). *Reefscape: Reflections on the Great Barrier Reef.* St. Leonards, Australia: Allen & Unwin.

Malouf, David (2014). *A First Place.* Sydney: Knopf/Random House.

Malpas, J. (2011). Place and the Problem of Landscape. In J. Malpas (Ed.), *The Place of Landscape: Concepts, Contexts, Studies* (pp. 3–26). Cambridge, MA: The MIT Press.

Marr, David (Ed.) (1994). *Patrick White: Letters.* Milsons Point, Australia: Random House Australia.

Mason, W., and Mason, M. (1993). *Kurangee: Cape Tribulation Pioneers.* Mareeba, Australia: Pinevale Publications.

Matthews, Brian (2008). Life in the Eye of the Hurricane: The Novels of Thea Astley. In Susan Sheridan and Paul Genoni (Eds.), *Thea Astley's Fictional Worlds* (pp. 42–63). Newcastle upon Tyne, UK: Cambridge Scholars Publishing.

McCalman, Iain (2016). *The Reef: A Passionate History.* Penguin Random House Australia.
McConnel, Ursula (1957). *Myths of the Munkan.* Melbourne: Melbourne University Press.
McLaren, Jack (1923). *My Odyssey.* London: Jonathan Cape.
McMahon, Elizabeth. (2016). *Islands, Identity and the Literary Imagination.* London: Anthem Press.
Merren, Terri (2005). *Hurricane Ivan Survival Stories.* Kingston, Jamaica: The Mill Press.
Moore, David (1978). *Islanders and Aborigines at Cape York.* ACT, Australia: Australian Institute of Aboriginal Studies/Humanities Press Inc.
Moses, Dick and Dixon, Bob (1991). *Buda:dji Miya-Miya-Djada* (Carpet Snake and the Nautilus Shells). National Aboriginal Language Programme.
Mountford, Charles P. (1978). The Rainbow Serpent Myths of Australia. In Ira R. Buchler and Kenneth Maddock (Eds.). *The Rainbow Serpent: A Chromatic Piece* (pp. 23–98). Paris: Mouton Publishers.
Mudrooroo (1995). *Us Mob: History, Culture, Struggle: An Introduction to Indigenous Australia.* Sydney: Angus & Robertson.
Murray, John A. (Ed.) (1991). *The Islands and the Sea: Five Centuries of Nature Writing from the Caribbean.* New York: Oxford University Press.
O'Leary, Stephen D. (1994). *Arguing the Apocalypse: A Theory of Millennial Rhetoric.* New York: Oxford University Press.
Oliver-Smith, Anthony (2002). Theorizing Disasters: Nature, Power and Culture. In Susanna M. Hoffman and Anthony Oliver-Smith (Eds.), *Catastrophe & Culture: The Anthropology of Disaster* (pp. 23–47). Santa Fe, New Mexico: School of American Research Press.
Operation Recovery Task Force Team (Ed) (2007). *Taken By Storm: Cyclone Larry 20/3/2005.* Brisbane, Australia: Queensland Government.
Paley, Morton (1986). *The Apocalyptic Sublime.* London: Yale University Press.
Palmer, Nettie (1988). *Nettie Palmer.* (Vivian Smith, Ed.). St. Lucia, Australia: University of Queensland Press.
Palmer, Vance, and Palmer, Nettie (1977). *Letters of Vance and Nettie Palmer 1915–1963.* (Vivian Smith, Ed.). Canberra, Australia: National Library of Australia.
Parker, K. Langloh (1905). *The Euahlayi Tribe: A Study of Aboriginal Life in Australia.* London: Archibald Constable & Co.
The Pearling Disaster, 1899: A Memorial (1899). Brisbane, Australia: Outridge Printing.
Piddington, Henry (1860). *The Sailor's Horn-Book for the Law of Storms* (3rd Ed). London: Williams & Norgate.
Popol Vuh: The Mayan Book of the Dawn of Life (1996). (Tedlock, Dennis, Trans.). New York: Touchstone/Simon & Schuster.
Potteiger, Matthew, and Purinton, Jamie (1998). *Landscape Narratives: Design practices for telling stories.* New York: J. Wiley.
Prieto, Eric (2013). *Literature, Geography, and the Postmodern Poetics of Place.* New York: Palgrave Macmillan.
Ratcliffe, Francis (1963). *Flying Fox and Drifting Sand: The Adventures of a Biologist in Australia.* Sydney: Sirius Books/Angus & Robertson.
Ravi, Srilata (2017). Tropical Cyclones in Mauritian Literature. In Anne Collet, Russell McDougall, and Sue Thomas (Eds.), *Tracking the Literature of Tropical Weather: Typhoons, Hurricanes and Cyclones* (pp. 25–44). Cham, Switzerland: Palgrave Macmillan/Springer International Publishing.
Reid, Robert (2003). *Under A Dark Moon: True Murders and Mysteries From North Queensland.* Cairns, Australia: Blue Heeler Books.
Relph, Edward (1976). *Place and Placelessness.* London: Pion.

Reynolds, Henry (2003). *North of Capricorn: The Untold Story of Australia's North*. Crows Nest, Australia: Allen & Unwin.
Roth, W.E. (1984). *The Queensland Aborigines* (Vols. I, II and III). Aboriginal Studies Series No. 4. (K.F. MacIntyre, Ed.). Carlisle, Australia: Hesperian Press.
Roughsey, Dick (1971). *Moon and Rainbow: The Autobiography of an Aboriginal*. Sydney: A.H. & A.W. Reed.
Ryken, Leland (1974). *The Literature of the Bible*. Grand Rapids, MI: Zondervan Publishing.
Schama, Simon (1996). *Landscape and Memory*. London: Fontana Press.
Schwartz, Stuart B. (2015). *Sea of Storms: A History of Hurricanes in the Greater Caribbean from Columbus to Katrina*. Princeton, NJ: Princeton University Press.
Seddon, G. (1997). *Landprints: Reflections on Place and Landscape*. Melbourne: Cambridge University Press.
Sharp, Nonie (2002). *Saltwater People: The Waves of Memory*. Crows Nest, Australia: Allen & Unwin.
Shaw, Sir William Napier (1928). *A Manual of Meteorology Vol. II*. London: Cambridge University Press.
Sheahan-Bright, Robyn, and Glover, Stuart (2002). *Hot Iron Corrugated Sky: 100 Years of Queensland Writing*. St. Lucia, Australia: University of Queensland Press.
Sheets, Bob, and Williams, Jack (2001). *Hurricane Watch: Forecasting the Deadliest Storms on Earth*. New York: Vintage Books/Random House.
Sheridan, Susan (2016). *The Fiction of Thea Astley*. Amherst, NY: Cambria Press.
Skilton, Liz (2019). *Tempest: Hurricane Naming and American Culture*. Louisiana State University Press: Baton Rouge.
Spirn, Anne Whiston (1998). *The Language of Landscape*. New Haven, CT: Yale University Press.
Stanner, W.E.H. (1991). *After the Dreaming*. Crows Nest, Australia: ABC Enterprises.
Strang, Veronica (1997). *Uncommon Ground: Cultural Landscapes and Environmental Values*. Oxford, UK: Berg.
Tal, Kali (1996). *Worlds of Hurt: Reading the Literatures of Trauma*. New York: Cambridge University Press.
Trezise, Percy (1993). *Dream Road: A journey of discovery*. Crows Nest, Australia: Allen & Unwin.
Tuan, Yi-Fu (1976). Literature, Experience and Environmental Knowing. In Gary T. Moore and Reginald G. Golledge (Eds.), *Environmental Knowing: Theories, Research, and Methods* (pp. 260–272). Stroudsburg, PA: Dowden, Hutchinson & Ross.
Tuan, Yi-Fu (1977). *Space and Place: The Perspective of Experience*. London: Edward Arnold.
Twain, Mark (1967). Old Times on the Mississippi. In Justin Kaplan (Ed.), *Great Short Works of Mark Twain* (pp. 1–78). New York: Harper& Row.
Vanclay, Frank, Higgins, Matthew, Blackshaw, Adam (Eds) (2008). *Making Sense of Place: Exploring concepts and expressions of place through different senses and lenses*. Canberra, Australia: National Museum of Australia Press.
Vollen, Lola, and Ying, Chris (2008). *Voices From the Storm: The People of New Orleans on Hurricane Katrina and Its Aftermath*. San Francisco: Voice of Witness/McSweeney's Books
Von Humboldt, Alexander (1849). *Cosmos, A Sketch of a Physical Description of the Universe* (Vol.1) (E.C. Otté. Trans.). London: Henry G. Bohn.
Walker, David (1976). *Dream and Disillusion: A Search for Australian Cultural Identity*. Canberra, Australia: Australian National University Press.
Watson, Lyall (1984). *Heaven's Breath: A Natural History of the Wind*. London: Hodder and Stoughton.

Waugh, Alec (1930). *Hot Countries*. New York: The Literary Guild.
Weil, Simone (1973). *Waiting for God*. New York: Harper & Row.
Welty, Eudora (1968). Place in Fiction. In Shiv K. Kumar and Keith McKean (Eds.), *Critical Approaches to Fiction* (pp. 249-264). New York: McGraw-Hill. [Originally published in 1956 in *The South Atlantic Quarterly*55(1), pp. 57-72].
White, Patrick (1981). *Flaws in the Glass: A Self-portrait*. London: Jonathan Cape.
White, Patrick (1990). Patrick White. In Peter Wolfe (Ed.), *Critical Essays on Patrick White* (pp. 24-28). Boston, MA: G.K. Hall & Co.
Willbanks, Ray (2008). Thea Astley: Interview. In Susan Sheridan and Paul Genomi (Eds.). *Thea Astley's Fictional Worlds* (pp. 21-35). Newcastle upon Tyne, UK: Cambridge Scholars Publishing.
Wilson, Helen. H. (1980). *Cyclone Coasts: Australia's North-West Frontier*. Melbourne: Rigby.
Winton, Tim (1993). *Land's Edge*. Sydney: Pan Macmillan.
Zapf, Michael Kim (2009). *Social Work and the Environment: Understanding People and Place*. Toronto, Canada: Canadian Scholars' Press.

Articles

Ablett, R. (2018). "Doris, You Old Slag": The Sexist and Gendered-Ageist Discourses of Twitter Users Concerning a Female-Named UK Storm. *Trent Notes on Linguistics*, Vol. 1, 75-88.
Astley, Thea (1970). The Idiot Question. *Southerly*, 30(1), 3-8.
Astley, Thea (1976). Being a Queenslander: A Form of Literary and Geographical Conceit. *Southerly*, 36(6), 252-264.
Beatson, P.R. (1974). The Skiapod and the Eye: Patrick White's *The Eye of the Storm*. *Southerly*, 34(3), 219-232.
Beston, John (2006). Why Are Epiphanies So Important in Patrick White's Novels? *AUMLA: Journal of the Australasian Universities Modern Language Association*, 105, 109-121.
Buckridge, Patrick (1995). Queensland Literature: The Making of an Idea. *Queensland Review*, 2(1), 30-41.
Casey, Edward S. (2001). Between Geography and Philosophy: What Does It Mean to Be in the Place-World? *Annals of the Association of American Geographers*. 91(4), 683-93.[online] http://www.jstor.org/stable/3651229. Accessed: 23-11-2017.
Charlton-Perez A. J., Vukadinovic Greetham D., Hemingway R. (2019). Storm Naming and Forecast Communication: A Case Study of Storm Doris. *Meteorological Applications*, 1-16. https://doi.org/10.1002/met.1794
Daley, Linda (2016). Alexis Wright's Fiction as World Making. In *Contemporary Women's Writing*, 10(1), 8-23.
Devlin-Glass, Frances (2007). Review Essay: Alexis Wright's 'Carpentaria.' *Antipodes*, 21(1), 82 84.
Devlin-Glass, Frances (2008). A Politics of the Dreamtime: Destructive and Regenerative Rainbows in Alexis Wright's "*Carpentaria.*" *Australian Literary Studies*, 23(4), 392-407.
Evans, Raymond (2008). A Queensland Reader: Discovering the Queensland Writer, *Queensland Review*, 15(2), 69-80.
Genoni, Paul (2007). Thea Astley Makes Something Out of Nothing [online]. *Antipodes*, 21(1), 35-40.
Gildersleeve, Jessica (2012). Trauma, Memory and Landscape in Queensland: Women Writing "a New Alphabet of Moss and Water." *Queensland Review*, 19(2), 205-216. doi: 10.1017/qre.2012.23.

Gingell-Beckman, Susan (1982/3). Seven Black Swans: The Symbolic Logic of Patrick White's *The Eye of the Storm*. *Journal of Post-Colonial Writing (World Literature Written in English), 21*(2), 315–325.

Goldsworthy, Kerry (1983). Thea Astley's Writing: Magnetic North. *Meanjin, 42*(4), 478–485.

Green, Donna, Billy, Jack, and Tapim, Alo (2010). Indigenous Australians' Knowledge of Weather and Climate. *Climate Change, 100*, 337–354. doi 10.1007/s10584-010-9803-z

Harding, S. (2011). The Tropical Agenda. *Journal of Tropical Psychology. 1*(1), 2–5. doi: 10.1375/jtp.1.1.2.

Hawthorne, Susan (2010–11). Ecology in Poetry/Poetry in Ecology. In Mohit Prasad (Ed.), *Dreadlocks: Oceans, Islands and Skies*. Proceedings of the Oceans, Islands and Skies Oceanic Conference on Creativity and Climate Change. Vol 6/7. pp. 101–126.+

Jordan, Deborah (2010). Environment and Colonial Shadows: Green Island 1932. *LiNQ. 37*, 142–158.

Jordan, Deborah (2011). Heeding the Warnings: 'Sucking up the seas' in Vance Palmer's *Cyclone. etropic, 10*, 20–31.

Loomes, Louise (2014). Armageddon Begins Here: Apocalypse in Alexis Wright's *Carpentaria*. *LiNQ, 21*, 124–138.

Lovell, Sue (2004). The "Psychic Space" of Queensland in the Work of Janette Turner Hospital. *Queensland Review, 11*(2), 11–23.

McKellar, John (1954). Vance Palmer as Novelist. *Southerly, 15*(1), 16–25.

Mullaney, William (2008). Her Eyes Were Watching Katrina: Unnatural Deaths in a Natural Disaster. *Obsidian, 9*(1). 124–136.

Nott, Jonathan (2000). How High Was the Storm Surge from Tropical Cyclone Mahina? *Australian Journal of Emergency Management, 15*(1), 11–13.

Nott, Jonathan, and Hayne, M. (2001). High Frequency of "Super-Cyclones" Along the Great Barrier Reef Over the Past 5000 Years. *Nature, 413*, 508–512.

Nott, Jonathan, Green, C., Townsend, I., and Callaghan, J. (2014). The World Record Storm Surge and the Most Intense Southern Hemisphere Tropical Cyclone: New evidence and Modelling. *American Meteorological Society, 95*(5), 757–765. doi: 10.1175/BAMS-D-12-00233.1.

Nott, Jonathan, Smithers, Scott, Walsh, Kevin, and Rhodes, Ed. (2009). Sand Beach Ridges Record 6000 Year History of Extreme Tropical Cyclone Activity in Northeastern Australia. *Quaternary Science Reviews, 28*(15–16), 1511–1520.

O'Neill, Graham (1999). Cyclone Warning. *Ecos, 99*, 20–22.

Plater, Diana (2011, May 27). A Dance for Winds. *Australian Geographic*. Retrieved from: http://www.australiangeographic.com.au/topics/history-culture/2011/05/a-dance-for-the-winds/

Pocock, Celmara (2005). Blue Lagoons and Coconut Palms: The Creation of a Tropical Idyll in Australia. *The Australian Journal of Anthropology, 16*(3), 335–349.

Priya, B. Siva (2012). Illumination of Elizabeth Hunter: A Study of Patrick White's "*The Eye of the Storm.*" *The Criterion, 3*(4), 2–8.

Ravenscroft, Alison (2010). Dreaming of Others: Carpentaria and Its Critics. *Cultural Studies Review, 16*(2), 194–224.

Sharrad, Paul (2009). Beyond Capricornia: Ambiguous Promise in Alexis Wright. *Australian Literary Studies, 24*(1), 52–65.

Shoemaker, Adam (2008). Hard Dreams and Indigenous Worlds in Australia's North. *Hecate, 34*(1), 55–62.

Skertchly, Allan, and Skertchly, Kristen (1999–2000). Traditional Aboriginal Knowledge and Sustained Human Survival in the Face of Severe Natural Hazards in the Australian Monsoon Region: Some Lessons from the Past for Today and Tomorrow. *Australian Journal of Emergency Management, 14*(4), pp. 42–50.

Sovka, Jordan (2013). The Right to Write About It: Literature After Katrina, *The Quarterly Conversation, 33.* Retrieved from http://quarterlyconversation.com/the-right-to-write-about-it-literature-after-katrina
Specht, Raymond L., and McCarthy, Frederick D. (2005). The "Snake Woman Story" of Hemple Bay, Groote Eylandt: An Enindilyakwa Legend of a Tsunami in the Gulf of Carpentaria [online]. *Proceedings of the Royal Society of Queensland,* 112, 77–82.
Swee, Hannah (2017). Assembling Local Cyclone Knowledge in the Australian Tropics. *Nature and Culture,* Vol. 12 (1), pp. 8–26.
Taylor, Cheryl (2001). Shaping a Regional Identity: Literary Non-Fiction and Short Fiction in North Queensland. *Queensland Review,* 8(2), 41–52.
Tuan, Yi-Fu (1991). Language and the Making of Place: A Narrative-Descriptive Approach. *Annals of the Association of American Geographers,* 81 (4), 684–696.
Wilson, James E. (2001). The Origin and Odyssey of Terroir. *Geoscience Canada,* 28(3), 139–141.
Windschuttle, Keith, and Gillin, Tim (2002). The Extinction of the Australian Pygmies. *Quadrant,* 46(6), 7–18.
Wright, Alexis (2002). Politics of Writing. *Southerly,* 62(2), 10–20.
Wright, Alexis (2007b). On Writing Carpentaria. *Harpers Gold: Heat,* 13, 1–17.
Wright, Alexis (2011). Deep Weather. *Meanjin,* 70(2), 70–82.

Papers

Holland, Greg J. (1983). *Tropical Cyclones in the Australian/Southwest Pacific Region: Department of Atmospheric Science Paper No. 363* [Paper]. Fort Collins, CO: Colorado State University.
Salter, Christopher L., and Lloyd, William J. (1977). *Landscape in Literature.* Washington, D.C.: Association for American Geographers.
State of the Tropics (2014). *State of the Tropics 2014 Report* [Whitepaper]. Cairns, Australia: James Cook University.

Newspaper Articles

A.B.P. (1921, January 1). In Cyclone and Coincidence. *Chronicle* [Adelaide], p. 37.
A-For-Annie (1955, March 10). *Central Queensland Herald,* p. 1.
Atmospheric Disturbances (1898, 24 February). *The Brisbane Courier,* p. 5.
Barrier Reef Expedition: Well-Known Author as Organiser (1933, June 6). *Newcastle Sun,* p. 6.
The Bishop of North Queensland (1903, June 1). *The Mercury* [Hobart], p. 6.
Chatty Mackay Letter (1918, March 22). *Chronicle and North Coast Advertiser,* p. 3.
Clement Wragge at Home (1894, September 8). *Sydney Mail,* p. 491.
Current Notes (1896, February 8). *The Capricornian,* p. 9.
Cyclone and Floods: The Fate of Mackay (1918, February 1). *Kalgoorlie Miner,* p. 5.
Cyclones and Other Evils (1920, February 4). *The Cairns Post,* p. 4.
Destructive Tornado at Cairns, Queensland (1878, 23 March). *Sydney Evening News,* p. 3.
Editorial (1896, February 5). *The Northern Miner,* p. 2.
Favenc, E. (1903, March 18). Cyclones in North Queensland. *The Mercury* [Hobart], p. 7.
The Floods in Brisbane (1887, February 2). *The South Australian Advertiser,* p. 6.
Francis, Nancy (1933, 15 July). In the Fury of a Cyclone, *The Brisbane Courier,* p. 19.
Hurricane at Mackay (1898, February 9). *The Telegraph* (Brisbane), p. 2.
In Queensland This Week (1963, February 7). *Canberra Times,* p. 2.
In Queensland This Week (1963, February 9). *Canberra Times,* p. 2.
Jolly, Norman (1903, 26 March). The Townsville Cyclone. *The Register* [Adelaide], p. 3.

The Law of Storms (1870, January 3). *South Australian Register,* p. 5.
The Mackay Disaster (1918, January 28). *The Cairns Post,* p. 4.
McDonald, Tom (1934, March 16). Airman's Thrilling Story of Search for Cyclone Survivors. *The Courier Mail,* p. 13.
Men Join Women (1975, November 20). *Hamersley News,* p. 1.
Meteorology of Australasia and Oceania (1894, April 4). *The Brisbane Courier,* p. 3.
Meteorology of Australasia and Oceania (1894, February 20). *The Brisbane Courier,* p. 3.
Meteorology of Australasia and Oceania (1898, February 19). *The Brisbane Courier,* p. 3.
Meteorology of Australasia and Oceania (1898, February 2). *The Brisbane Courier,* p. 5.
Meteorology of Australia and Oceania (1897, October 23). *Brisbane Courier,* p. 3.
Meteorology of Australia and Oceania (1899, March 7). *The Brisbane Courier,* p. 3.
Mr Clement Wragge: The Weather Prophet. *The Australian Star* (1894, May 26), p.7.
Mr. Wragge's Disturbances (1895, October 11), p. 6.
Mr Wragge's Forecasts (1894, 26 April). *The Maitland Daily Mirror,* p. 3.
North Queensland Cyclone: History of a Former Disaster (1918). *The Armidale Chronicle,* page 3
A Northern Pilgrimage (1893, October 14). *The Queenslander,* p. 750.
Palmer, Nettie (1932, June 4). On a Coral Island: Living in Arden. *The Age,* p. 9.
Palmer, Nettie (1934, March 31). The Cyclone of the North: A Haunting Peril. *The Argus,* p. 4.
Palmer, Vance (1932, July 2). Life on a Coral Island. *The Brisbane Courier,* p. 20.
Palmer, Vance (1934, April 9). Good Comrade, Good Seaman: Tribute to Captain of Missing Launch. *The Cairns Post,* p. 6.
Palmer, Vance (1938, March 11). An Amateur Robinson Crusoe. *Henty Observer and Culcairn Shire Register,* p. 4.
Queensland Cyclone: Sermon by Dr Mercer at Holy Trinity Church (1903, June 15). *The Examiner* [Launceston, Tasmania], p. 5.
The Ravages of "Nerva" (1899, October 7). *Sydney Mail and New South Wales Advertiser,* p. 847.
Rhodes. F. Ungentle Annie (1955, March 17). *The Central Queensland Herald,* p. 3.
A Storm in the Pacific (1910, February 17). *The Advertiser* [Adelaide], p. 9.
Terrible Gale at Cleveland Bay (1867, March 23). *The Brisbane Courier,* p. 5.
Theory of Cyclones (1849, February 3). *The Sydney Morning Herald,* p. 3.
Tit-Bits from Hansard (1902, August 20). *Dubbo Liberal and Macquarie Advocate,* p. 1.
The Townsville Cyclone: Speech by Bishop Frodsham (1903, May 19). *The Advertiser* [Adelaide], p. 6.
The Two Greatest Storms on Record (1877, May 26). *Freeman's Journal* (Sydney), pp. 17–18.
The Weather (1901, December 28). *The Telegraph* (Brisbane), p. 8.
The Weather (1902, August 2). *The Telegraph* (Brisbane), p. 6
The Weather (1902, June 3). *The Telegraph* (Brisbane), p. 3.
The Weather (1902, June 7). *The Telegraph* (Brisbane), p. 8.
Wragge, Clement (1898, February 22). The Weather: "Sana" and "Blastus." *Gympie Times,* p. 3.
Wragge, Clement (1898, February 24). Atmospheric Disturbances: Grand Meteorological Opera. *The Brisbane Courier,* p. 5.

Film

deHeer, Rolf, and Djigirr, Peter (Directors). (2006). *Ten Canoes* [Motion picture]. Australia: Fandango/SBS/Vertigo.

Index

A la recherche du temps perdu 25
Aborigine, Australian 3, 11, 47, 52, 70, 85, 86, 120, 121, 132, 133, 136–154, 164, 168, 169; *see also* Indigenous
The Acolyte 84, 159
Adam and Eve 30, 123
Adelaide 49
After the End 10, 66
"After Yasi" (poem) 160–161
Ahab 73, 77; King 147
air 10, 21, 28–29, 30, 32, 46, 71, 72, 80, 81, 82, 97, 105, 120, 122, 123, 130, 131, 133, 135, 143, 145, 150, 157, 162, 168
America 5, 16, 49
apocalypse 2, 3, 9, 10, 17, 18–19, 20, 43, 64, 66, 67, 74, 78, 80, 81, 82, 87, 90, 91, 95, 96, 106, 107, 115, 116, 121, 125, 128, 135, 136, 140, 144, 148, 152, 153, 154, 159, 160, 163, 164, 165, 166, 169, 170; as cyclone 78, 80, 116, 153, 163; as storm 152, 160; sublime 17
Arabian Sea 16
archetype 102, 103, 108, 145, 162, 163, 164, 165
Aristotle 13, 121
Armageddon 135, 136
Arnhem Land 9, 47
Astley, Thea 2, 5, 6, 9, 11, 12, 16, 31, 32, 33, 34, 36, 37, 38, 49, 51, 52, 54, 84–97, 101, 105, 133, 136, 157, 159, 160; *see also The Acolyte*; "Being a Queenslander" (essay); *A Boat Load of Home Folk*; *A Descant for Gossips*; *Girl with a Monkey*; "The Idiot Question" (essay); *It's Raining in Mango*; *A Kindness Cup*; *The Multiple Effects of Rainshadow*; *Slow Natives*; *The Well Dressed Explorer*
Atlantic 16, 17
Australia 2, 3, 5, 6, 9, 12, 15, 16, 34, 35, 36, 37, 38, 39, 41, 49, 51, 52, 53, 54, 56, 58, 59, 60, 61, 63, 70, 86, 88, 89, 109, 128, 130, 137, 144, 146, 147, 153, 154, 155, 158, 164; coast 33, 36–37, 58, 61, 157, 158; bush 36; identity 158; imagination 37; literature 2, 36, 147; tropical cyclones 15, 58; tropics 2, 37, 71; writers 11, 36, 118
Australian Aborigine *see* Aborigine, Australian

author 2, 6, 7, 10, 17, 35, 65, 70, 99, 121, 132; Queensland 31, 33

Bachelard, Gaston 163; *see also Earth and Reveries of Repose*
"The Ballad of the Calliope" (poem) 17, 118
Banfield, E.J. 120, 121; *see also* Dunk Island
Bate, Sir Andrew Jonathan 117, 134
Battle of Parramatta Park 71
Bathurst Bay 10, 38, 53; *see also* Cyclone Mahina
Bathurst Island 9
beach 36, 37, 75, 77, 78, 79, 94, 107, 108, 114, 115, 126, 153, 166; Airlie 42; Mission 61, 62, 63, 120, 123, 132
Becke, Louis 31
being (entity) 21, 23, 29, 30, 34, 51, 62, 63, 78, 100, 102, 103, 112, 116, 121, 124, 135, 140, 141, 142, 143, 145, 146, 148, 151, 153, 163, 164, 169
being (state of existence) 3, 24, 25, 35, 45, 48, 104, 117, 134, 160, 164, 165; being-in-the-world 25
"Being a Queenslander" (essay) 35; *see also* Astley, Thea
Bender, Barbara 167
Berger, James 10, 66
Bermuda 14, 17
Berndt, Catherine 141, 142, 153
Berndt, Ronald 141, 142, 153
Beston, John 106
The Bible 29–30, 77, 138, 147; *see also* God; Jesus; Job; Jonah
Biblical 12, 26, 68, 76, 77, 89, 104, 106, 123, 139, 144, 146, 147, 149, 162
"The Big Wind" (story) 65, 71, 79, 82; *see also* Palmer, Vance
biosphere 16, 171
birth 1, 18, 56, 57, 67, 96, 102, 141, 145
Blanchot, Maurice 18, 23
A Boat Load of Home Folk 2, 11, 31, 84–97, 101, 105, 136, 157, 159; *see also* Astley, Thea
Bolton, Roxcy 59–60
book 1, 5, 6, 10, 14, 17, 20, 27, 29, 47, 48, 56, 86, 87, 99, 112, 123, 124, 137, 156
Booth, William 32

193

Index

Bowen 37, 42, 59
Bradbury, Ray 81, 82; see also *Something Wicked This Way Comes*
Braithwaite, Edward Kamau 17
breath/e 28, 29, 31, 47, 61, 73, 107, 117, 121, 123, 124, 128, 133, 134, 140, 141, 157, 164
breathless 1, 119, 121, 133
Brisbane 9, 38, 49, 54
brumbies 107–108
Brumby Island 98, 107–108, 109, 110, 111, 112, 114, 165
Bryant, William Cullen 17, 120
Bufi, Barbara 11, 61, 62
Bundaberg 54, 55
Bureau of Meteorology (Australia) 15, 59
Burke, Edmund 17, 18, 55–56, 125, 148–9, 155
"Burnt Norton" (poem) 103

Cader, Teresa 17
Cairns 11, 32, 38, 39, 58, 61, 64, 66, 67, 68, 70, 71, 81, 142, 143
Callahan, David 33–34
Callander, Kim 167
Campbell-Lloyd, Kate 157
Cape Melville 10, 38; Tribulation 51, 64, 70; York 9, 53, 55, 59, 69, 143
Capote, Truman 35
Cardwell 42, 59, 61
Caribbean 16, 35
Carpentaria 3, 120, 121, 135–154, 157, 164–165, 168–170
Casey, Edward 24
cassowary 129
catalyst 2, 5, 66, 83, 86, 96, 150, 159
catastrophe 5, 7, 9, 11, 12, 13, 17, 39, 43, 50, 66, 67, 83, 127, 128, 157, 158–159, 162, 170; cyclone 18–23; nature 6, 9, 10, 18, 19, 22, 42, 156, 158, 161, 162, 170; weather 10, 42, 158, 159, 168
catharsis 1, 20, 66
chaos 5, 7, 10, 11, 13, 22, 39, 43, 44, 45, 54, 60, 63, 67, 73–75, 76, 78, 79, 80, 81, 83, 85, 89, 100, 114, 117, 118, 122, 126, 127, 133, 134, 155, 156, 158, 160, 162, 163, 168
character 2, 3, 5, 11, 12, 18, 19, 21, 31, 33, 45, 46, 51, 53, 56, 57, 59, 60–67, 70, 71, 72, 77, 78, 79, 80, 81, 82, 83, 84, 85, 86, 88, 89, 90, 91, 95, 96, 100, 101, 103, 106, 133, 136, 139, 140, 147, 148, 159, 160, 161
characteristics 12, 14, 15, 21, 31, 33, 45, 48, 56, 73, 79, 144, 157
"Chasing the Storm" (short story) 11
China Sea 17
circle 32, 75, 101, 102, 121, 122, 136, 150, 163–164, 165, 166
Clemens, Samuel 27; *see also* Twain, Mark
Clifford, Maureen 62
climate 2, 6, 7, 13, 27, 30, 31, 121, 131, 136, 162
cloud 27, 29, 30, 69, 117, 121, 131, 140, 150, 151, 157, 163, 164
coast 9, 15, 17, 31, 36–37, 42, 47, 50, 51, 52, 58, 68, 147, 148, 158; of Australia 33, 37, 58; culture of 157; Queensland 5, 15, 37, 38, 51, 54, 61, 64, 69, 70, 71, 72, 80, 107, 122, 136, 142, 157
The Coast Dwellers 37
Coleridge, Samuel Taylor 139
common 1, 7, 11, 23, 29, 63, 84, 85, 96, 122, 127, 128, 132, 144, 167, 168,
communion 37, 96, 98, 105, 107, 156
community 7, 9, 10, 11, 12, 13, 15, 20, 28, 37, 38, 40, 42, 43, 46, 60, 62, 69, 80, 83, 85, 88, 89, 90, 95, 96, 127, 128, 143, 144, 157, 159, 167, 170, 171
concept 21, 22, 23, 24, 25, 26, 44, 55, 57, 78, 112, 136, 138, 139, 159, 161,
Condon, Matthew 36
connect 7, 17, 22, 23, 24, 25, 26, 28, 34, 40, 43, 56, 77, 82, 84, 85, 86, 88, 95, 104, 119, 120, 121, 122, 124, 129, 130, 132, 142, 150, 154, 156, 157, 163, 164
Conrad, Joseph 15, 17, 32; see also *Heart of Darkness*; *Typhoon*
Contested Landscapes 167
Cooktown 33, 38, 51, 69, 70, 142
cope 2, 5, 6, 15, 20, 43, 63, 65, 83, 96, 100, 125, 168
Coral Sea 15, 16
Cosgrove, General 40
cosmos 101, 165
country 36, 61, 82, 88, 120, 121, 124, 128, 132, 135, 138, 140, 141, 142, 143, 144, 145, 148, 150, 151, 152, 153, 154, 155, 158, 164, 169, 170; of the mind 167
Crane, Hart 17
creation 1, 2, 3, 12, 15, 16, 22, 24, 26, 28, 30, 35, 40, 43, 45, 46, 64, 83, 91, 76, 114, 118, 121, 123–124, 128, 130, 133, 134–136, 138, 140–143, 147–149, 152–154, 157, 160, 163, 164, 168; Biblical 26, 123; creation spirits 151, 152, 160; re-creation 30, 40, 43, 84, 129, 134, 154
creativity 6, 37, 44, 45, 63, 136, 138, 140, 157, 171
creator 67, 142, 152, 170
Crest of the Wave (boat) 9, 10
"Cry of the Wild Wind" (short story) 10–11
Cuba 16
culture 2, 5, 7, 12, 13, 15, 21, 24, 35, 37, 38, 43, 45, 46, 47, 48, 68, 102, 120, 123, 124, 127, 134, 135, 137, 138, 139, 144, 147, 155, 157, 158, 159, 160, 161, 162, 165
cultural 2, 3, 10, 11, 12, 17, 20, 21, 34, 35, 37, 46, 47, 48, 49, 73, 101, 102, 120, 132, 137, 139, 140, 147, 157, 159, 161, 162, 165; consciousness 170; history 20, 46; identity 157, 162; mythos 3, 161–166; perception 29
cycle 6, 9, 14, 15, 18, 40, 47, 56, 67, 100, 101, 105, 118, 121, 123, 124, 126, 130, 131, 132, 135, 136, 147, 153, 154, 163, 164; life 57, 102, 161, 165, 168; poetry 3, 10, 118, 119, 123, 129, 132, 133, 136, 144, 163
cyclone: as animal 12, 68–69, 73, 75, 80, 94;

as apocalypse 10, 64, 66, 78, 80, 81, 82, 95, 106, 116, 153, 154, 159, 160, 161, 169; as catalyst 2, 86, 159; categories 15; as chaos 10, 13; character of 2, 5, 45, 51, 56, 61, 63, 168; and community 11; as disaster 18, 22, 158; edge 11, 84, 86, 90, 96, 133, 157, 159, 160; experience 7, 14, 16, 22, 29, 42, 44, 62, 63, 78, 83, 90, 110, 111, 124, 128, 131, 160, 166, 167, 170; eye 14, 51, 84, 93, 95, 98–116, 124, 126, 159, 165, 166, 170; gender 2, 58–59, 61, 62, 63, 168; history 37, 38, 39, 51, 61, 71; literary 2, 6, 7, 10, 11, 12, 18, 31, 40, 61, 71, 84, 88, 119, 135, 136, 154, 161, 167, 168; literature 7, 17, 29, 39, 40, 88, 135, 136, 154, 159, 161, 167; as monster 66, 94, 121, 163; as mythos 124, 161
Cyclone 7; *see also* Holthouse, Hector
Cyclone 2, 11, 64–83, 121, 144, 157, 163; *see also* Palmer, Vance
"Cyclone" (story) 65–66, 71, 80–81
"Cyclone, Aftermath" (poem) 130
"A Cyclone at Sea" (poem) 17
Cyclone Larry: Tales of Survival 12
Cyclone Yasi: Our Stories 12
cyclone name: Ada 42; Agnes 58; Annie 58; Audrey (Little Audrey) 59; Bangladesh 132; Bertha 58; Bessie 59; Beta 38, 51, 52; Cairns 1878 39; Cape Tribulation 1934 69, Clara 59; Connie 59; Debbie 15; Dora 59; Eline 53; Flora 59; Gertie 59; Gladstone 1854 37; Harry 11; Larry 12, 15, 29, 40, 44, 60–61, 117–134, 160; Leonta 39, 51; Harry 11; Ita 15; Leda 145, 154; Mackay 1918 39, 87, 169; Mahina 9, 10, 38, 53, 61, 66; Marcia 15; Maria 17, 21; Monica 15; Nargis (Burma) 133; Port Douglas 1911 38; Sana 54–55; Sigma 51; Townsville 1903 39; Tracy 14, 59; Ului 15; Yasi 5, 11, 12, 15, 42, 61–62, 63, 155, 157, 167; Zeta 51
cyclone naming 2, 5, 16, 20–21, 44–63, 58–59, 63, 168; North Queensland 7, 22, 37–40, 60, 67, 160, 162; origin of term 16–17; as part of place 2, 18, 28, 40, 66, 155, 157, 158; personal experience of 14, 56, 67, 167, 170; as revelation 83, 84, 95, 171; rotation 14–15; season 13, 38, 68, 69, 70, 71; Severe Tropical (STC) 5, 15, 37, 60, 69, 120; spirituality of 3, 84, 135, 141, 151–152, 154, 164, 165, 169, 170; stories 40, 82, 120, 144, 161, 162, 167; as storm 2, 5, 7, 10, 12, 13, 14, 15, 16, 17, 29, 33, 37, 44, 46, 48, 49, 51, 53, 54, 80, 85, 97, 99, 102, 109, 114, 118, 119, 122, 130, 132, 135, 151, 152, 153, 155, 157, 159, 160, 162, 164, 165, 166, 169, 170, 171; as trauma 42, 128; as trope 2, 6, 7, 17, 18, 22, 40, 67, 73, 87, 88, 96, 136, 155, 158, 161, 163, 164, 166, 168; tropical 2, 3, 6, 9, 13, 15, 21, 31, 37, 39, 53, 58, 59, 86, 91, 98, 135, 155–156, 158, 159, 161, 168, 170; as weather 5, 6, 9, 14, 15, 20, 29, 31, 39, 42, 46, 51, 56, 62, 135, 143, 154, 155, 157, 168; within 3, 29, 43, 84, 96, 117, 119, 128, 129, 133, 157, 160, 267; writing about 6, 11, 46, 62, 162

Darwin 9, 14, 59
dasein 24
death 2, 11, 18, 19, 30, 33, 37, 56, 61, 64, 67, 70, 75, 77, 78, 80, 86, 90, 92, 93, 95, 98, 99, 100, 102, 103, 105, 106, 108, 109, 110, 111, 112, 113, 114, 115, 116, 118, 121, 129, 130, 141, 143, 147, 149, 150, 151, 154, 163, 164, 165, 166
DeBlieu, Jan 46, 48, 123–124, 155; *see also Wind*
Defoe, Daniel 17, 162; *see also The Storm*
A Descant for Gossips 85; *see also* Astley, Thea
desert 29, 41, 139, 147, 148, 158
Desperance (town) 145, 146, 147, 148, 149, 151, 152, 153, 169; *see also Carpentaria*; Wright, Alexis
destiny 18, 19, 39, 44, 67, 81, 93, 101, 103, 113
destruction 1, 2, 3, 5, 6, 7, 10, 12–19, 20–22, 26, 33, 38, 40, 42, 45, 50–51, 53, 57–63, 66–67, 70, 74–75, 78, 81–87, 93, 95, 96, 100, 105, 108, 112–113, 116, 118, 120–122, 124, 126–131, 134–135, 142, 144, 149, 151–152, 154–155, 159, 160, 162–165, 168, 170
disaster 2, 18, 19, 23, 35, 40, 59, 62, 73, 79, 80, 83, 84, 88, 89, 91, 118, 120, 127, 128, 156, 161; meaning 7, 156; name 2, 44–63; nature 6, 18–23, 38, 73, 74, 170; story 144; understanding 22, 156; writing about 23, 60
disorder 1, 19, 73, 75, 118; *see also* chaos; order
Divine Wind 5
Donolly, Fay 65, 66, 74–75, 78, 82, 85, 94, 121, 163
the Dreaming 138, 140–141, 142, 145, 146, 148, 150
Drew, Phillip 37, 158
Dubliners 104; *see also* Joyce, James
Dunk Island 9, 69, 70; *see also* Banfield
Dutton, Geoffrey 99

earth 13, 18, 27, 28, 29, 33, 74, 77, 80, 105, 117, 118, 121, 123, 124, 126, 128, 129, 130, 132, 133, 134, 136, 139, 141, 142, 144, 148, 157, 164, 167
Earth and Reveries of Repose 163
earthquake 18, 48, 131
Earth's Breath 3, 10, 14, 44, 117–134, 136, 144, 160, 163–164; *see also* Hawthorne, Susan
Eco, Umberto 11–12
ecosystem 3, 133, 157
Eden (garden) 30, 53, 68, 69, 71, 74–75, 80, 93, 94, 121, 163, 164; *see also* Adam and Eve; the Bible; creation
Eliade, Mircea 101
Elias Smith *see Carpentaria*; Smith, Elias; Wright, Alexis
Elijah 147, 149, 151
Eliot, T.S. 98, 103, 126, 165; *see also* "Burnt Norton"; *Four Quartets*
Emanuel, Kerry 5; *see also Divine Wind*
Enata (people) 47
England 16, 17, 23, 26, 31, 32, 49, 50, 56, 66, 77, 122, 148, 167
*Enuma Eli*sh 124, 140

Index

environment 1, 5, 6, 11, 19, 20, 22, 23, 28, 30, 34, 43, 44, 45, 46, 49, 54, 60, 63, 64, 67, 68, 74, 80, 82, 94, 117, 118, 119, 120, 122, 126, 128, 132, 134, 137, 139, 141, 144, 152, 154, 156, 157, 160, 161, 169, 170
epic 25, 72, 80, 124, 137, 138, 145, 153, 164
epiphany 3, 10, 17, 56, 66, 78, 80–81, 83, 89, 90, 91, 92, 93, 98–116, 119, 125, 126, 133, 135, 150, 151, 153, 159, 165, 166, 170, 171
An Essay Concerning Human Understanding 23
Euahlayi (people) 47
Eucharistic 105; *see also* communion
existence 3, 19, 22, 27–29, 32–34, 42, 67, 69, 78, 84–85, 91, 93, 98, 100, 103, 105, 106, 111, 113, 115, 121, 123–124, 127–128, 133–136, 138, 141, 144, 147, 152, 155, 157, 160, 164–165, 167, 168
eye 32, 80, 81, 84, 89, 92, 98, 104, 105, 106, 111, 114, 118, 122, 128, 129, 155; of cyclone 14, 51, 61, 63, 84, 93, 95, 98, 99, 100, 103–116, 124, 126, 165, 166, 170; eyewall 14, 115, 126; of needle 98, 110; spiritual 104, 113, 114, 115, 116, 125, 166; of storm 85, 89, 93, 98, 106, 107, 109, 110, 111, 114, 124, 125, 150, 159; of typhoon 102, 109; of universe 103, 105, 113, 116, 124
The Eye of the Storm 3, 10, 84, 93, 98–116, 125, 136, 157, 165–166; see also Patrick White

faith 3, 18, 19, 56, 75, 92, 94, 100, 101, 107, 110, 116, 118, 131, 146, 148, 149
Far North Queensland 2, 5, 6, 10, 13, 22, 40, 70
fate 11, 18, 19, 63, 67, 85, 91, 93, 109, 130, 168
Faulkner, James 35
Favenc, Ernest 37
fear 2, 11, 21, 42, 43, 44, 45, 46, 62, 65, 71, 73, 75, 78, 79, 80, 82, 83, 91, 93, 108, 112, 113, 125, 126, 128, 149, 153, 157, 163
Finch, Anne 17
fire 21, 48, 58, 72, 73, 93, 104, 128, 143, 144, 149, 164
Fishman, Mozzie 138–139, 140, 146, 149; see also *Carpentaria*; Wright, Alexis
Fitzroy Island 9, 69
Flaws in the Glass (1981) 99, 106; *see also* White, Patrick
flood 11, 15, 31, 33, 39, 47, 48, 50, 51, 58, 59, 60, 69, 70, 73, 78. 121, 130, 132, 133, 142, 143, 144, 148, 151, 153, 161, 164, 168, 169; the Flood 123, 162; flood-making 142, 164
Four Quartets 103; *see also* Eliot, T.S.
frigate bird 71, 82, 122, 126
Frodsham, George 39, 52
Frye, Northrop 74, 76, 77, 162
Fury, Tom 81, 82; *see also* Bradbury, Ray; *Something Wicked This Way Comes*

Galeano, Pamela 160–161
gender 2, 12, 48, 49, 51, 53, 57, 58, 60, 62, 63, 66, 156, 168,
genius loci 166

The Georgics 117, 122
Getting Back Into Place 24
Gidjingarli (people) 47
Gingell-Beckman, Susan 105
Girl with a Monkey 85; *see also* Astley, Thea
Gladstone 37
god/God 1, 3, 9, 29–30, 32, 68, 76, 77, 82, 92, 94, 100, 101, 103, 104, 106, 109, 117, 118, 123, 124, 139, 144, 146, 147, 148, 149, 152, 153, 162, 165, 168, 170; of cyclone 51, 124; hidden 100, 103, 165, 166; in-dwelling 103, 165, 166; of nature 9, 10; search for 100, 165; of wind 16, 97, 124
Great Barrier Reef 32, 68, 69, 70, 71; *see also* reef
Green Island 9, 32, 64, 67, 68, 69, 70, 71, 82; *see also* Palmer, Nettie; Palmer, Vance
groper (fish) 147, 149–150
Gross Manndrenke (storm) 50
Gulf of Carpentaria 9, 15, 69, 121, 136, 140, 142, 143, 144, 145, 147, 149, 150, 154, 164
Gulpilil, David 138; see also *Ten Canoes*
gyres 102–103, 105; *see also* Yates, W.B.

habitat 28, 156, 157
habitudes 24–25, 31
habitus 2, 24–25, 31, 34, 161
Halcro, Hugh 11
Happy Valley (2014) 104; *see also* White, Patrick
Harding, Sandra 16
Harris, Alexandra 7, 31; see also *Weatherland*
Hawthorne, Susan 3, 10, 14, 29, 44, 117–134, 136, 144, 157, 160, 163–164; see also *Earth's Breath*
Haynes, William Hamilton 17
Head, Ivan 125
Heaney, Seamus 166–167; *see also* country of the mind
heart 33, 36, 45, 53, 62, 77, 78, 88, 89, 95, 100, 101, 109, 114, 116, 117, 120, 124, 131, 133, 143, 144, 151
Heart of Darkness 32; *see also* Conrad, Joseph
Heat-Moon, William Least 102, 121
Heaven's Breath (1984) 47
Heidegger, Martin 25; see also *dasein*
helix 136, 139, 140, 160, 168
Heseltine, Harry 64
High Wind in Jamaica 17
history 2, 5, 13, 16, 17, 21, 24, 26, 28, 41, 45, 46, 48, 49, 53, 61, 64, 120, 123, 129, 132, 138, 139–140, 145, 152, 154, 157, 158, 164, 170; cultural 20, 46; of cyclones 7, 48, 51; oral 41, 150
"History of Hurricanes" (poem) 17
Hobart 50
Hoffman, Susanna 17, 73, 158, 171
Holthouse, Hector 7; *see also* Cyclone
Holy Wind (nilch'i) 124
Homer 1
hope 34, 100, 101, 114, 126, 127, 131, 132, 135, 136, 140, 146, 147, 148, 151, 152, 153, 165, 169, 170

Index

Hope (character) 136, 138, 139, 151, 152, 153, 154; see also *Carpentaria*; Wright, Alexis
Hope, A.D. (poet) 147
Hopi 102
Horace 1
horses 107–108
Hosking, Rick 36
Hosking, Sue 36
Hospital, Janette Turner: "Litany for the Homeland" 34, 36; "The Second Coming of Come-By-Chance" 34; "You Gave Me Hyacinths" 33
Hot Countries 35–36
Houston, James M 43
Hudson, William Henry 44–45
Hughes, Richard 17
human 2, 3, 5, 10, 12, 19, 21, 23, 24, 32, 39, 40, 42, 43, 45, 48, 56, 57, 58, 60, 61, 66, 70, 72, 74, 82, 84, 85, 100, 102, 103, 106, 108, 117, 118, 122, 123, 124, 128, 130, 133, 134, 135, 136, 140, 145, 147, 154, 157, 158, 159, 160, 162, 163, 165, 167, 170, 171; beings 21, 23, 34, 62, 63, 100, 102, 111, 116, 121, 124, 145, 153; characteristics 12, 15; experience 12, 96, 134, 170
humanity 10, 11, 19, 27, 28, 30, 45, 84, 85, 88, 88, 101, 115, 117, 123, 124, 134, 153, 158, 160, 159
Humboldt, Alexander Von 18–19, 31, 32, 131
Hunter, Sir Basil 98–116
Hunter (de Lascabanes), Dorothy 98–116
Hunter, Elizabeth 3, 93, 98–116, 130, 150, 165
huracan 46
Huracan (book) 17
"The Hurricane" (Bryant poem) 17
"The Hurricane" (Crane poem) 17
hurricane 2, 5, 7, 10, 12, 13, 14, 15, 16, 17, 20, 38, 45–46, 48, 50, 58–60, 90, 120, 121, 124, 130, 132, 162; Bathurst Bay 10, 38; Camille 60; Debbie 60; Ivan 12; Katrina 12, 130, 132; naming 45–46, 59–60; Okeechobee 17, 132
Hurricane Ivan: Survival Stories 12
Hurston, Zora Neale 17, 132, 133; *Their Eyes Were Watching God* 17, 132
hurucan 16

identity 2, 16, 22, 23, 24, 46, 56, 89, 132, 139, 140, 145, 146, 157, 158, 161, 162, 166, 168
"The Idiot Question" (essay) 88
image 2, 3, 13–14, 16–19, 22, 29, 30, 41, 54, 60, 77, 78, 82, 105, 111, 112, 130, 163
imagination 5, 6, 14, 17, 21, 24–28, 30–33, 37, 40, 46, 54, 55, 56, 63, 69, 71, 83, 86, 92, 100, 104, 108, 112, 117, 120, 135, 136, 144, 145, 156–157, 160–162, 164–170
In Darkest England 32; see also Booth, William
Indian Ocean 15, 16, 36
Indigenous 3, 16, 40, 47, 88, 135, 136, 137, 138, 139, 142, 143, 145, 147, 150; see also Aborigine, Australian
Ingold, Tim 15
Innisfail 40, 60, 61, 69

integrate 5, 7, 13, 15, 18, 22, 38, 41, 42, 48, 112, 120, 161, 162
interconnect *see* connect
Ishmael 12, 77; see also Ahab; Melville, Herman; *Moby Dick*
island 9, 14, 17, 31, 35, 36, 47, 50, 53, 56, 59, 67, 68, 69, 71, 82, 85, 87, 88, 89, 90, 91, 93, 94, 95, 98, 100, 105, 107, 108, 109, 110, 113, 116, 120, 126, 140, 155, 159; see also Bathurst; Brumby; Caribbean; Cuba; Dunk; Fitzroy; Green; Jamaica; Lord Howe; Marquesas; New Caledonia; Palm; Puerto Rico; Tahiti; Whitsunday
It's Raining in Mango 31, 86

Jackson, John Brinkerhoff 25, 28
Jamaica 17
James Cook University 6
Jardine, Frank 54–55
Jesus 77–78; see also *The Bible*; Jonah
jewel 105, 106, 109, 110, 113, 114, 115
Job 12, 29–30, 76, 82
Jonah 77, 78, 145
Jordan, Deborah 66
journey 1, 49, 68, 80, 82, 93, 98, 101, 102, 103, 104, 136, 142, 149, 150, 151, 153, 164, 165, 166
Joyce, James 104–105; see also *Dubliners*; *Stephen Hero*
Jurukan 16

Kangaroo (1994) 85
Kennedy, Victor 118
Kimberleys 9, 157
Kincaid, Jamaica 35
kindness 85, 88, 93, 95
A Kindness Cup 85
King Lear 9
Knight, Esther 11
Kreps, Dr. Juanita 60

labyrinth 14, 77, 99, 111
Lake, Father 94–95
Lamb, Karen 87
land 1, 9, 13, 14, 26, 27, 29, 30, 35, 37, 39, 40, 43, 63, 72, 76, 118, 120, 129, 132, 133, 135, 136, 137, 139, 141, 142, 143, 144, 145, 148, 151, 153, 154, 155, 157, 158, 164, 168, 170
landfall 5, 10, 14, 15, 37, 50, 51, 58, 59, 60, 61, 62, 73, 118, 155
landscape 2, 15, 21, 24, 25, 26, 27, 28, 32, 33, 42, 46, 73, 76, 84, 111, 119, 121, 127, 129, 139, 140, 147, 154, 157, 160, 162, 165, 166, 167, 168, 169, 170; cultural 35; language of 31, 44; literary 168, 169, 170; etymology of 26; of imagination 27, 33–34; of literature 168; of memory 27, 33; of the mind 43, 111, 170; personal 25, 119, 160, 167, 168; of place 42–43; tropical 33–34
language 12, 20, 22, 26, 27, 29, 39, 41, 43, 46, 47, 48, 52, 117, 143, 158, 161; of landscape 25, 27, 31, 44; literary 31; of place 9, 25, 26, 27

Larner, S.G. 11
Lawrence, D.H. 85; see also *Kangaroo*
Leviathan 2, 66, 73, 74–76, 77, 78, 79, 81, 94, 121, 144, 163
life 2, 5, 9, 10, 13, 15, 16, 17, 18, 19, 22, 24, 26, 27, 30, 32, 33, 34, 36, 37, 38, 39, 40, 41, 42, 43, 44, 47, 51, 58, 60, 61, 62, 63, 64, 65, 66, 67, 68, 69, 70, 73, 74, 75, 76, 77, 78, 79, 80, 82, 83, 84, 85, 86, 87, 88, 89, 90, 92, 98, 99, 100, 101, 103, 104, 105, 106, 107, 110, 111, 112, 113, 114, 115, 116, 118, 119, 121, 123, 125, 128, 129, 130, 131, 132, 139, 143, 147, 148, 149, 150, 151, 154, 155, 159, 160, 163, 164, 168, 170, 171; creating 133, 141; cycle of 40, 56, 57, 102, 161, 165, 168; end of 166; human 19, 170; tropical 39, 67; way of 2, 20
"Litany for the Homeland" (story) 34
literary 2, 5, 7, 14, 23, 31, 39, 40, 43, 53, 68, 73, 76, 84, 88, 141, 156, 163, 167, 168; cyclone 7, 10, 11, 18, 161; experience 7, 171; imagination 2, 5, 6, 18; place 40, 157; storm 155, 171; studies 5; trope 1, 161, 170; works 2, 6, 136
literature 1, 2, 3, 5, 6, 7, 14, 15, 17, 20, 21, 22, 27, 28, 29, 31, 40, 48, 73, 97, 104, 135, 137, 141, 153, 156, 157, 158, 161, 162, 163, 167, 168, 170, 171; Australian 36, 147; cyclone 7, 29, 39, 40, 48, 161; of place 156, 158; Queensland 6, 7, 11, 17, 18, 40, 67, 87, 159, 170; storm 6; of trauma 20; of weather 29
"Little Sigma" (short story) 11
littoral 36–37, 40, 157, 158
living 6, 11, 15, 29, 32, 35, 47, 66, 68, 76, 84, 90, 92, 107, 108, 113, 118, 124, 131, 133, 139, 140, 141, 142, 144, 151, 155, 157, 159, 160, 164, 171
Locke, John 23; *An Essay Concerning Human Understanding* 23
London 30, 49, 87, 99
Lopez, Barry 26, 155
Lord Howe Island 38, 51
love 3, 37, 70, 85, 89, 90, 91, 92, 102, 104, 108, 109, 110, 111, 113, 114, 115, 116, 132, 143
Love, Rosaleen 32
Lucretius 1

Mackay 38, 39, 53, 58, 61, 87, 169
Malouf, David 34, 35
"Man Building" (poem) 118
mandala 99, 100, 101–102, 104, 165, 166
A Manual of Meteorology (1928) 56
Maria (storm) 17, 21, 56, 57, 162
Marquesas Islands 47
Masigalgal (people) 47
Mayan 16, 124
McCauley, Diana 17
McCullers, Carson 35
McDonald, Tom 70
meaning 6, 7, 10, 12, 16, 18, 19, 20, 22, 23, 25, 26, 28, 31, 33, 41, 42, 43, 47, 51, 64, 98, 112, 106, 118, 123, 125, 136, 152, 156, 157, 158, 159, 161, 162, 165, 168; of life 98, 106, 110, 111, 114, 116, 161; of place 28, 157; search for 11, 18, 64, 66, 83, 101, 102, 107, 114, 159, 165, 170; spiritual 103, 165
meaningless 6, 7, 81, 162. 165
Melbourne 34, 52, 67, 69, 70, 71
Melville, Herman *see Moby Dick*
memory 23, 24, 25, 26, 27, 28, 41, 45, 50, 57, 69, 104, 137, 139, 140, 145, 146, 147, 149, 150, 152, 153
Merren, Terri 12
Metamorphoses 1
metaphor 12, 17, 19, 20, 22, 30, 43, 54, 55, 62, 65, 74, 81, 86, 131, 134, 170
Meteorologica 13
meteorology 1, 6, 10, 16, 20, 30, 38–39, 45, 48, 49, 50, 51, 52, 54–57, 71, 72, 119, 130–131, 155, 161, 162, 166, 168; Bureau of 15, 59
Midsummer Night's Dream 68
Millard, Bill 64–65, 69, 70–71
Milton, John *see Paradise Lost*
miracle 71, 145, 153
Mission Beach (Hull River) 61, 62, 63, 86, 120, 123, 132
Moby Dick 12, 73, 76; *see also* Ahab; Ishmael; Melville, Herman
monsoon 11, 33, 47, 118, 160
"Monsoon Two" (short story) 11
monster 2, 21, 60, 65, 66, 73–74, 75, 76, 77, 78, 79, 80, 81, 82, 94, 144, 145, 155, 163, 164
The Multiple Effects of Rainshadow 31, 86, 120
myth 2, 19, 21, 34, 40, 41, 62, 64, 72, 73, 74, 76, 77, 78, 80, 94, 101, 106, 112, 115, 121, 122, 124, 131, 139, 141, 142, 144, 153, 161, 162, 163, 164, 168
mythology 73, 121, 141, 142, 144, 145, 153, 162, 163, 164, 167

name 5, 12, 16, 17, 20, 21, 22, 38, 44, 45, 46, 47, 48, 49, 50–54, 56, 57, 58, 59, 60, 61, 62, 63, 71, 73, 76, 79, 94, 104, 107, 119, 122, 132, 134, 139, 143, 145, 146, 147, 152, 162, 168; cyclones 2, 46, 49, 58, 59, 60, 61, 63, 168; disaster 44–63; naming 21, 45, 56, 58, 60; storms 2, 15, 20, 45, 48, 51, 52, 53, 54, 56, 57, 58; weather 20–21; wind 46
The Name of the Rose 12
narrative 2, 3, 11, 19, 33, 40–43, 46, 77, 117, 136, 140, 155
narrator 84, 144, 146, 148, 159
National Hurricane Center 60
National Organization for Women 59–60
National Weather Service 60
Native American 102, 121
natural 6, 9, 18, 21, 22, 45, 48, 49, 60, 62, 73, 78, 82, 117, 118, 122, 123, 128, 129, 131, 144, 163, 164, 168; environment 22, 43, 46, 49, 132, 154, 160; world 26, 103, 134, 141, 152, 160, 170
nature 3, 6, 9, 10, 12, 13, 18, 19, 21, 24, 30, 31, 32, 33, 37, 39, 40, 43, 44, 48, 55, 56, 62, 63, 64, 66, 67, 72, 73, 78, 85, 87, 89, 91, 94, 95, 101, 105, 107, 108, 112, 117, 118, 119, 122, 123, 128,

Index 199

129, 130, 131, 134, 142, 145, 158, 160, 164, 167, 168, 170; catastrophe 2, 6, 10, 18, 19, 22, 42, 48, 156, 161, 162; cyclone 3, 38, 39, 121, 158, 163; disaster 6, 18, 38, 74, 170
Navajo 124
"A New Beginning" (poem) 62, 63
New Caledonia 39, 50, 53, 55
New South Wales 38, 41, 47, 52
A Night at the Pink Poodle 36
nilch'I (Holy Wind) 124
Norse 121, 137, 144, 163
North Queensland 2, 5, 6, 10, 11, 13, 15–16, 22, 28, 31–35, 37–39, 42, 51, 61, 64, 66–68, 70–72, 83, 118, 142–143, 155, 157, 164, 166–168; cyclone 37–40; *see also* Far North Queensland
Nott, Jonathan 37
novel 2, 3, 10, 11, 17, 21, 36, 41, 56, 57, 58, 64, 65, 66, 67, 71, 72, 75, 79, 80, 81, 83, 84, 87, 88, 90, 92, 95, 96, 99, 100, 101, 104, 106, 113, 120, 121, 125, 135, 136, 137, 142, 144, 150, 152, 154, 159, 163, 164, 170

O'Connor, Flannery 35
O'Connor, Mark 118
The Odyssey 1
Old Times on the Mississippi 27
order 1, 6, 7, 11, 12, 22, 30, 43, 54, 59, 73–76, 80, 100, 105–106, 117–118, 127–128, 134, 158, 160, 162–163, 168; *see also* disorder; pattern
origin 3, 27, 29, 41, 55, 58, 62, 76, 100, 123, 138–140, 146, 147, 159
original 2, 3, 26, 27, 58, 66, 68, 77, 99, 100, 136, 146, 153, 159,
Orlando 30–31, 157
Ovid 1

Pacific (Ocean) 16, 22, 36, 47, 50, 53, 55, 58, 87, 122, 159; South Pacific 16, 159
Paint Your Wagon (musical/film) 57, 58
Paley, Morton 17
Palm Island 9, 69, 70, 86, 120
Palmer, Nettie 32, 64–83
Palmer, Vance 2, 11, 64–83, 85, 94, 121, 144, 157, 163; "The Big Wind" (story) 65, 71, 79, 82; *Cyclone* 2, 11, 64–83, 121, 144, 157, 163; "Cyclone" (story) 65–66, 71, 80–81; "Tempest" (story) 65–66, 71, 81
paradise 30, 31, 32, 36, 68, 69, 75, 80, 83, 85, 94
Paradise, Verna 90, 92–96
Paradise Lost 30, 76, 157
Paterson, A.B. "Banjo" 17, 118; "The Ballad of the Calliope" (poem) 17, 118
pattern 1, 2, 3, 14, 27, 28, 32, 41, 53, 54, 58, 61, 99, 100, 101, 102, 103, 106, 121, 122, 125, 135, 136, 138, 139, 142, 154, 165, 166, 168; *see also* order
peace 83, 99, 100, 107, 109, 115, 165
The Pearling Disaster 1899 10
people 1, 2, 3, 5, 6, 10–13, 15–20, 22–24, 27, 29, 30–31, 34, 35, 37–64, 66, 67, 69–74, 76,
78–82, 86, 88–89, 91, 92, 94–96, 101–102, 105, 110–114, 116–120, 122–124, 127–133, 135, 138–155, 157–162, 164, 166, 168, 169, 171; and place 23–26, 31, 40–63, 117, 118, 134, 155–157, 160, 161, 166, 167, 171
perception 11, 18, 19, 23, 31–33, 43, 46, 74, 87, 99, 117, 145, 162, 166, 171; of cyclone storm 14, 45, 46, 48, 57, 62, 162; of place 26, 29, 32, 41, 42, 157, 161, 167; of self 23, 26, 27, 28, 96, 98, 106, 157; of weather 29, 54
personality 2, 51, 53, 57, 63, 68, 87, 103
Phantom, Norm 136–154
Phantom, Will 136–154, 169–170
A Philosophical Enquiry 17, 55
Piddington, Henry 16–17
pilgrimage 35, 147
place 2, 3, 5, 6, 9–11, 13, 16–19, 22–30, 34, 40–43, 45, 48, 54, 61, 63, 64, 68, 72, 75, 78, 81, 86, 88, 94, 101, 103, 108, 110, 117, 118, 121, 122, 125, 126, 129–132, 134, 136, 140, 150, 154–159, 161, 162, 166, 167, 169, 170; coastal 36–37, 157–158; cultural place 11, 47, 123, 161, 162, 165; ego-centered 166; and identity 23–24, 161; imagined place 24, 165, 167; language of 9–43, 158; literary 40, 157; literature of 40, 156, 158; narrative of 40–43; and people 2, 5, 6, 17, 19, 23, 25, 26, 31, 40–43, 61, 71, 117, 118, 134, 160, 161, 166, 167, 171; perception of 23–24, 28, 29, 41, 157; Queensland 6, 31, 33, 36, 40, 49, 66, 68, 83, 122, 166, 167; regional 11, 13, 27–29, 120, 154, 164; sacred 147, 150–152; and self 24; semiotics 25; sense of 17, 24, 27–29, 44, 162, 166, 167; spirit of 66, 166; spiritual 165–170; story place 144, 165, 167; tropical 5, 13, 18, 31–37, 64, 66, 67, 83, 155, 159, 160
Place and Placelessness 23
poetry 3, 5, 10–12, 17, 20, 29, 40, 43–44, 60, 61–63, 76, 108, 117–134, 136, 144, 147, 156–157, 160, 161, 163, 165
Popol Vuh 124, 140
Port Douglas 37
Porter, Mrs 9, 10, 66
prophet 135, 145, 146, 147, 148, 149, 151, 154, 165
prose 5, 12, 20, 33, 54, 60, 156, 160, 161
Proust, Marcel 25
Puerto Rico 50
python 75, 122, 142, 143; *see also* serpent; snake; taipan

Queensland 5, 6, 7, 9, 10, 13, 15, 16, 18, 22, 29, 31, 33, 34, 35, 36, 38, 48, 49, 50, 51, 58, 59, 60, 62, 63, 68, 70, 71, 97, 98, 117, 118, 120, 142, 143, 150, 155, 159, 164, 168, 170; coast 5, 15, 37, 38, 54, 61, 64, 71, 72, 107, 157; cyclone 7, 10, 22, 37–40, 59, 60, 61, 67, 71, 72, 98, 155, 160, 161, 162, 170; cyclone naming 49; difference 35; Gothic 34–35; literature 6, 7, 11, 17, 18, 33–34, 40, 67, 87, 88, 97, 156, 159, 160, 170; place 6, 17, 28, 31,

Index

40, 68, 83, 122, 166, 167; tropics 2, 7, 31–34, 38; weather 31
Queenslander (person) 6, 10, 16, 17, 21, 28, 35, 36, 38, 39, 62, 168; *see also* Far North Queenslander; North Queenslander

rain 13, 15, 28, 29, 30, 31, 33, 42, 44, 47, 52, 54, 58, 60, 62, 80, 93, 100, 102, 118, 122, 127, 135, 142, 144, 147, 153, 157, 164, 164
"The Rainbow Serpent" (poem) 118
rainforest 33, 34, 129
Random, Michael 147–8; *see also* Stow, Randolph; *Tourmaline*
re-create 10, 30, 40, 43, 84, 129, 134, 154, 160
Redfield, William 16
reef 32, 53, 54, 67, 68, 69, 70, 71, 75, 91, 121, 150; *see also* Great Barrier Reef
Reefscape 32
region 6, 7, 10, 15, 16, 27, 33, 38, 46, 47, 61, 68, 69, 131, 132, 133, 140, 142, 143, 144, 154, 156, 157, 158, 161, 164, 167, 168, 170; North Queensland 7, 34, 66; regional identity 16, 46, 157; regional imaginary 13, 162; regional place 11, 13, 28, 120, 164; tropical 6, 7, 9, 13, 15, 31, 71, 164, 168, 171
Reid, Robert 31–32
religion 94, 100, 101, 102; religious 3, 32, 99, 106, 141
Relph, Edward 23
renewal 3, 18, 19, 63, 64, 67, 78, 79, 81, 105, 116, 123, 126, 153, 154, 159, 160, 162, 165
research 6, 14, 36, 48, 56
resilience 43, 83, 137, 170
resurrection 2, 64, 75, 76, 78, 79, 80, 121, 163
revelation 2, 3, 10, 17, 18, 20, 31, 43, 64, 66, 67, 80–85, 87, 88, 95–98, 103, 104, 106, 107, 114, 117–119, 125, 126, 152, 154, 155, 157, 159, 160, 162, 165, 166, 170, 171
Rich, Adrienne 17, 131
Rockhampton 38, 58
Royal Meteorological Society 49

Saffir-Simpson Scale 15,
saga 137, 138, 140
Sailor's Hornbook 16
salvation 109, 113, 147
Scarborough, Dorothy 21–22, 133, 148; see also *The Wind*
scope 7, 18, 20, 22, 45, 64, 73, 121, 164
sea 1, 15–17, 22, 30, 32, 36, 37, 47–49, 51, 53, 55, 68–70, 72, 74–81, 85, 86, 93, 94, 107, 112, 121–124, 133, 136, 138, 145–154, 157, 158, 163, 168
Sea Venture (ship) 14, 17
Seabrook, Gerald/Kathleen 91, 95, 96
search 7, 10, 11, 19, 20, 29, 36, 64, 66, 70, 79, 81, 83, 100–103, 111–114, 132, 136, 138, 147, 153, 156, 159, 165, 168, 170
season 2, 3, 6, 9, 13, 15, 30, 32, 38, 47, 68–69, 71, 73–74, 102, 118, 122, 143, 149–150, 168
"The Second Coming" (poem) 103

"The Second Coming of Come-By-Chance" (story) 34
Seddon, George 44–45
self 2, 23–28, 36, 52, 66, 79, 85, 89–92, 94–96, 101, 102, 105, 106, 109, 111–113, 115, 125, 129, 132, 136, 141, 149, 157, 165
sense (of) 7, 13, 23, 24, 26, 32, 35, 36, 44, 62, 77, 79, 80, 85, 86, 90, 96, 103, 107, 115, 120, 127, 131, 135, 154, 156, 161, 164, 166–168, 171; of place 13, 17, 24, 27–28, 43, 44, 122, 162, 166, 167; of self 24, 36, 96, 141; of *terroir* 2, 23, 158
senses 14, 25, 34, 36, 40, 100, 112, 122, 125, 128, 132
serpent/s 6, 14, 35, 36, 69, 75–76, 80, 94, 121, 151, 152, 163–164; ancestral 169, 141, 142, 164, 169; creative 135, 136, 140; Midgardorm 121, 144, 163; monster 2, 73, 163; ouroboros 121, 122, 144, 163–164; python 122, 142; Rainbow Serpent 47, 118, 121, 140, 142–144, 152, 154, 164; serpent-bird (Quetzalcoatl) 144, 164; serpent dragon 144, 164; taipan 142, 143; tempting 121, 163; winged 121, 163; *see also* python; snake; taipan
Shakespeare, William 1, 17, 68, 166; *see also* *King Lear*; *Midsummer Night's Dream*; *The Tempest*
"Shar: Hurricane Poem" 17
Shaw, Sir William Napier 56
sing 89, 120, 134, 136, 154, 161, 170
skiapod 112, 114,
Skilton, Liz 7, 45–46
sky 7, 13, 27, 30, 32, 35, 68, 73, 79, 80, 118, 124, 126, 140, 143, 149, 150, 151, 163, 169
Slow Natives 90–91, 92; *see also* Astley, Thea
Smith, Elias 136, 138, 146, 147, 148, 149, 150, 151, 153, 154, 169
snake 14, 16, 68, 75, 76, 142, 143, 144, 164; *see also* python; serpent
society 5, 11–12, 18, 20, 26, 36, 64, 73–74, 81, 108, 139, 143–144, 156–157, 162, 170–171
Something Wicked This Way Comes 81
song 57, 58, 134, 155, 160, 170; cycle 47; songline 142, 168
The Song of the Earth 118
South America 131, 144, 164
South Australia 55
Southern Ocean 36
space 7, 22, 28, 32, 34, 36, 40, 81, 86, 87, 119, 120, 126, 133, 137, 141, 145, 152, 155, 167, 170
Space and Place 23
speak 5, 9, 10, 25, 31, 32, 47, 57, 62, 76, 82, 119, 128, 132, 137, 147, 153, 160, 161, 163
spiral 6, 14, 16, 82, 84, 102, 103, 110, 119, 122–125, 127, 130–131, 133, 136, 140, 157, 160, 165, 168
spirit 1, 21, 35, 39, 63, 66, 89, 111, 120, 123, 135, 137, 140–143, 145, 146, 148–152, 154, 166; spirit being 142, 143, 151
spiritual 3, 10, 28, 30, 78, 84, 85, 98–101, 103–109, 112, 115–116, 120, 123, 125, 132, 137, 140,

141, 144–147, 149–151, 153–154, 157, 164–166, 168–170; spirituality 3, 64, 89, 141, 142, 170
Spirn, Anne Whiston 25–27
Stanner, W.E.H. 153
Stephen Hero 104; *see also* Joyce, James
Stevenson 89–90, 93, 160
Stewart, George Rippey 17, 21, 56; *see also* *Storm*
still 72, 81, 82, 93, 103, 105, 133, 147, 170; air 82, 123; center 99, 100, 109, 165; eye 100, 165; point 98, 103, 115, 124, 126, 150, 165
storm 1, 3, 9–13, 15, 20, 21, 30, 31, 37, 39, 43, 45, 46, 48, 52, 54, 68, 85, 79, 90, 93–96, 98–100, 105–110, 112–116, 118–122, 124, 125, 127, 128, 130–132, 142–146, 148, 150, 151, 154, 159–162, 166, 169; Aleph (Aus) 52; apocalyptic 152, 160; Barton (Aus) 52; Conroy (Aus) 52; cyclonic 2, 5, 7, 12–17, 29, 38, 44, 46, 48, 49, 51, 56, 61–63, 66–67, 69–71, 75, 78–84, 86, 88, 89, 97, 118, 131, 132, 151, 155, 162, 166, 168, 170, 171; Deakin (Aus) 52; Doris (UK) 48; eye of 85, 109–110, 114, 150, 151, 159; language of 12; Leda 145; Leonta (Aus) 51; literary 6, 85, 86, 88, 155, 171; making 152; Maria (US) 21, 56–57; naming 2, 15, 20, 45–58; personify 12, 46, 57; rotating 14, 16, 17, 155; Royal Charter 50 (UK); Sana 55 (Aus); trope 1, 7; tropical 5, 16, 46, 48, 51, 52, 53, 58, 73, 132, 164
Storm 56–58; *see also* Stewart, George Rippey
The Storm 17, 162; *see also* Defoe, Daniel
"Storm Warnings" (poem) 17, 131
story 2, 3, 5, 12, 13, 15, 16, 20, 21, 25, 27, 33, 40–43, 46, 56, 60, 64–68, 73, 77, 78, 120, 127, 133, 135–141, 143–147, 154, 158–159, 161–162, 164–166, 169, 170; of creation 123, 140, 141, 146, 147, 152, 164; cyclone 46, 82, 162; epic 145, 146, 153; oral 138; place 144, 164, 167; short 10, 11, 33, 34, 64, 65– 67, 71, 79–82, 104, 162
storytelling 3, 7, 12, 20, 40, 73, 136, 137, 141, 158, 162, 163; oral 137–138
Stow, Randolph 147–8; *see also Tourmaline*
Strachey, William 13; *see also True Reportory of the Wracke*
structure 2, 3, 10, 11, 12, 15, 33, 40, 41, 56, 73, 88, 119, 127, 129, 162, 163
sublime 2, 17, 55, 56, 86, 125, 166; apocalyptic 17; sense of 32, 125
suffer 11, 36, 51, 61, 82, 99, 101, 103, 104, 107, 108, 110, 113, 114, 143, 147, 165
survival 5, 9–12, 14, 17, 20, 27, 39, 40, 60, 61, 65, 67, 70, 77–81, 84, 88, 89, 95, 96, 116, 118, 120, 123, 126–128, 132, 133, 138, 139, 144, 151–153, 157, 159
swans 98, 105, 108, 114, 115, 116, 126, 127; *see also The Eye of the Storm*; Stewart, Patrick
Swee, Hannah 14
Sydney 39, 111
symbol 2, 20, 22, 30, 33, 37, 64, 66, 74, 75, 79, 85, 86, 90, 94, 99–102, 104–105, 107–108, 112, 121, 122, 126, 127, 136, 147, 158, 163–165, 169–170

Tahiti 36, 53
taipan 142, 143; *see also* python; serpent; snake
Tal, Kali 11, 19, 20
tempest 1, 14, 98, 121, 128, 151, 159
"Tempest" (story) 65–66, 71, 81
The Tempest (play) 1, 17; *see also* Shakespeare, William
Tempest: Hurricane Naming 7, 45–46
Ten Canoes (2006, film) 138; *see also* Gulpilil, David
terroir 2, 23, 27–29, 33, 34, 40, 41, 43, 46, 47, 66, 83, 157, 158, 159, 161, 162, 166, 167
Their Eyes Were Watching God 17, 132; *see also* Hurston; Nora Zeal
theme 6, 37, 71, 77, 78, 80, 101, 170
"They Call the Wind Mariah" (song) 57, 58; *see also* Stewart, George Rippey; *Storm*
time 1, 3, 7, 12, 13, 17, 23, 24, 26, 27, 29, 32, 33, 41, 43, 44, 46, 48, 54, 60, 71, 72, 73, 76, 78, 83, 85, 91, 92, 98, 103, 105, 106, 107, 109, 111–116, 118, 120, 121, 122, 123, 124, 126, 127, 128, 129, 130, 131, 133, 136–139, 141, 144, 145–147, 149, 152, 153, 154, 155, 162, 164, 165, 166, 168
topography 2, 22, 45, 57, 164, 167, 168
tornado 2, 17, 37, 73, 162
Torres Strait 9, 16, 38, 47, 53, 86
Tourmaline 147–8; *see also* Random, Michael; Stowe, Randolph
Tourmaline (town) 147–8
Tournier, Paul 43
Townsville 37, 38, 39, 51, 58, 61, 70, 120
Traherne, Meredith 10
transformation 2, 3, 34, 76, 103, 104, 111, 123, 132, 145–146, 154, 166, 170
trauma 11, 14, 19, 20, 22, 42, 61, 62, 63, 96, 119, 127, 128
The Tree of Man 106; *see also* White, Patrick
trope 3, 17, 19, 22, 29, 34, 96, 144, 147, 155, 159, 161, 170; of catastrophe 20, 22, 159; cyclone 2, 6, 7, 17, 18, 22, 40, 67, 73, 87, 88, 97, 136, 156, 158, 161, 163, 164, 166, 168, 170; literary 1, 17, 22, 156, 159; of place 3, 155; storm 1, 7, 97
Tropic of Cancer 13
Tropic of Capricorn 9, 13
tropical 13, 14, 16, 32, 33, 34, 35, 39, 56, 67, 82, 91, 92, 94, 118, 121, 128, 142, 164, 171; cyclone 2, 3, 5, 9, 11, 13, 15, 21, 31, 37, 39, 48, 51, 53, 58, 59, 60, 61, 62, 69, 86, 91, 98, 136, 155, 156, 158, 159, 161, 168, 170; Gothic 34–35; landscape 33, 34; place 5, 13, 18, 31, 32, 33, 34, 64, 66, 67, 155, 159, 160; North Queensland 34, 38; region 6, 7, 9, 13, 15, 71, 164, 168, 171; storm 5, 16, 46, 48, 51, 52, 53, 58, 73, 83, 132, 164; "Tropical Cyclone Yasi" (poem) 62; weather 28, 31, 35; world 16; zone 7, 31, 171
tropics 2, 7, 13, 16, 31–32, 33, 34, 36, 37, 55, 67, 68, 71, 122, 155, 166, 170

True Reportory of the Wracke 14; see also Strachey
Trumper, Kitty 90, 91, 92–93, 94, 95; see also Astley; Thea
Tuan, Yi-Fu 22, 23, 45
"Tully Under Cyclone" (poem) 125
Twain, Mark 27; see also Clemens, Samuel; *Old Times on the Mississippi*
The Twyborn Affair 106; see also Patrick White
Typhoon 15, 17; see also Conrad; Joseph
typhoon 13, 14, 15, 16, 20, 45–46, 48, 102, 109, 162

understanding 10, 13, 16, 18–22, 25–27, 29, 31, 40, 41, 43, 60, 63, 67, 78, 83, 97, 98, 100, 101, 103, 105, 107, 109, 110, 112, 114, 115, 119, 127, 131, 134, 136, 138, 140, 149, 150, 152, 153, 158, 162, 165–168, 170, 171
"Upon the Hurricane" (poem) 17

Varo, Remedios 133
Vaughan, Linda J. 62, 63
violent 5, 6, 7, 9, 14, 17, 21, 31, 34, 44, 57, 59, 61, 62, 63, 66, 67, 69, 71, 72, 74, 81, 86, 87, 93, 95, 96, 118, 151, 168, 170
Virgil 1, 117, 118, 122; see also *The Georgics*
visualization 14, 60, 66, 74, 125
The Vivisector 113
voice 3, 12, 27, 40, 72, 78, 86, 94, 104, 128, 133, 137, 141, 147, 152, 153, 154
Voices from the Storm 12
volcano 73, 93, 94, 95,
Voss 101, 113, 116, 147

Watson, Lyall 47
Waugh, Alec 35–36
weather 1, 5–7, 9, 10, 13–15, 22, 25, 27–31, 35, 37–40, 42–43, 47, 58, 61, 63–64, 66–68, 73–74, 80–81, 86–87, 96, 113, 118–119, 122, 126, 131, 136, 142, 154–156, 158, 161, 164, 171; catastrophe 5, 42, 168; events 5, 6, 10, 12, 14, 20, 22, 42, 45, 48, 57, 59–60, 66, 69, 82, 84, 155, 158, 161–163, 168, 171; forecasting 9, 49–56; moral dimension of 30; part of place 29–30, 157, 165; tropical 31, 35; within us 29, 131, 157

Weatherland 7, 28, 29, 31, 157
Weil, Simone 104
The Well Dressed Explorer 85
Welty, Eudora 162, 166
whirlwind 76, 117, 147, 149
White, Patrick 3, 10, 84, 93, 98–116, 125–126, 130, 136, 147, 150, 157, 159, 165–166; see also *The Eye of the Storm*; *Flaws in the Glass*; *Happy Valley*; *The Tree of Man*; *The Twyborn Affair*; *The Vivisector*; *Voss*
white whale 73, 77
Whitsunday Islands 9
Wilson, James E 28, 157
wind 1, 2, 6, 12–17, 21–22, 27–30, 37, 42, 44–46, 55–56, 59–62, 65, 70, 72–74, 79–80, 82, 86, 93, 95, 102, 118–124, 127, 129–134, 144, 147–148, 150–151, 155, 162, 164; cyclonic 33, 51; names 20, 47–48, 57–58; sound of 128; within 129, 130, 133, 157
Wind (DeBlieu) 46, 48, 123–124
The Wind (Scarborough) 21–22, 133, 148
Woolf, Virginia 30–31, 157
The Wonderful Wizard of Oz 109
world 18, 23–29, 31, 33, 35, 36, 39, 42–44, 49, 52, 56, 58, 59, 66, 74, 76, 78, 81, 82, 88, 90, 95, 96, 98, 103, 104, 117, 118, 121–123, 126–128, 130, 131, 134–136, 138, 140, 143, 144, 146, 149–154, 162–165, 168, 169, 171; being in the world 25; natural 26, 134, 152, 160, 170; place 25, 28; weather 29
Wragge, Clement 2, 38–39, 49–56, 58
Wright, Alexis see *Carpentaria*
Wright, Judith 130
writer 6, 10, 12, 16, 20, 22, 23, 25, 26, 27, 29, 32, 34, 35, 36, 46, 54, 60, 62, 65, 67, 72, 79, 118, 123, 134, 139, 159, 162, 166; Australian 11, 36; Queensland 11, 62

"Yasi Tried" (poem) 62
Yeats, W.B. 102–103, 105, 165; see also gyres
"You Gave Me Hyacinths" (story) 33

Zapf, Michael K 28
zoomorphism 12, 21, 80
zonda 48, 162

www.ingramcontent.com/pod-product-compliance
Ingram Content Group UK Ltd.
Pitfield, Milton Keynes, MK11 3LW, UK
UKHW041938210426
5322IPUK00016B/241